D1596161

**Victims of
Personal Crime:
An Empirical
Foundation For a
Theory of Personal
Victimization**

Victims of Personal Crime: An Empirical Foundation For a Theory of Personal Victimization

Michael J. Hindelang
Michael R. Gottfredson
James Garofalo

Ballinger Publishing Company ● Cambridge, Mass.
A Subsidiary of J.B. Lippincott Company

This book is printed on recycled paper.

International Standard Book Number: 0-88410-793-0

Library of Congress Catalog Card Number: 77-15981

Printed in the United States of America

Library of Congress Cataloging in Publication Data

Hindelang, Michael J
  Victims of personal crime.

  Bibliography: p. 309
  Includes index.
  1. Victims of crimes—United States. 2. Victims of crimes surveys—United States. I. Gottfredson, Michael R., joint author. II. Garofalo, James, joint author. III. Title.
  HV6250.3.U5H57   364   77-15981
  ISBN 0-88410-793-0

To Debbie, Karol, and Eugenia.

Contents

List of Tables

List of Figures

Preface

The systematic study of criminal victimization has, until recently, received only scant attention. With the advent of the LEAA-Census surveys of personal, household, and business victimization the basic data required to undertake studies of criminal victimization are gradually becoming available. Our own research using these data began in 1973,[1] resulting in the publication of *Criminal Victimization in Eight American Cities: A Descriptive Analysis of Common Theft and Assault* (Hindelang, 1976) and several other papers.[2] As a consequence of intensive research on

1. This early research was largely supported by two grants from the statistics division of the Law Enforcement Assistance Administration to the Criminal Justice Research Center in Albany, New York. The first was entitled, "Analysis of National Crime Survey Data" (74–SS–99–6001) and the second, "Analysis of NCP Attitude and Victimization Data" (75–SS–99–6002). The fact that the statistics division of the Law Enforcement Assistance Administration provided financial support for some of the activities resulting in these publications does not necessarily indicate their concurrence with the statements or conclusions contained herein.
2. Michael Gottfredson and Michael Hindelang, "Victims of Personal Crimes: A Methodological Disquisition," in *Proceedings of the Social Statistics Section of the American Statistical Association* (Washington, D.C.: American Statistical Association, 1975); Michael Hindelang and Michael Gottfredson, "The Victim's Decision Not to Invoke the Criminal Process," in William McDonald, ed., *The Victim and the Criminal Justice System*, (Beverly Hills: Sage, 1976); Michael Gottfredson and Michael Hindelang, "Bodily Injury to Victims of Personal Crime," in W. Skogan, ed., *Sample Surveys of the Victims of Crime*, (Cambridge, Mass.: Ballinger Publishing Co., 1976); Michael Gottfredson and Michael Hindelang, "A Consideration of Memory Decay and Telescoping Biases in Victimization Surveys." *Journal of Criminal Justice*, 1977; Michael Gottfredson, "An Empirical Classification of Victims of Personal Crimes" (Paper read at the 1976

the survey methods and results over a long period of time, we have become familiar with both the potential and the limitations of these data. In addition, in-depth analyses of these data using a wide variety of analytic techniques have given us an appreciation not only for the tremendous complexity of the data set, but also for the empirical regularities in the data. For many of the most important *patterns* in the data, relationships maintain with surprising consistency across geographic areas and across time, regardless of the statistical methods employed in analyzing the results.

As a result of our earlier work, we decided that it was essential to give more detailed attention to particular important aspects of personal victimization. Specifically, we believed that it was necessary to focus sharply on bodily injury, financial loss, and attitudes and beliefs of respondents toward crime and related topics and to explore in more detail the question of victimization risk. In the course of analyzing these phenomena, the patterns and relationships that emerged began to suggest to us a theoretical model that would help to explicate many of the most central findings. Although this "lifestyle/exposure" model is in an early stage of development, we believe that it has considerable potential for explaining differential risks of personal victimization.

The data analyzed and presented in this book are from surveys conducted by the Bureau of the Census in the cities of Atlanta, Baltimore, Cleveland, Dallas, Denver, Newark, Portland, (Oregon), and St. Louis in 1972. We chose this eight-city data set because much of the basic descriptive information had been previously published (Hindelang, 1976). In various places throughout this volume, data from LEAA-Census victimization surveys conducted in other cities are used. For those who are unfamiliar with the LEAA-Census victimization surveys, we suggest beginning by consulting Appendix A, which contains the survey instruments, and reading Appendix B, which provides a general background of the survey and the sampling and data collection procedures.

In Chapter 1, some of the highlights from earlier analyses are presented in order to lay the foundation for subsequent chapters. In this chapter, the relationships between demographic characteristics of respondents and rates of victimization are briefly reviewed. Following this introduction and review, the book is divided into four

---

annual meetings of the American Society of Criminology, Tucson, Arizona); James Garofalo, *Public Opinion About Crime: The Attitudes of Victims and Nonvictims in Selected Cities*, Law Enforcement Assistance Administration, National Criminal Justice Information and Statistics Service, Analytic Report SD-VAD-1 (Washington, D.C.: Government Printing Office, 1977).

parts. Part I (Chapters 2, 3, and 4) examines bodily injury and financial loss in personal victimizations, regardless of the type of crime in connection with which these consequences occurred. Chapter 2 outlines the strategy for analysis that is used in the two subsequent chapters. This strategy suggests that analysis within a priori legal categories such as rape, robbery, assault, and larceny may be less informative than an analytic approach that focuses on types of personal harm, irrespective of legal categories. Specifically, Chapter 3 uses this approach to explore in detail bodily injury to victims in personal crimes. Such topics as the role of weapons, the victim-offender relationship, and use of self-protective measures by the victim are analyzed in relation to an injurious outcome. Financial loss is examined in a parallel fashion in Chapter 4.

In Part II (Chapters 5 and 6) the focus shifts away from an emphasis on the event to an emphasis on characteristics of respondents that are differentially associated with risks of victimization. In Chapter 5, we attempt to discover which segments of the population are most likely to be personally victimized. We examine this question for risks of bodily injury, financial loss, and total personal victimization. In Chapter 6, we look more closely at the question of personal victimization risk by isolating those respondent characteristics associated with multiple victimization (i.e., being victimized two or more times within the reference period). We examine models of victimization in order to test some competing hypotheses about "victimization proneness." Of particular interest is an analysis of the conditional likelihood of being a victim of a particular type of crime, given that the respondent reported being a victim of another type of crime.

Attitudes, beliefs, and opinions of respondents toward crime and related topics are presented in Part III (Chapters 7, 8, 9, and 10). The first two of these chapters analyze perceptions of the crime problem and how these perceptions are related to demographic characteristics and to victimization experiences. Chapter 9 examines the limitations on behavior that respondents report as a result of crime. In Chapter 10, we take a look back upon our analyses in all of the preceding chapters and attempt to assess their limitations and strengths. Specifically in this methodological postscript we reflect on limitations of the data and the analytic methods used throughout.

A theoretical model of personal victimization is presented in Part IV (Chapter 11). Within this "lifestyle/exposure model" we postulate an explanation for variations in risks of personal victimization as a function of personal characteristics. In developing this model we have endeavored to account for the major findings resulting from studies of victims of crime.

We believe that victimization survey results are an important source of criminological data that, in this first decade of their availability, are only beginning to be tapped. It is our hope that this book will stimulate interest not only in using victimization survey results to explore problems of central concern to criminology and criminal justice but also in investigating methodological aspects of surveying victimization. As more researchers begin to do so, we anticipate that an increasingly strong empirical foundation for studying crime and victimization will be developed. This foundation will help us to understand and respond to the phenomenon of criminal victimization and also to elucidate patterns of offending behavior.

As with all books, this one results not only from the effort of the authors, but from the efforts of many others as well. The victimization survey data are available as a result of the sustained interest that the Statistics Division of LEAA and the Demographic Surveys Division of the Bureau of the Census have devoted to this area of inquiry. Further, the Statistics Division of LEAA has supported large portions of the analytic work upon which this book rests. In this regard we are grateful to Benjamin Renshaw, Charles Kindermann, Dawn Nelson, Patsy Klaus, and Sue Lindgren, all of LEAA's Statistics Division, as well as to Linda Murphy of the Demographic Surveys Division of the Bureau of the Census, for the assistance that they have provided throughout the life of our research. Computer programming assistance was provided by Dan Pappenfus and Terry Quinn and secretarial services by Marianne Hammond, Barbara Meilinger, Stephanie Brooks, and Kim McClure.

In addition, we are particularly grateful to Maynard Erickson, Sherwood Zimmerman, and Gary Gottfredson for reading and commenting on early versions of the manuscript. It has benefitted considerably as a result of their critical comments. We are also indebted to John Gibbs, John Goldkamp, Alan Harland, David van Alstyne, Joseph Weis, and Vernetta Young for their helpful comments on various portions of the manuscript.

※ *Chapter 1*

Introduction

In *Criminal Victimization in Eight American Cities: A Descriptive Analysis of Common Theft and Assault* (Hindelang, 1976), the history and development of victimization surveying and a description of the results of the 1972 surveys conducted in the "eight Impact Cities"[1] were presented in detail. This volume builds upon that earlier work, which should be consulted by those interested in the development of the National Crime Survey (NCS) victimization studies or a detailed presentation of the survey results in the eight Impact Cities. This chapter, which draws heavily from the earlier volume, will briefly highlight the development of victimization surveying and some substantive results that are useful and necessary for examining the findings presented in this book.

In the United States, crime statistics have historically been generated as a by-product of administrative data collected by operational criminal justice agencies, primarily the police. Only recently have attempts been made, through victimization surveys, to generate, independently of operating criminal justice agencies, statistics about the nature and extent of crime. In some very fundamental respects, victimization surveys differ from police statistics. In data collection programs like the FBI's Uniform Crime Reporting program, an attempt is made to collect a limited number of data elements about all crimes of interest that are known by the police to have occurred. Because the volume of crimes is so large and because the voluntary cooperation of so many police departments is required, it is not feasible to collect more than a very few data

1

elements about each event. In addition, again because of the volume of crimes, the data are collected in summary "tally" form. In victimization surveys on the other hand, extensive information is collected about each victimization. This is possible because victimization surveys involve an important tradeoff: rather than attempting to collect a few basic elements about all victimizations, a wide variety of data elements about a *representative sample* of victimizations is collected.

In victimization surveys, representative samples of the general population are asked to report to survey interviewers any crimes that they have suffered during the reference period, typically the six- or twelve-month period preceding the interview. The first nationwide victimization surveys in the United States were sponsored by the President's Commission on Law Enforcement and Administration of Justice (Biderman, Johnson, McIntyre, and Weir, 1967; Reiss, 1967; Ennis, 1967). Of the three victimization surveys sponsored by the President's Commission, the most widely known is the national survey conducted by the National Opinion Research Center (Ennis, 1967). In this survey, interviews were conducted in 10,000 households (containing 33,000 eligible persons) in the continental United States. In each household, a knowledgeable household respondent was asked a series of short "screen" questions[2] about victimizations that might have been suffered by any member of the household. When a household respondent reported that any household member had been a victim of one of the included crimes, the victim was personally interviewed. This national study indicated that the estimated rate of victimization for index crimes was more than twice the rate indicated by the *Uniform Crime Reports.* Despite this, the 33,000 respondents included in the sample reported to survey interviewers only fourteen rape incidents and thirty-one robbery incidents. Thus, serious crimes —even when measured by victimization surveys—are statistically rare phenomena. This statistical rarity of serious criminal victimizations has three crucial and interrelated implications. First, in order to generate reliable estimates of serious criminal victimizations, it is necessary to use massive samples of respondents. Second, these large sample requirements have the effect of making such surveys very expensive. Third, the large sample size requirement and the concomitant expense mean that it is simply not feasible to use victimization surveys to make estimates either for small areas (e.g., groups of census tracts) or at frequent intervals. In light of these constraints, it is apparent that victimization surveys will not displace police statistics. They are simply too costly for that. Yet victimization survey results can provide critical information about victimization experiences and risks of victimization that is nowhere else available.

The NCS instruments, design, and procedures currently in use evolved through a series of pilot studies undertaken during the early 1970s (U.S. Bureau of the Census, 1970a, 1970b, undated; LEAA, 1972, 1974, undated).[3] The pilot studies investigated the nature and extent of memory decay (including the failure of respondents to mention victimizations to survey interviewers), forward telescoping (the tendency of respondents to report events as occurring more recently than they actually occurred), as well as questionnaire wording and survey procedures. Among the survey procedures studied were whether each eligible household member must be personally interviewed (the self-respondent method) or whether a knowledgeable household member could sufficiently answer screen questions for all eligible household members (the household-respondent method); whether respondents could be asked screen questions by mail; and what constituted the optimal reference period length. The NCS instruments and procedures were developed on the basis of these pilot results.

A detailed description of the LEAA–Bureau of the Census National Crime Survey methods and procedures used to collect the data reported in the following chapters is presented in Appendix B. Most of the results reported herein are from interviews conducted in Atlanta, Baltimore, Cleveland, Dallas, Denver, Newark, Portland (Oregon), and St. Louis during 1972. In each of these cities, representative samples of about 22,000 persons were interviewed about victimizations that they may have suffered within the twelve months preceding the interview. The crimes that fell within the scope of the survey are rape, robbery, assault, larceny from the person, burglary, household larceny, and motor vehicle theft. In this book the focus will be almost exclusively on personal victimizations.

HIGHLIGHTS OF VARIATION IN RATES OF PERSONAL VICTIMIZATION

When our analytic work first began, we expected to find substantial variation from city to city in personal characteristics associated with risks of criminal victimization and in characteristics of criminal incidents. We were surprised to find that personal characteristics associated with risks of victimization were rather stable across cities. For example, in all of the cities in which surveys have been done, younger persons had much greater rates of personal victimization than did older persons; similarly, males had higher rates than did females, and single persons had higher rates than married persons. Although it is true that *levels* of victimization showed considerable heterogeneity across cities, the patterns of association between victimization and most demographic characteristics were strikingly similar regardless of the individual city examined. This was not only true for personal characteristics that are associated with risks of victimization, but also for many characteristics of the incidents themselves—the extent of reporting to the police, the nature and extent of physical injury and financial loss, and so on—particularly when the focus is on the correlates of these characteristics.

In this book, the emphasis is on *patterns* of risk factors associated with criminal victimization and on correlates of characteristics of criminal incidents rather than on absolute *levels* of victimization. Because we found that most of the phenomena of immediate interest showed similar *patterns* across the eight cities, we have aggregated these data. As a practical matter, most of the analyses undertaken herein could not have been executed reliably on a city-by-city basis; the phenomena of interest are simply too rare for that luxury. On an empirical basis, the aggregation of data across cities is warranted because of the similarity in patterns of relationships across cities.[4]

Because this volume builds upon substantive findings reported in an earlier work (Hindelang, 1976), it will be useful to highlight some of the major results of that research. Throughout, rates of victimization will be reported per 1,000 persons twelve years of age or older, unless otherwise noted. The survey results indicate that rates of victimization are closely linked to the characteristics of victims—especially to age, sex, marital status, family income, and race. Personal victimizations are those suffered by individual victims who, at least in some sense, come into contact with the offender. Personal victimizations include crimes that threaten or actually result in personal injury to the victim[5] (such as assault), crimes in which an offender confronts the victim and takes or attempts to take property from the victim's possession by force or threat of force, and crimes in which property is taken (including attempts) from the victim's person by stealth (such as pocket picking).

In the earlier work, personal victimizations were analyzed using a threefold classification scheme for personal victimization. The first category, "assaultive violence without theft," includes assaults and rapes in which property theft was not attempted or completed. "Personal theft without injury" includes robberies without injury to the victim and larcenies from the person, such as pocket picking and purse snatching without force. "Assaultive violence with theft" includes robberies with injury and rape with theft or attempted theft.[6]

Family Income and Race
In general, it was found that for both whites and black/others,[7] rates of personal victimization decreased as family income increased. Among whites, the rate of total personal victimization decreased from a high of 83 in the under $3,000 category to 51 in the $7,500 to $9,999 category but then *increased* to 59 in the $10,000 to $14,999 category, finally decreasing gradually to 51 in the $25,000 or more category. Among black/others, the rate of total personal victimization decreased steadily from 72 in the under $3,000 category to 49 in the $15,000 to $24,999 category, before rising sharply to 64 in the $25,000 or more category (Hindelang, 1976: Table 5-6).[8] Despite this up-swing in the total personal victimization rate at the highest income level of the black/others, the generally decreasing pattern in the total personal victimization rate for black/others is more consistent than is the pattern for whites.

The rate of assaultive violence without theft for whites was about one and one-half times greater than for black/others, while for personal theft without injury the rate for black/others was about one and one-half times greater than the rate for whites. These differences maintained with about the same strength even when income was controlled.[9] Furthermore, rates of assaultive violence with theft were higher for black/others than for whites, a relationship that generally held across income categories (Hindelang, 1976: Table 5-6).

In sum, within each racial group, the rate of personal victimization involving theft generally decreased as income increased—except that the rate for black/others in the highest income group showed an upturn. For personal theft without injury in particular, black/others had higher rates than whites in each income group; in fact, black/others in the higher income groups endured personal theft without injury at rates comparable to those endured by whites in the lower income groups. On the other hand, rates of assaultive victimization not involving theft were higher for whites than black/others in each income category, and for both whites and black/others, rates of assaultive violence without theft showed a U-shaped pattern: the rate in the $7,500 to $9,999 income group was the lowest and the rates at the income extremes were higher.

Age

Age was strongly associated with personal victimization. As Table 1-1 shows, total personal victimization peaked in the sixteen to nineteen year old age group and declined monotonically as age increased beyond that point. The table reveals, however, that the pattern for total personal victimizations is determined almost wholly by the pattern for assaultive violence without theft; although the rate of assaultive violence without theft for those in the sixteen to nineteen year old group was 76 per 1,000, the rate in the sixty-five or older group was only 6 per 1,000. It might be argued that this gulf between victimization rates for the age extremes reflects, in part, the relatively minor altercations that are common among adolescents. However, because the assaultive violence without theft victimization rate in the twenty-five to thirty-four year old group, an age group well beyond adolescence, was *three* times greater than that in the fifty to sixty-four year old group and *six* times greater than that in the sixty-five or older group, more than simple "schoolyard" fights account for the generally decreasing rates of assaultive violence without theft as age increased.

For those under thirty-five years of age, theft without injury showed a pattern similar to, though much less exaggerated than, that of assaultive violence without theft. The rate of victimization for theft without injury increased slightly from the twelve to fifteen year old to the sixteen to nineteen year old groups and then decreased gradually with age for the next two age groups before leveling off. Assaultive violence with theft shows a similar general pattern; the rate of assaultive violence with theft victimization was about one and one-half times as great in the twenty to twenty-four age group as in the sixty-five or older group.

Table 1-1 shows not only that *rates* but also that the *patterns* of personal victimization are strongly related to age. For the four age groups made up by those less than thirty-five years old, assaultive violence without theft was the modal personal victimization suffered; about six out of ten victimizations involved assaultive violence without theft. For those in the thirty-five to forty-nine, fifty to sixty-four, and sixty-five or older age groups the respective percentages of total personal victimizations that involved assaultive violence without theft were 40 percent, 30 percent, and 20 percent. Although assaultive violence with theft made up a slightly greater percentage of total personal victimizations in the older age groups than in the younger age groups, theft without assault constituted a *markedly* higher proportion of total victimizations in the three older age groups (from about one-half to two-thirds) than in the four younger

Table 1-1. Estimated Rates (per 1,000 Persons) and Percentage Distribution of Personal Victimization, by Age of Victim and Type of Victimization, Eight-City Aggregate, 1972[a]

| | Age of Victim | | | | | | | |
	12-15	16-19	20-24	25-34	35-49	50-64	65 or Older	Total
Population base	351,168	330,848	399,377	573,416	685,542	668,817	471,280	3,480,445
Assaultive violence with theft	8%[b]	7%	7%	8%	13%	16%	14%	10%
	[7][c]	[8]	[6]	[5]	[6]	[6]	[4]	[6]
	(2,503)[d]	(2,729)	(2,324)	(2,866)	(4,033)	(4,089)	(1,951)	(20,494)
without theft	62%	67%	67%	59%	40%	30%	20%	53%
	[54]	[76]	[58]	[37]	[18]	[11]	[6]	[32]
	(18,803)	(25,228)	(23,235)	(20,969)	(12,475)	(7,641)	(2,777)	(111,127)
Personal theft without injury	30%	26%	27%	33%	47%	54%	65%	37%
	[26]	[29]	[23]	[20]	[21]	[21]	[19]	[22]
	(9,264)	(9,716)	(9,342)	(11,483)	(14,368)	(13,953)	(8,970)	(77,098)
Total personal victimization	100%	100%	100%	100%	100%	100%	100%	100%
	[87]	[114]	[87]	[62]	[45]	[38]	[29]	[60]
	(30,569)	(37,673)	(34,901)	(35,318)	(30,875)	(25,684)	(13,699)	(208,718)

[a]Subcategories may not sum to total because of rounding.
[b]Column percent.
[c]Rates appear in brackets.
[d]Numbers in parentheses are number of victimizations.

Source: Michael J. Hindelang, *Criminal Victimization in Eight American Cities: A Descriptive Analysis of Common Theft and Assault* (Cambridge, Mass.: Ballinger Publishing Co., 1976), p. 113. Reprinted by permission.

age groups (from about one-quarter to one-third). These data suggest, then, that for persons thirty-five years or older, personal victimization tends to be directed against the victim's property rather than the victim's person. In personal victimizations involving persons under thirty-five years of age, assaultive violence was much more likely to be an element of the victimization than it was for the personal victimization of older persons.

Sex and Marital Status

Males in both racial groups had rates of personal victimization that were substantially greater than those of their female counterparts. Among whites, for example, the rate for males was 77 compared with a rate of 45 for females; among black/others the respective rates were 74 and 51. In general, these race-specific sex differences held for each age group except that the magnitude of the sex difference decreased with age (Hindelang, 1976: Table 5-5).

Marital status was strongly related to rates of personal victimization. Persons who were never married (90) or who were divorced or separated (90) had total personal victimization rates that were more than twice the rates found for those who were married (39) or widowed (42). These differences persisted across subcategories of total personal victimization with varying degrees of intensity. Under assaultive violence without theft, for example, those who were never married had a rate that was more than two and one-half times that found for those who were married (54 versus 20), whereas for personal theft without injury the rate for those who were never married was slightly less than twice as great as the rate for those who were married (28 versus 15). Further, when the age of the victim was controlled, these differences in victimization rates among the various categories of marital status continued to hold (Hindelang, 1976: Table 5-7).

SERIOUSNESS-WEIGHTED RATES

One limitation of examining rates of victimization in this fashion is that each victimization reported to survey interviewers is given equal weight; a minor assault and a serious assault both contribute equally to the total personal victimization rate. In order to avoid this shortcoming of using raw rates of total personal victimization, the Sellin-Wolfgang (1964) seriousness-weighting scheme was used to calculate seriousness-weighted rates of total personal victimization. Sellin and Wolfgang have developed a scaling technique designed to provide a composite seriousness score for delinquency incidents.

Their seriousness scoring system takes into account: (1) the number of victims of bodily harm and the extent to which they are injured; (2) the number of victims of forcible sexual intercourse; (3) the number of victims intimidated verbally or with a weapon; (4) the number of premises unlawfully entered; (5) the number of motor vehicles stolen; and (6) the value of property stolen, damaged, or destroyed (1964: Appendix F). Each of these elements is weighted according to the nature and the extent of the injury or loss involved. For example, if a victim receives minor injuries requiring no professional medical attention, the seriousness score is one. If the victim is treated and discharged, the seriousness weight is four, and if the victim is hospitalized, the weight is seven. In the event that the victim dies, the seriousness weight is twenty-six. Similarly, seriousness weights are attached to the value of properly lost; these weights range from one for losses of less than $10, to three for losses of $251–$2,000, to seven for losses in excess of $80,000.

Under the Sellin-Wolfgang scheme, each element is scored; therefore, if a rape also involves injuries requiring hospitalization and a theft of property, the seriousness score of each element is cumulated. Further, because the Sellin-Wolfgang procedure is designed to gauge the seriousness of *incidents*, the injuries and losses suffered by each victim in a given incident are summed to yield an incident score. In our application of their method, only the consequences suffered by the victim interviewed were scored, and that score was not dependent on the number of co-victims (if any). Thus, the seriousness-weighted rates (per 1,000 persons twelve years old or older) of total personal victimization were computed by summing (across victims) the seriousness score for each victimization reported, times 1,000, divided by the number of persons at risk. A comparable procedure has been illustrated by Sellin and Wolfgang (1964: Table 70) and used by Wolfgang, Figlio, and Sellin (1972: Table 5-5). The result of using this procedure is that victimizations are differentially weighted according to their estimated seriousness.

Table 1-2 shows seriousness-weighted rates of total personal victimization by age, race, and sex. As earlier results foreshadowed, the seriousness-weighted rates of total personal victimization are closely linked to age. Within each of the four race-sex groups, the rate increased from the youngest to the sixteen to nineteen age group and then declined monotonically for each age group thereafter.[10] This table shows that males had a higher seriousness-weighted rate than females; for most age groups the ratio of the male to the female rates was about 2:1 for whites and about 3:2 for black/others. Finally, Table 1-2 indicates that for both males and females

Table 1-2. Estimated Seriousness-Weighted Rates (per 1,000 Persons) of Total Personal Victimization, by Age, Sex, and Race of Victim, Eight-City Aggregate, 1972[a]

| | Age of Victim | | | | | | | |
	12-15	16-19	20-24	25-34	35-49	50-64	65 or Older	Total
Male:								
White	348 (90,859)[b]	506 (89,350)	380 (119,531)	245 (180,130)	182 (199,051)	144 (215,022)	98 (139,549)	239 (1,033,492)
Black/other	253 (85,004)	435 (67,426)	386 (59,003)	314 (84,143)	271 (107,122)	229 (80,965)	130 (43,413)	291 (527,076)
Female:								
White	185 (89,638)	251 (98,258)	195 (135,880)	140 (183,040)	88 (226,441)	75 (268,414)	66 (229,664)	121 (1,231,332)
Black/other	135 (85,667)	209 (75,813)	244 (84,961)	183 (126,104)	169 (152,929)	134 (104,416)	93 (58,654)	169 (688,547)

aSubcategories may not sum to total because of rounding.
bNumbers in parentheses are the population bases on which the rates were computed.
Source: Michael J. Hindelang, Criminal Victimization in Eight American Cities: A Descriptive Analysis of Common Theft and Assault (Cambridge, Mass.: Ballinger Publishing Co., 1976), p. 144. Reprinted by permission.

under twenty years of age the rate for whites exceeded that for black/others; however, for those twenty years of age or older this pattern is reversed.

In Table 1-3, seriousness-weighted rates of total personal victimization are shown by family income and race. The data in this table indicate that the seriousness-weighted rates of total personal victimization for black/others exceeded those for whites in each income group. Overall, the rate for the former was about one-quarter again as great as that for the latter. Within each racial group, the trend was for the seriousness-weighted rate of total personal victimization to decrease as income increased. One notable finding in Table 1-3 is that the rate for black/others in the $25,000 or more income category showed a marked upturn to 209 after having declined monotonically from 268 in the lowest income category to 165 in the second highest income category. As noted earlier, however, only 1 percent of the black/others are found in the highest income group.

What happens to the race and income findings when age is controlled? Table 1-4 shows the joint effects of income, age, and race. For each of the three groups, within both races, there was a generally decreasing seriousness-weighted rate of victimization as income increased, except that the highest income group tended to show an upswing in the rate. One exception to the inverse relationship between income and seriousness-weighted rates of personal victimization is that black/others in the youngest age group showed a U-shaped pattern of victimization such that those in the extreme income groups had the highest seriousness-weighted rates of personal victimization. Once again, the small number of black/others in the highest income group should be noted.

The familiar inverse relationship between age and victimization held when income and race were controlled. Table 1-4 further suggests that, when income is controlled, whether whites or black/others had higher seriousness-weighted rates of total personal victimization is dependent on age. Among twelve to nineteen year old respondents, whites in each income category except the $25,000 or more had higher rates than black/others. For respondents who were twenty to thirty-four years of age, the racial differences were small; only for those with incomes between $7,500 and $9,999, where the rate for black/others was higher, was there a large difference. Finally, for respondents who were thirty-five years of age or older, black/others in each income category had seriousness-weighted rates of victimization that were greater than those of whites. This table emphasizes that, even when income is controlled, racial differences are age-contingent.

Table 1-3.   Estimated Seriousness-Weighted Rates (per 1,000 Persons Twelve Years of Age or Older) of Total Personal Victimization, by Family Income and Race of Victim, Eight-City Aggregate, 1972[a]

	Family Income[b]							
	Under $3,000	$3,000–7,499	$7,500–9,999	$10,000–14,999	$15,000–24,999	$25,000 or more	Not Ascertained	Total
Race:								
White	246 (236,811)[c]	202 (541,595)	153 (289,221)	168 (530,967)	143 (318,075)	134 (120,158)	147 (227,997)	175 (2,264,824)
Black/other	268 (223,422)	237 (446,319)	197 (146,322)	182 (179,837)	165 (83,082)	209 (11,996)	210 (124,648)	222 (1,215,625)

[a]Subcategories may not sum to total because of rounding.

[b]Family income during previous twelve months was defined as all money income of the household head plus that of all household members twelve years of age or older at the time of the interview.

[c]Numbers in parentheses are the bases on which the rates were computed.

Source: Michael J. Hindelang, *Criminal Victimization in Eight American Cities: A Descriptive Analysis of Common Theft and Assault* (Cambridge, Mass.: Ballinger Publishing Co., 1976), p. 145. Reprinted by permission.

Table 1-4. Estimated Seriousness-Weighted Rates (per 1,000 Persons) of Total Personal Victimization, by Family Income, Age, and Race of Victim, Eight-City Aggregate, 1972[a]

	Family Income[b]							
	Under $3,000	$3,000–7,499	$7,500–9,999	$10,000–14,999	$15,000–24,999	$25,000 or More	Not Ascertained	Total
Age:								
12–19								
White	458 (32,096)[c]	375 (75,916)	248 (42,850)	335 (96,416)	265 (61,791)	283 (24,658)	252 (34,371)	321 (368,097)
Black/other	268 (56,046)	261 (127,223)	215 (35,882)	242 (42,797)	256 (18,199)	431 (2,099)	200 (31,661)	249 (313,906)
20–34								
White	359 (46,165)	291 (149,865)	189 (101,025)	188 (168,155)	182 (85,070)	219 (22,820)	227 (45,474)	229 (618,574)
Black/other	366 (51,350)	283 (128,696)	237 (48,151)	181 (61,683)	204 (28,353)	243 (3,694)	261 (32,280)	262 (354,207)
35 or older								
White	170 (158,542)	118 (315,803)	99 (145,342)	95 (266,389)	79 (171,213)	57 (72,682)	99 (148,150)	107 (1,278,121)
Black/other	224 (116,020)	190 (190,393)	157 (62,285)	149 (75,354)	89 (36,528)	114 (6,201)	187 (60,704)	180 (547,486)

[a] Subcategories may not sum to total because of rounding.
[b] Family income during previous twelve months was defined as all money income of the household head plus that of all household members twelve years of age or older at the time of the interview.
[c] Numbers in parentheses are the bases on which the rates were computed.

Source: Michael J. Hindelang, *Criminal Victimization in Eight American Cities: A Descriptive Analysis of Common Theft and Assault* (Cambridge, Mass.: Ballinger Publishing Co., 1976), p. 147. Reprinted by permission.

The seriousness-weighted rates of total personal victimization by marital status and age in Table 1-5 are striking for their consistency. Almost without exception, there was a substantial decline in the seriousness-weighted rate of total personal victimization as age increased for each of the marital status groups. Further, generally in each age group except the youngest, those who were divorced or separated had the highest seriousness-weighted rate, followed in turn by those who were never married, those who were widowed, and finally, by those who were married.

It is clear that rates of personal victimization are associated with characteristics of victims. Although some of these characteristics have been examined jointly in relation to rates of victimization, the polychotomous nature of many of these victim characteristics, in conjunction with the relative rarity of victimization, puts stringent limitations on the extent to which conventional tabular analysis can be useful in disentangling the effects of these interrelated independent variables. In later sections of this book we undertake multivariate analyses of victimization risks as they are associated with configurations of personal characteristics of respondents. First, however, it will be instructive to give close attention to the dependent variable itself. Specifically, it is necessary to explore the nature of victimizations reported by the respondents to the interviewers.

NOTES

1. These cities (Atlanta, Baltimore, Cleveland, Dallas, Denver, Newark, Portland, (Oregon), and St. Louis) participated in the Law Enforcement Assistance Administration's high-impact crime reduction program. In this program about $20 million was allocated to each of the cities in an attempt to reduce burglary and stranger-to-stranger homicide, rape, and robbery.

2. Screen questions are a series of short questions asking respondents whether they have been victims of any of the crimes on which the survey focuses. See Appendix A.

3. Also see a discussion of the Quarterly Household Survey, Victim Supplement, in Dodge and Turner (1971).

4. One exception to the cross-city similarity of personal characteristics associated with victimization risks is the race of the victim. See Hindelang (1976:114-16).

5. Specifically excluded is murder.

6. See Hindelang (1976: ch. 4) for further details.

7. Black/others is a designation used to encompass blacks and persons of other races. About 90 percent of the persons in this group are black, and hence persons of "other" races are too few to analyze separately. According to Bureau of the Census conventions, persons of Spanish heritage are counted as white.

8. It should be noted that a relatively small proportion (1 percent) of

Table 1-5. Estimated Seriousness-Weighted Rates (per 1,000 Persons) of Total Personal Victimization, by Marital Status and Age of Victim, Eight-City Aggregate, 1972[a]

| Age: | Marital Status of Victim | | | | | |
	Never Married	Married	Divorced or Separated	Widowed	Not Ascertained	Total
12-19	287 (639,712)[b]	326 (31,443)	326 (3,793)	125 (1,667)	186 (5,403)	288 (682,016)
20-34	284 (300,076)	185 (551,195)	414 (106,871)	229 (9,050)	208 (5,604)	241 (972,793)
35-49	200 (54,191)	123 (491,958)	304 (108,887)	208 (27,683)	323 (2,926)	162 (685,542)
50-64	200 (45,866)	88 (457,460)	236 (71,722)	181 (91,591)	267 (2,177)	125 (668,817)
65 or older	129 (34,306)	61 (217,402)	214 (24,297)	87 (193,071)	103 (2,205)	85 (471,280)

[a]Subcategories may not sum to total because of rounding.
[b]Numbers in parentheses are the bases on which the rates were computed.
Source: Michael J. Hindelang, Criminal Victimization in Eight American Cities: A Descriptive Analysis of Common Theft and Assault (Cambridge, Mass.: Ballinger Publishing Co., 1976), p. 148. Reprinted by permission.

black/others had incomes in excess of $25,000; the reliability of the estimated rate for this group is less than that of other rates reported.

9. The only reversal was for personal theft without injury in the under $3,000 category, in which the rate for black/others was only slightly larger than the rate for whites (35 versus 31).

10. For the black/other females, the peak is in the twenty to twenty-four year old group.

The Victimization Event

We begin our detailed analyses with a study of the correlates and consequences of personal victimization. Before
analyzing in detail the probabilities of personal victimization, it is informative to study the dependent variable—personal
victimization. Part I is primarily concerned with an exploration of
the victimization event.

An adequate understanding of victimization experiences requires
an analytic strategy that can uncover the significant patterns in
these complex data. The traditional approach is to study the correlates of *legalistically* categorized events. For reasons outlined in
Chapter 2, we find this approach to be problematic and instead
adopt what is termed a "classification approach" to the study of
victimization. Some of the logic and rationale for this approach, as
well as the statistical technique that will be used, are discussed in
Chapter 2. Additionally, Chapter 2 describes our decision to focus
this portion of our inquiry on observable harm to the victims of
personal crimes.

The remaining chapters in Part I analyze harm to the victim—
defined as bodily injury and property loss—in some depth. The
classification approach to studying these harms follows a descriptive analysis of the incident characteristics related to an outcome of
either injury (in Chapter 3) or the loss of property (in Chapter 4).

Chapter 2

A Classification Approach to the Analysis of Victimization

CLASSIFICATION AS AN ANALYTIC STRATEGY

One unique feature of the National Crime Survey victimization data is that a number of standard and specific elements are collected about each event reported to the interviewer. These data elements can be studied in their raw uncategorized form. Rather than necessarily studying the correlates of victimization categorized by offense type, the researcher may variously define subsets of events (e.g., bodily injury) that are worthy of study, regardless of the legal categories into which they fall.

In American criminological research, a classification of events, such as that used in the *Uniform Crime Reports*, is usually taken for granted, with research preceding from that point. Thus, the crimes of robbery (Conklin, 1972; Normandeau, 1968), rape (Amir, 1971; MacDonald, 1971), homicide (Wolfgang, 1958; Pokorny, 1965), and aggravated assault (Pittman and Handy, 1964; Pokorny, 1965) have all served as the basis for investigation. Rather than studying specific crimes, however, a useful research strategy would be to use the process of classification, which simply means to group crimes on the basis of similarities and differences, as a mechanism by which criminal events may profitably be explored. By searching for components that are common across events we may be led to hypotheses concerning why regularities occur. On the other hand, if we base our research only on a preexisting legal classification scheme, we may limit the potential of these data for uncovering important aspects of criminal victimization.

These concerns suggest that before we launch into a data analysis effort, it may be important to give some attention to the ways we typically organize crimes for study. We should critically examine existing systems to see whether they pose impediments to a broader understanding of the correlates of criminal victimization. Because the way we organize events so substantially influences what we may discover about them and because the NCS provides us with fairly refined data elements that are uncategorized, we should explore some of the logic and method of classification, the use of which has led to important work in many areas of science. We can start this inquiry with a brief look at the basis of the *Uniform Crime Reports*, the most common crime classification system in use today.

The Uniform Crime Reports—A Legalistic Classification System

In 1974, the *Uniform Crime Reporting Handbook* (Kelley, 1974b: 14), defined robbery as "the taking or attempting to take something of value from the care, custody, or control of a person or persons by force or threat of force or violence and/or putting the victim in fear." Nearly two hundred years earlier, in his *Commentaries on the Laws of England*, Blackstone (1778:188-243) defined robbery as "the felonious and forcible taking, from the person of another, of goods or money to any value, by violence or putting him in fear." Such parallels between modern definitions of offenses and those found in older texts are unmistakable; for example, the *Uniform Crime Reports* (1974b:6-30) definition of rape is "the carnal knowledge of a female, forcibly and against her will," while Blackstone's reads "the carnal knowledge of a woman forcibly and against her will"; the *Uniform Crime Reports* definition of burglary is "the unlawful entry of a structure to commit a felony or a theft," while in his *Pleas of the Crown* (1678:79), Sir Matthew Hale stated the common law definition of burglary as "where a person in the night-time breaketh and entreth into the Mansion-House of another, to the intent to commit some felony within the same, whether the felonies intent be executed or not." Clearly, although there are certainly differences between historical and modern offense classification systems, there are striking similarities as well. The questions arise, then, as to why these specific categories of behavior came to be defined as they are, and why they remain as the central organizational format for the modern systems that have served as the basis for so much recent research.

One of the earliest and most fundamental classifications of offenses was based on the distinction between felonies and misdemeanors (Stephen, 1883). Although the precise origins of the classification are disputed, Pollock and Maitland (1898:465) trace the origin of felony to around the year 1200, where it derived from the Latin *fell-, fel*, "the original sense being one who is full of bitterness or venom. When the adjective *felon* first appears it seems to mean cruel, fierce, wicked, base." However, an exact definition of what constituted a felony at common law was never given; "one could do no more than enumerate the felonies" (Pollock and Maitland, 1898: 466). At common law, those crimes that were not felonies (or treason) were misdemeanors (Clark and Marshall, 1967). Although "felony" could not be defined precisely, it seems clear that a major classificatory distinction between the felonies and misdemeanors was indicated by the nature of the punishment prescribed for the offense:

> . . . if we place ourselves in the first years of the thirteenth century some broad statements seem possible. (i) a felony is a crime which can be prosecuted by an appeal, that is to say, by an accusation in which the accuser must as a general rule offer battle. (ii) the felon's lands go to his lord or to the king and his chattels are confiscated. (iii) if a man accused of felony flies, he can be outlawed. (Pollock and Maitland, 1898:466)

Within the broad common law distinction of felony, a number of subcategories of offensive behavior were defined, most of which closely parallel those used in the classification systems employed today by social scientists. In general, the common law provided a number of definitions and general principles that were followed throughout the lengthy transformation from common law to statutory law. Where modifications or additions were made, it was almost exclusively that some factor aggravated or mitigated the common law definition, and therefore an alternative punishment was deemed appropriate (Clark and Marshall, 1967).

The number of felonious offenses increased constantly from the earliest records onward. According to Stephen (1883:197–206), Glanville (circa 1187) discussed five felonies—concealment of treasure trove, homicide, arson, robbery, and rape—while Bracton (circa 1250) specified eleven felonies—adding such crimes as mayhem, false imprisonment, and theft. By Blackstone's time (1778) the number of felonies had increased to 160 (Stephen, 1883). Although some modifications of the definitions have naturally occurred between 1778 and 1974, Table 2-1, which places Blackstone's definitions in juxtaposition to the index crimes described by the *Uniform Crime Reports*, demonstrates substantial comparability. There were, of course, a number of felonies defined at common law that have now disappeared or have been incorporated into more general statutory categories. Perhaps a prime example is the category "mayhem," defined by Blackstone (1778:205) as "the violently depriving another of the use of such of his members as may render him the less able in fighting, either to defend himself, or to annoy his adversary." And, naturally, new categories of criminal offenses that were not found in common law, such as motor vehicle theft, have emerged as society has changed technologically.

Table 2-1. Definitions of Selected Crimes in the FBI's *Uniform Crime Reports* and Blackstone's *Commentaries*

Uniform Crime Reports	Blackstone
Criminal Homicide (pp. 6–9) 1. Murder and nonnegligent manslaughter: The willful (nonnegligent) killing of one human being by another.	*Felonious Homicide* (pp. 188–90) 1. Murder: Whenever a person, of sound memory and discretion, unlawfully killeth any reasonable creature in being, and under the king's peace, with malice aforethought, either express or implied.
2. Manslaughter by negligence: The killing of another person through gross negligence.	2. Manslaughter: The unlawful killing of another without malice either express or implied.
Forcible Rape (p. 12) The carnal knowledge of a female forcibly and against her will.	*Rape* (p. 209) The carnal knowledge of a woman forcibly and against her will.
Robbery (p. 14) The taking or attempting to take anything of value from the care, custody, or control of a person or persons by force or threat of force or violence and/or by putting the victim in fear.	*Robbery* (p. 243) The felonious and forcible taking from the person of another, of goods or money to any value, by violence or putting him in fear.
Aggravated Assault (p. 18) An unlawful attack by one person upon another for the purpose of inflicting severe or aggravated bodily injury. This type of assault usually is accompanied by the use of a weapon or by means likely to produce death or great bodily harm.	*Assault*[a] An attempt to offer, with force and violence, to do a corporal hurt to another.

Table 2-1 continued

Uniform Crime Reports	*Blackstone*
Burglary (p. 22) The unlawful entry of a structure to commit a felony or a theft.	*Burglary* (p. 218) He that by night breaketh and entereth into a mansion-house, with intent to commit a felony.
Larceny (p. 26) The unlawful taking, carrying, leading, or riding away of property from the possession or constructive possession of another.	*Larceny* (p. 229) The felonious taking and carrying away of the personal goods of another.
Motor Vehicle Theft (p. 30) The theft or attempted theft of a motor vehicle.	

[a] Assault was not a felony at common law and no distinction was drawn between aggravated and simple assault, although Clark and Marshall (1927:719) note that the former was punished more severely.

Source: U.S. Department of Justice, Federal Bureau of Investigation, *Uniform Crime Reporting Handbook* (Washington, D.C.: Government Printing Office, 1966); William Blackstone, *Commentaries on the Laws of England,* 8th ed. (Oxford: Clarendon Press, 1778).

The continuity in offense classifications from the early thirteenth century to modern times appears to stem from the functional necessity for criminal law to define broad and generic categories of human conduct so that the categories can incorporate continuously emerging forms of behavior. The great heterogeneity of criminal conduct and the almost endless variations in behavior are extremely difficult to specify completely. Legal classifications of offenses confront this issue by using broad categories of conduct that minimally specify the activities in the class.

The great diversity of conduct subsumed under legal categories has long been recognized; for example, Stephen (1883:195) wrote:

> there are many crimes which, from the nature of the case, must differ almost infinitely in the degree of guilt and danger which they involve. Burglary may be a trifling form of theft, as for instance, if a man opens the door of a back-kitchen of a house in a street in London at 9:30 P.M., and steals a loaf of bread without alarming anyone. It may be a crime of the greatest atrocity, as for instance, if armed men break into a lonely dwellinghouse in the country, rob the owners of all their property, and frighten and ill-use them. So robbery with violence may mean something close upon murder, or something hardly differing from a common assault.

Thus, because of the infinite number of possible combinations of illegal conduct and the requirement that a legally oriented classification system be able to incorporate it all, broad and somewhat ambiguous definitions of categories may be well-suited to legal purposes. It does not necessarily follow, however, that they suit the purposes of the criminologist equally well.

The Classification of Offenses for
Statistical Purposes

Because crime statistics arose as an adjunct to the administration of justice, the legal definitions of offenses first served as the basis for the classification of offenses in criminal statistics (Sellin and Wolfgang, 1964). The history of crime statistics shows that the systematic collection of crime statistics was undertaken primarily for the benefit of the legislature. One of the earliest proponents of the compilation of these data, Jeremy Bentham, recommended in 1778 that criminal courts be required to report statistics on convictions and that prisons be required to report statistics on prisoners:

> The ordering of these returns is a measure of excellent use in furnishing data for the legislature to work upon. They will form altogether a kind of *political barometer*, by which the effects of every legislative operation relative to the subject may be indicated and made palpable. It is not til lately that legislators have thought of providing themselves with these necessary documents. They may be compared with the bills of mortality published annually in London; indicating the moral health of the country (but a little more accurately it is hoped) as these latter do the physical.[1]

The early link between legislative purpose and the collection and classification of crime statistics was also evident in France, as reflected in the first annual report of criminal justice published in 1827. In the introduction to that series, Guerry de Champneuf wrote that these statistics would "assist in determining the circumstances which cooperate in increasing or diminishing the number of crimes."[2]

Thus, the collection and classification of data about crime were first initiated to serve a legislative function. Collecting information in legislatively prescribed classes of offenses was thought to serve the utilitarian function of determining how penalties set forth in legislation were reflected in the amounts and kinds of offensive behavior. The practice of collecting and classifying data about crime as a by-product of legislative and law enforcement operations has continued up to the present day.

Although some American states began systematically to collect information about crime in the 1800s, the first significant development in American statistics on criminal offenses came in 1930, when the International Association of Chiefs of Police devised and implemented a system of data collection and offense classification, *The Uniform Crime Reports* (UCR), that remains the offense classification system most often used in American criminological research. The primary purpose of the system, as expressed in the most recent manual of rules for classification, is that "the information collected under the UCR program should be a portion of the data a law enforcement agency compiles for its own effective and efficient operation" (Kelley, 1974b:1). Because current systems of offense classification have their origins in common law distinctions and because concern for the collection of data about crime stems from a legislatively linked purpose, it should not be surprising that the UCR classification of offenses currently in use may not be optimal for many of the research needs of the criminologist. Indeed, the criminological literature is replete with objections to using the *Uniform Crime Reports* classification of offenses for many research purposes. Because a substantial literature concerning the limitations of the UCR exists (see especially, Wolfgang, 1963; Robison, 1966; Doleschal and Wilkins, 1972), it is not necessary to explore these problems in depth here. Rather, the limitations of the classification approach used by the UCR for our present purposes may be briefly summarized: (1) it ignores a good deal of possibly relevant criminological information about offenses; (2) it utilizes broad legal labels that mask the variety of offenses within categories; (3) it includes attempted and completed offenses in many classes; (4) it fails to distinguish multiple events; (5) it fails to distinguish adequately between amounts of property loss and destruction; (6) it inhibits analysis of amounts and types of violence and personal harm involved; and (7) it allows for numerous types of classification errors.

Although the shortcomings of statutory type offense classifications have been noted by criminologists for quite some time, there have been remarkably few attempts to classify criminal behavior into more meaningful categories for research purposes. A major exception to this generalization is the research carried out by Sellin and Wolfgang (1964) in *The Measurement of Delinquency* as part of their research into quantifying the seriousness of delinquent behavior. Sellin and Wolfgang presented descriptions of events to groups of students, police, and judges and asked them to rate the offenses in terms of their seriousness according to magnitude estimation procedures. The derived scale scores were then used as weights to be applied in the construction of an index. The Sellin-Wolfgang seriousness scale is an alternative method of classifying offenses (e.g., by seriousness) for research purposes, a method that is not based on a legal classification of the criminal event.

With the exception of the Sellin-Wolfgang work, relatively little research attention has focused on the elements of criminal events independent of legal classifications of such events. For example, although several researchers have studied personal injury in the crime of robbery (Normandeau, 1968; Conklin, 1972), virtually none has studied personal injury irrespective of the crime in conjunction with which it occurs. It therefore would appear desirable to focus on the *elements* of criminal victimization. One way that this may be facilitated is *via* numerical classification techniques.

The Aims of the Classification Method

There are numerous purposes for embarking on a classification analysis (see Sneath and Sokal, 1973; Sokal, 1974). One major aim of numerical classification techniques is the exploration and reduction of data. Put another way, a major goal of most classification efforts is the achievement of economy of memory. In one sense, all entities are unique: no two people are alike in all respects, no two crimes are exactly similar, no two criminologists hold exactly similar views. Yet, despite these individual differences, persons, crimes, and criminologists may be grouped together such that a description of the taxon to which each has been assigned is, in a way, a description of each of the individual entities: "to classify an individual and then to describe the class to which he had been assigned is to some extent to describe that individual" (Macnaughton-Smith, 1965).

An economy of memory is served if we may refer to a group of individuals as "criminologists" and spare ourselves from considering a vast series of ideas about subject matter, type of science, research methods, principal areas of interest, and so forth. Of course, a limitation of classification as a tool is immediately apparent; in the process of simplification, we trade off detail, information, and, to some, a respect for individual differences. A point to be stressed is that this tradeoff has two distinct components. There is simplification that is internal to the system, that is, among the classification variables. Thus, the wide variety of interests of "criminologists" and their particular research methods may be masked by our classification. We also simplify, however, by not considering individual variation on attributes not in our system. Thus, such attributes as sex, age, and weight may not be systematically taken into account in our classification of criminologists. It is essential, then, for the taxonomist to be constantly aware of the tradeoffs implicit in the classification method; by grouping together there is necessarily a reduction of some types of information. Additionally, the inevitably artificial boundaries of the taxa need to be kept clearly in mind. Without being more explicit, our classification of criminologists may not include such persons as police detectives, sociologists of deviance, or defense lawyers. Their inclusion would, of course, depend on our purpose apart from the economy of memory. It should be stressed, however, that without some form of information summary, our ability to operate in both the everyday and the scientific worlds would be greatly impaired. If, at the extreme, we treat every case as unique, we lose the ability to see patterns and to operate on general levels of abstraction.

Another purpose of classification, and one which is growing in use in criminological research, is prediction. There are two principal ways in which numerical classification techniques may be employed for a predictive purpose. The first, and in many respects preferable, technique is to form groups on the basis of the relations between characteristics of entities and the criterion to be predicted. The resulting classes may then be used to identify other entities not included in the original classification and to infer their scores on the criterion on the basis of group membership. The second method is to form a classification system without regard to a criterion, but rather solely on the basis of empirical similarities and differences on other variables. The resulting groups are then compared on the criterion, with the expectation that differences among the various taxa in classification attributes will be reflected in differences among them with respect to the criterion.

Although economy of memory and prediction may serve as the aim for classification, the general purpose of all analytical classifications, and the central purpose of our work here, is the generation of meaningful hypotheses. In fact, as Sokal (1974:1118) points out:

> the principal scientific justification for establishing classifications is that they are heuristic (in the traditional meaning of this term as "stimulating interest as a means of further investigation") and that they lead to the stating of a hypothesis which can then be tested. A classification raises the question of how the perceived order has arisen. . . .

A classification may be considered useful if it serves to generate hypotheses regarding the nature of relationships and to stimulate research designed to explicate the empirical patterning of entities.

CLASSIFICATION AND ANALYSIS OF OFFENSES—A FUNCTION-SPECIFIC APPROACH

In his critique of the reliance by criminologists on legal categories for research purposes, Sellin (1938:24) wrote that "the acceptance of specific forms of 'crime' and 'criminal' as laid down in law renders criminological research theoretically invalid from the point of view of science." The important question arises, then, as to how offenses should be classified—and illegal behavior and its effects should be analyzed—so as to enhance, as much as possible, criminological knowledge.

A number of criminologists have addressed the problem of exactly what the focus of offense classifications should be. In their study of delinquency measurement, Sellin and Wolfgang (1964:145) wrote that an offense classification "should function to give social relevance to the forms of delinquency, facilitate efficiency in statistical compilation, and promote an analytical theory that can be tied to empirical data." In accordance with these data, and as a result of their search for a sociological classification, Sellin and Wolfgang focused on the concept of harm to the victim in the form of physical injury, property loss, or property destruction.

There are advantages, both at the empirical and theoretical levels, in isolating *harm to the victim* for analytical explorations of these NCS data. By focusing on harm to the victim, attention is directed to elements of criminal events that are objectively observable. Physical injury and property loss can be both rigorously described and measured in a relatively consistent fashion. In addition, a specific analytic examination of harm to victims of crime would be expected to expand our substantive knowledge in the areas of personal injury and property loss. Because most criminological research has attended primarily to correlates of specific predefined legalistic categories of behavior such as rape, robbery, and assault, we have only narrow and unconnected knowledge concerning how characteristics of criminal events are related to the outcome of the incident. A careful examination of the correlates of personal injury and property loss and of the interrelationships among the correlates could add important knowledge about the nature of harm suffered by victims of crime. An important contribution of classificatory analysis should be a broadening of our substantive knowledge about the correlates of personal harm in criminal victimization.

A focus on personal harm in the form of physical injury and property loss raises the question as to whether a single analytic endeavor will adequately inform about both bodily injury and property loss. To a significant extent, this is an empirical question: How much information contained in these data about these harms would be lost if a single versus a multiple classification were to be developed? In the absence of constructing numerical taxonomies for both physical injury and property loss there is no entirely satisfactory answer to this question. However, some indication of the relative utility of the independent versus the joint approach can be sought by asking the question: How interdependent are injury and loss in the empirical distribution of criminal victimizations? If loss and injury were found to occur jointly in a significant proportion of victimizations, then there may be substantial rationale for the construction of a single analytic system. Conversely, if the two types of harm were found to be relatively independent in personal victimization, then a more satisfactory analytic procedure would be to analyze each type of harm separately and to compare the resulting systems for any differences that might emerge.

An inquiry into this question may begin by examining the distribution of harms in personal victimizations as reflected in our data. A description of how injury and loss are related may prove valuable in deciding how best to proceed. Figure 2-1 presents the relationship between bodily injury and property loss in the eight-city sample. The estimated number of personal victimizations in the

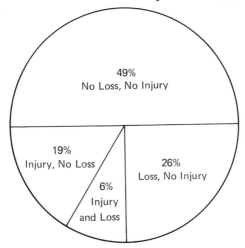

Figure 2-1. Distribution of Injury and Loss in All Personal Victimizations, Eight-City Aggregate, 1972[a]

[a]The total estimated number of personal victimizations is 208,719.

aggregated population is 208,719, of which 25 percent (19 percent plus 6 percent) resulted in some bodily injury to the victim and 32 percent (6 percent plus 26 percent) resulted in some financial or property loss. As Figure 2-1 clearly indicates, when all personal victimizations are the focus of interest, nearly one-half resulted in neither physical injury nor property loss to the victim—that is, they involved only *attempted* theft or *attempted* assault. This figure also shows that only 6 percent of all personal victimizations resulted in *both* bodily injury and property loss. Thus, a large proportion of all victimizations involve no "harm" as defined by the presence of physical injury or property loss, and only an extremely small proportion of cases involved both forms of harm.

This evidence of the relative independence of injury and loss suggests that some substantive knowledge about the similarities and differences in the offense correlates of these harms may be gained by an in-depth examination of each separately. For example, separate analyses of these harms would demonstrate whether there are basic differences between loss and injury in terms of the influence of weapons, the time and place of occurrence, the victim-offender relationship, and the victim's behavior during the incident. Such differences might be obscured if injury and loss were jointly analyzed. Thus, rather than an analysis of specific crimes, we will examine injury and loss regardless of how they cut across legal categories of victimization. Our analyses will be function-specific, focusing first on physical injury and then on property loss. A systematic study of these phenomena independent of restrictive legal labels has yet to be performed, and therefore a major aim of this research is to expand and refine what is known about the nature of injury and loss.

The Selection of an Analytic Technique

What we are seeking is an analytic method that allows us to uncover the major patterns of victimization in these data. We need a method of analysis by which we can group victimization elements objectively and in such a way that in the process of doing so we better understand the correlates and consequences of criminal victimization. Earlier research with these data suggests strongly that multivariate numerical methods may be useful. And, we are looking for a method that is compatible with the function-specific approach, a way to organize the data around harm to the victim, conceptualized as property loss or bodily injury.

There is a rapidly expanding literature, particularly in the biological sciences, on numerical taxonomic methods (Sneath and

Sokal, 1973; Sokal, 1974; Cormack, 1971; Simpson, 1961). Without embarking on a comprehensive review of this literature here, we can say that there are several major advantages to applying numerical methods to the problems at hand. Numerical taxonomic methods strive for both objectivity and replicability. They are objective in that they employ precise statistical definitions of similarity and thus leave little room for the researcher's intuition or preconceived theoretical notions of how the observable entities are related. They are replicable in that precise rules and methods are described in detail and the data are fully displayed so that others may reproduce the findings or apply the method to other samples. While it is true that both objectivity and replicability are relative terms—probably no study could be both *perfectly* objective and replicable—central aims of numerical methods of classification are to remove theoretical bias as far as possible and to provide to other researchers the information needed to replicate the study. The variables are quantified in an explicit fashion and the algorithms are specified in detail so that replicability is feasible. The approach is primarily empirical, and as such, "the fundamental test of the validity . . . must be whether it can be used as a consequential and consistent method for arranging organized nature" (Sneath and Sokal, 1973:9).

Because our analytic classifications are to be criterion-based—that is, victimizations will be grouped according to how the offense elements found in the NCS data relate to the criteria of injury or loss—they are analogous to predictive classifications. In predictive classifications, the aim is to organize the attributes in such a way as to form subgroups that have differing probabilities of manifesting a given criterion. In this case, because injury and loss are the criteria to be predicted, the aim is to form subgroups of offenses that have differing probabilities of resulting in injury or in loss to the victims involved. A review of the numeric taxonomic methods suggests that one method appropriate for addressing this problem is predictive attribute analysis. Originally developed by Macnaughton-Smith (1963), this method has received some application in recent criminological research (Wilkins and Macnaughton-Smith, 1964; Turner, 1969; Simon, 1971; Gottfredson, Gottfredson and Garofalo, 1977). Predictive attribute analysis (PAA) is a divisive hierarchical classification technique in which subgroups are formed in a stepwise fashion according to the strength of association between attributes and the criterion. The criterion is dichotomous (e.g., injury versus no injury), as are the predictors to be used in the classification.

The clustering process works from a vector of associations (e.g., phi coefficients). First, the association of each attribute with the criterion is examined and the sample is split on the attribute that has the highest association with the criterion. This split defines the first two subgroups. For example, if attributes A through Z are used as predictors and F has the highest association with the criterion, the sample cases are subdivided into F and non-F groups. It can be seen that by employing such a clustering rule, the resulting subgroups will differ in relation to the criterion moreso than if any other attribute in the set had been used to subdivide the sample. Each of these two subgroups is then treated as an entity, and division proceeds within each group separately. Within the first group (F) a new vector of associations is formed, and the group is split on the attribute that has the highest association with the criterion (e.g., attribute S) forming two subgroups. Within the second group (*non-F*), a vector of associations is formed and the group is split on the attribute that has the highest association with the criterion (e.g., attribute K). The first and second groups, of course, will not necessarily subdivide on the same attribute, so that the division of each successive subgroup results in a hierarchical classification system designed to produce groups that are heterogeneous in relation to the criterion.

PAA is criterion-based and thus useful for function-specific analyses. The method takes into consideration overlap among the attributes in their relation to the criterion; once a division has been made on a particular attribute, further divisions are made within groups. This is essentially the same as saying that the first attribute will be "held constant" in later constructions of the vector of associations. PAA displays the joint effects of the attributes that emerge in the solution, an important consideration for these data.

Reliability of the Analyses

A significant problem with all of the stepwise numerical taxonomic methods is that they are vulnerable to random variations. That is, most stepwise techniques such as PAA, operating on the basis of sample statistics, select the largest similarity measures present in the matrix. However, given that these statistics are only estimates, and that splits are made only on a subset of the available predictors, the selection of predictors will be subject to the error variation in the statistics themselves, and thus PAA will capitalize on chance variation. In such hierarchical classification methods, the selection decisions are irrevocable, and the entire structure is dependent upon the earliest decisions. Thus the problem of error variation, especially when the associations with the criterion are relatively homogeneous, is substantial.

The general problem of capitalization on chance variations is not unique to PAA. This is a difficulty that is shared by stepwise procedures, including stepwise multiple regression. The problem of capitalization on chance variation is particularly acute when sample size is small and/or when selection of predictors is made from a larger set of predictors (McNemar, 1969:208–209; Kerlinger and Pedhazur, 1973:282–84). The traditional means of assessing the extent to which the obtained solution has capitalized on chance variations is cross-validation. When cross-validation is used, clustering operations must *necessarily* be two stage analyses, consisting of both a construction stage and a validation stage. Thus, the standard method of cross-validation will be used throughout our PAA analyses. The entire sample of victimizations will be randomly split into two groups, with the first half sample serving as the construction sample on which the classification system will be derived. The second sample will serve as the validation sample on which the structure from the construction sample will be forced. By comparing the construction sample and forced validation sample results, the reliability of our results can be determined.

Another method that will be employed for assessing the stability of the solution uses data collected in another set of victimization surveys, the five largest cities samples, as the validation sample. Thus the consistency of the results will be assessed by a split-half cross-validation procedure and a procedure that assesses the generality of the solutions on an independent sample of cities.

The Utility of the Analyses

The question of how well our analytic solutions "work" can be addressed in two ways. First, the solutions can be evaluated in terms of how well they organize our knowledge concerning the phenomena of interest: Are meaningful and consistent subgroups of events formed that significantly differ in the probability of injury or loss? Do these subgroups then suggest hypotheses as to why the patterns that emerge are associated with the phenomena of interest? Thus, the solutions may be evaluated according to their contributions to substantive knowledge and their usefulness as heuristic devices.

Second, these solutions may be assessed in terms of how meaningful their external correlates are: Do they serve to order our understanding, in meaningful and consistent ways, of important criminological concerns other than injury and loss? Do the empirically derived subgroups of events also provide some insight into the characteristics of persons most likely to suffer that specific form of victimization? Linking aspects of offenses with characteristics of persons may lead to some hypotheses about why persons with particular characteristics may be found to be disproportionately victimized by offenses that exhibit particular objectively defined characteristics. If various combinations of offense elements are found to relate to various combinations of victim characteristics, then speculation as to why these configurations arise will be well grounded in research. There currently exist very few systematic empirical studies of victims of crimes of common theft and assault, and therefore such analyses may lead to a fuller understanding of the nature of victimization.

The function-specific approach described here would appear to have utility as a research strategy for the substantive analysis of elements of victimizations and characteristics of victims. The focus on harms in our analysis of elements of crimes promises to yield considerable substantive information not currently available. The impediments that legalistic offense classification systems erect for reseach into injury and loss, and the current lack of knowledge concerning the consequences of criminal victimization, combine to support the utility of the analytic approach that we have selected for the first part of this book. We begin our study with an analysis of bodily injury in personal victimizations.

NOTES

1. Bentham, "A View of the Hard Labour Bill," 1778, reported in Sellin (1951).
2. Reported in Sellin (1951).

Chapter 3

Bodily Injury to Victims of Personal Crimes[1]

We noted in Chapter 2 that there are numerous analytical and substantive advantages to isolating objectively observable suffering on the part of victims as a focus of study. Apart from the very important collateral consequences of personal crime—such as mental anguish, fears for personal safety, and so forth[2]—bodily injury as a result of a personal attack can be the most serious individual consequence of personal crime. Unfortunately researchers have discovered that injurious encounters are among the most difficult types of criminal events to study. Often interpersonal violence is a complex interactive process in which the temporal sequence of events and the specific environmental circumstances are of utmost importance (see Toch, 1969). Although the complexity of personal criminal violence is known, it is somewhat paradoxical to find that we are still unsure about many of the most fundamental correlates of victimizations resulting in injury. We are not without some informative data about injurious personal crimes; for example, the studies of Wolfgang (1958), Wolfgang and Ferracuti (1967), Normandeau (1968), Amir (1971), and Conklin (1972) give us numerous insights into the nature of physical harm to victims. However, all of these studies have not only been limited to official data but, more important to our present concern, they have only analyzed injury *within* selected crime categories, such as robbery. Further, none has focused *primarily* on the correlates of bodily injury. Thus, the fundamental correlates of bodily injury and the types of encounters most likely to climax in injury to the victim are not well known.

PRIOR INJURY-RELATED RESEARCH

Although it is true that personal injury is a consideration in the UCR classificatory scheme,[3] much potentially valuable information regarding the variability of injury within crime categories—and, therefore, perhaps important correlates of injury—cannot easily be determined from UCR type data. To some extent, the variability in injury to victims of personal crimes among the UCR classes of offenses is limited by the classification rules adopted by the UCR. For example, when robbery occurs, regardless of whether or not it is accompanied by physical injury such as broken bones or teeth, the event is classified simply as a robbery. Of course, one consequence of such a classificatory principle, given the heterogeneity in the extent and nature of injuries suffered by robbery victims, is that incidents differing widely in the extent and nature of injury suffered by the victim are grouped together. By treating all such crimes as the "same" and all others as "different," this within class heterogeneity is ignored. Further, crimes resulting in the same physical injury can, under the UCR classification rules, be classified as different crimes. For example, the victim could suffer nonfatal stab wounds in a rape, a robbery, or an assault. Clearly, for those interested in studying injury to victims, it is unfortunate that persons who have suffered the same physical injuries fall into different UCR crime categories.

What can prior research tell us about variations, both within and among crime categories, in the nature and extent of physical injury suffered by victims of crime? A number of studies have examined physical injury, primarily within the index offenses. For example, several studies, relying on police offense reports for data concerning injury to victims, provide valuable insights into injuries to victims of robbery. Normandeau drew a 10 percent random sample of all crimes of robbery listed by the police in Philadelphia between 1960 and 1966 which provided information on 1,785 victims. The extent of injury in his sample varied dramatically, with 44 percent receiving no injury, 26 percent minor injuries, and 30 percent receiving either medical or hospital treatment (Normandeau, 1968:116). Similar data are reported by Conklin, who studied all robbery incidents known to the Boston police in the first six months of 1964 and 1968. For the 1964 data, 68 percent of the victims received no injury, 11 percent experienced minor injury, and 21 percent received either medical or hospital treatment (Conklin, 1972:119). Conklin investigated not only the extent but also the nature of injuries suffered by robbery victims. He found that 4 percent of the 1964 victims were cut, stabbed, or shot; 21 percent were beaten, punched, or hit with a weapon; and 27 percent were shoved, pushed, or knocked to the ground. Thus, these findings suggest that within the same crime category (robbery) there is substantial variation in both the extent and nature of injuries suffered by victims.[4]

Studies using police offense reports to investigate victims of aggravated assault indicate that victim injury in assaultive crimes is also quite variable. For example, Pittman and Handy (1964), who reviewed a 25 percent random sample of the 965 crimes classified as aggravated assault by the St. Louis police during 1961, found that while the victim was injured to some degree in all of the sampled cases, 53 percent were "seriously wounded," but 47 percent were not "seriously wounded."[5] The President's Commission on Crime in the District of Columbia (1966), which studied police reports in Washington, D.C., found that of the 131 aggravated assault victims, 84 percent were injured and 35 percent required hospitalization.

Research has shown that nonindex offenses may also have serious consequences to victims in terms of injury, a finding that serves to emphasize the problematic nature of injury-related research that uses the UCR classification system as a basis for analysis. Sellin and Wolfgang reported that in their analysis of 145 juvenile offenses that resulted in some bodily injury to the victim, 62 percent would have been classified as nonindex offenses under the UCR classification rules. In addition, 28 percent of the bodily injury cases, classified by UCR rules as simple assaults and, hence, as nonindex offenses, were more serious in terms of harm to the victim than were 76 percent of those cases classified as aggravated assaults. Overall, offenses classified as simple assaults resulted in proportionately more serious physical harm to the victims than did robberies with personal violence (Sellin and Wolfgang, 1964:192).

One major limitation inherent in attempts to assess correlates of physical injury suffered by victims of personal crime is that the categories of crime under study may artificially limit the types of variables that may be considered. For example, theft-related variables (e.g., the amount of monetary loss) cannot be considered in assault victimizations if the UCR offense categories are used, because if theft was part of the victimization, then under the UCR classification rules the offense becomes robbery. On the other hand, if all crimes were separated into those involving and those not involving injury, variables such as amount of loss could be examined in relation to injury. Thus, although studies using the UCR classification scheme provide valuable information with regard to the heterogeneity of injury within crime categories, it is essential to assess the correlates of physical injury without regard to predefined categories in order to examine whether elements of victimizations are systematically related to victim injury.

THE NATURE OF INJURY
IN THE NCS SAMPLE

All victims of personal crime identified in the survey who were attacked were asked the questions: "What were the injuries you suffered, if any? Anything else?" Of the estimated 208,719 victims of personal crime in the eight cities, 25 percent reported that they had suffered some form of injury.[6] Table 3-1 presents the estimated number of victimizations resulting in specific types of injuries to victims, as well as the percentage of those injured suffering particular forms of injury. Although there is a great variety of forms of injury, ranging from rape injuries to gunshot wounds to bruises and black eyes, the vast majority of those injured reported that they received some minor injury such as bruises, black eyes, cuts, or scratches (78 percent).[7] The next largest proportion of those reporting injuries reported that they received "other" injuries (13 percent), followed by knife or gunshot wounds (8 percent), broken bones or teeth (7 percent), and internal injuries or were knocked unconscious (7 percent).

In order to examine the distribution of injury using traditional offense classification systems, victimizations were classified according to the *Uniform Crime Reports* classification and counting rules.[8] The data collected by the survey were designed so that they could be placed in the UCR format, and preliminary methods work indicates that a high degree of congruence can be obtained between survey classification into the UCR format and classifications made by the police.[9] The UCR personal crime categories that are amenable to study with these data include rape, robbery, aggravated assault, simple assault, and larceny from the person.[10] Consistent with the UCR procedures, attempts are included in each category.

With the exception of larceny from the person, in which, by definition, there can be no injury to the victim, each UCR crime category contains a substantial proportion of victims who suffered some form of injury. The greatest proportion of injured victims in any crime category was in the rape category, in which nearly one-half (48 percent) reported injury (in addition to the rape itself), followed by aggravated assault (35 percent), robbery (29 percent), and simple assault (22 percent).[11] Thus, along the single dimension of bodily injury, there is a good deal of variation both among and within each

Table 3-1. Type of Injury in Personal Victimizations, Eight-City Aggregate, 1972[a]

Total Personal Victimizations	Victimizations without injury[c]	Victimizations with Injury[c]	Type of Injury[b]						
			Rape Injury[d]	Attempted Rape Injury[d]	Knife or Gunshot Wounds	Broken Bones or Teeth	Internal Injuries or Knocked Unconscious	Bruises, Black Eyes, Cuts, or Scratches	Other
100% (208,719)	74% (155,506)	25% (53,213)	2% (1,286)	1% (647)	8% (4,459)	7% (3,772)	7% (3,711)	78% (41,253)	13% (6,693)

[a]Subcategories may not sum to total because of rounding.

[b]Multiple response question: Victims may have reported more than one type of injury and thus subcategories may sum to more than 100 percent. Percentages shown are based on the estimated 53,213 victimizations that resulted in injury to the victim.

[c]Percent of total personal victimizations.

[d]Rape and attempted rape injuries are injuries, in addition to the rape or attempted rape itself, suffered during the crime. Not all victims of rape or attempted rape received rape injuries.

UCR category in these data.[12] A more complete picture of the variability within and among the UCR classes in the extent and nature of physical injury is seen in Table 3-2, where the estimated numbers of victimizations within UCR categories involving various types of injury are presented. By far the greatest percentage of injuries in each type of crime category were relatively minor—bruises, black eyes, and cuts.[13] For the crimes of rape, robbery, aggravated assault, and simple assault, about one-quarter of the victims suffered such injuries. The utility of considering the actual injury suffered is nowhere more apparent than in aggravated assault. Sixty-five percent of these victims reported no physical injury, 6 percent were shot or knifed, and 4 percent received internal injuries or were knocked unconscious. Thus, nearly two-thirds of the aggravated assault victimizations resulted in no physical injury whatever. This comes about because an assault is aggravated when a deadly weapon is used, whather or not *any* bodily damage is actually inflicted.

CORRELATES OF PHYSICAL INJURY

Before an attempt is made to use predictive attribute analysis to investigate elements of victimizations that are most closely associated with physical injury, it may be informative to assess the relations betweeen various individual elements of victimizations and injury. Preliminary analysis will focus on the categorical variable "injury versus no injury," placing all victims who suffered *any* physical injury into one category (25 percent of all victims) and all others into the other category. The heterogeneity of types of injury subsumed under the general heading of injury requires that attention be given to alternative definitions of injury. This will be done later in this chapter.

As previously noted, the NCS victimization survey systematically collects extensive and detailed data on characteristics of personal victimization. Data concerning the time and place of occurrence, weapon use by the offender, the number of offenders and number of victims involved in each incident, the victim-offender relationship, and so forth are collected systematically about each victimization. Because the primary aim of this analysis is to explore elements of the victimization that are associated with injury, this discussion will focus upon aspects of the event itself rather than on characteristics of victims.[14]

Place and Time of Occurrence

The places in which the victimizations occurred were categorized as follows: "in own home," "vacation home," "inside commercial

Table 3-2. Type of Injury by *Uniform Crime Reports* Categories, Eight-City Aggregate, 1972[a]

Uniform Crime Reports Category	Total Personal Victimizations	Personal Victimizations without Injury	Personal Victimizations with Injury	Rape and Attempted Rape Injuries	Knife or Gunshot Wounds	Broken Bones or Teeth	Internal Injuries or Knocked Unconscious	Bruises, Black Eyes, Cuts, or Scratches
							(Type of Injury)	
Rape	100.0%[b] 3.3%[c] (6,829)	52.0% 2.3% (3,551)	48.0% 6.8% (3,278)	28.0% 100.0% (1,933)	0.7% 1.1% (51)	1.8% 3.2% (122)	4.1% 7.6% (283)	25.9% 4.3% (1,770)
Robbery	100.0% 31.7% (66,150)	71.0% 27.6% (46,967)	29.0% 36.8% (19,183)	0% 0% (0)	2.0% 29.6% (1,320)	2.5% 44.1% (1,664)	2.5% 44.2% (1,642)	23.2% 37.2% (15,361)
Aggravated Assault	100.0% 23.8% (49,601)	65.0% 22.6% (32,241)	35.0% 33.3% (17,360)	0% 0% (0)	6.2% 69.3% (3,088)	4.0% 52.7% (1,987)	3.6% 48.1% (1,786)	24.0% 28.8% (11,888)
Simple Assault	100.0% 26.8% (56,025)	78.0% 28.0% (43,791)	21.8% 23.5% (12,234)	0% 0% (0)	0% 0% (0)	0% 0% (0)	0% 0% (0)	21.8% 29.7% (12,234)
Larceny from the Person	100.0% 14.4% (30,113)	100.0% 19.3% (30,113)	0.0% 0.0% (0)	0% 0% (0)	0% 0% (0)	0% 0% (0)	0% 0% (0)	0% 0% (0)
Total	100.0% 100.0% (208,719)	75.0% 100.0% (156,630)	25.0% 100.0% (52,089)	0.9% 100.0% (1,933)	2.1% 100.0% (4,459)	1.8% 100.0% (3,772)	1.8% 100.0% (3,711)	19.8% 100.0% (41,253)

[a]Subcategories may not sum to total because of rounding. Victimizations in which an "other" injury was sustained are included in total but are not shown separately.
[b]Row percent.
[c]Column percent.

building or public conveyance," "inside office," "near own home," "on the street," and "inside school." Rates of injury showed little variation across place of occurrence categories with the exception of a difference in the injury rate between victimizations taking place inside commercial buildings or public conveyances and those taking place inside victims' homes. Eighteen percent of the victimizations occurring in commercial buildings or public conveyances and 32 percent of those occurring in the victim's home resulted in injury to the victim.

Of all personal victimizations, 48 percent occurred during the day (6 A.M. to 6 P.M.), 40 percent between 6 P.M. and midnight, and 11 percent between midnight and 6 A.M.[15] A greater percentage of those victimizations occurring at night resulted in injury to the victim than did those occurring during the day; whereas 22 percent received some injury during daytime victimizations, 28 percent of those in the 6 P.M. to midnight category and 32 percent of those in the midnight to 6 A.M. category were injured.

Weapon Use

One element of criminal victimization that is of potentially great relevance to victim injury is weapon use. Sellin and Wolfgang examined the use of weapons in relation to bodily injury in their analysis of 1,313 juvenile offenses in Philadelphia. Their hypothesis that more serious injury is likely to occur to the victim when the offender is armed than when he is not armed was confirmed by their data. They found that if any kind of weapon was present in a face-to-face offense, serious harm occurred in 72 percent of the cases, whereas if no weapon was present, serious harm occurred in only 20 percent of the cases (Sellin and Wolfgang, 1964:204). It is interesting to note that although they found the presence of a weapon to be associated with serious injury, they found no relationship between type of weapon and serious injury.

For each personal victimization elicited in the NCS surveys, the victim was asked, "Did the person(s) have a weapon such as a gun or a knife or something he was using as a weapon such as a bottle or a wrench?" If the respondent answered affirmatively, the type of weapon was ascertained. Overall, weapons were used by the offender in nearly one-half of all personal victimizations (47 percent).[16] Contrary to the findings reported by Sellin and Wolfgang on the basis of official statistics, survey victimizations in which weapons were used were found to result in injury to the victim only slightly more often than victimizations in which weapons were not used (30 percent versus 24 percent).[17] However, as shown in Table

3-3, there is important variation in the percentage of victims injured depending upon the *type* of weapon used.[18] Although only 17 percent of those victimizations in which the offender used a gun resulted in some injury, 28 percent of the victimizations in which knives were used, and fully one-half in which "other" weapons (such as clubs and bottles) were used, resulted in some injury. It is important to note that victimizations in which a gun was present had a slightly *lower* rate of injury than those in which no weapon was used.

Self-Protective Measures and the Victim-Offender Relationship

There is no longer much doubt that victimizations are dynamic events with outcomes often dependent upon the manner in which, and by whom, the victimization is instigated and also dependent on the interpersonal interaction that occurs between the victim and the offender as the event unfolds. Studies of violent personal victimizations by Wolfgang (1958), Amir (1971), Normandeau (1968), and Toch (1969) have indicated that who the victim *is* in relation to the

Table 3-3. Injury by Offender's Weapon Use, Eight-City Aggregate, 1972[a]

| | Injury | | |
	Yes	*No*	*Total*
Weapon[b]	30%[c] (24,961)	70%[c] (59,459)	47%[d] (84,421)
No Weapon	24% (23,333)	76% (72,159)	53%[d] (95,392)
Total	27% (48,195)	73% (131,618)	100%[d] (179,812)
Gun	17% (6,177)	83% (30,774)	44%[e] (36,952)
Knife	28% (6,688)	72% (17,081)	28%[e] (23,769)
Other	52% (13,090)	48% (12,208)	30%[e] (25,298)

[a]Subcategories may not sum to total because of rounding. Includes only those cases in which weapon use was ascertained.
[b]Multiple response question: Victims may have reported more than one type of weapon and thus subcategories may sum to more than 100 percent.
[c]Row percent.
[d]Percent of "total" victimizations.
[e]Percent of victimizations in which weapons were used.

offender and what the victim *does* during the event may have important implications for the outcome of the victimization.

The relation between victim behavior during the event and physical injury can be addressed partially by data provided in the survey. All respondents suffering a personal victimization were asked "Did you do anything to protect yourself or your property during the incident?" If an affirmative answer was received, victims were asked what it was that they did. In slightly more than one-half (51 percent) of all personal victimizations, the victim took some self-protective measure. As shown in Table 3-4, the use of weapons as a self-protective measure by victims is relatively rare; in only 4 percent of all personal victimizations did the victim report using a weapon. On the other hand, in 18 percent of the victimizations, the victim reported using physical force against the offender. The remaining types of self-protective measures were less frequently used: in 6 percent of the victimizations the victim threatened, argued, or reasoned with the offender; in 7 percent the victim tried to get help; in 14 percent the victim left the scene; in 3 percent the victim held onto his or her property; and in 10 percent the victim reported taking some other self-protective measure.

Those victims taking some form of self-protective measure were slightly *more* likely to be injured than those not taking self-protective measures (29 percent versus 21 percent). Although we will later discuss the important question of whether the victim's self-protective measure preceded or followed the injury, it should be noted that the question cannot be answered definitely with these data because the time sequence of events was not collected. Thus, many of those taking self-protective measures may have done so as a *result* of being attacked. Conversely, the use of self-protective measures may have *provoked* the offender into injuring the victim.

Table 3-4 also reflects that the *type* of self-protective measure employed is related to whether or not the victim suffered injury. Of those who said they used physical force as a self-protective measure, 53 percent were injured, and of those who reported trying to get help (screamed, yelled, etc.), 36 percent were injured. On the other hand, those who resisted without force (threatened, argued, or reasoned with the offender), took "other" self-protective measures, or held onto their property were less likely to be injured than those who did not take these self-protective measures. *The injury rate suffered by victims who used physical force in resistance was more than twice as great as the overall injury rate (53 percent versus 25 percent).*

The association between the victim-offender relationship and

Table 3-4. Injury by Victim's Use of Self-Protective Measures, Eight-City Aggregate, 1972[a]

	Injury		
	Yes	*No*	*Total*
No Self-Protective Measure Taken, Not Ascertained	21%[c] (21,767)	79%[c] (79,972)	49%[d] (101,739)
Some Self-Protective Measure Taken[b]	29% (31,446)	71% (75,533)	51% (106,979)
Total	25% (53,213)	75% (155,506)	100% (208,719)
Physical Force (Hit, Kicked)	53% (19,639)	47% (17,193)	18% (36,832)
Evasive Action (Left Scene)	16% (4,622)	84% (23,683)	14% (28,305)
Try to Get Help (Yelled, Screamed)	36% (5,175)	64% (9,084)	7% (14,259)
Resist Without Force (Argue, Threaten, Reason)	20% (2,541)	80% (10,124)	6% (12,665)
Weapon	27% (2,151)	73% (5,952)	4% (8,103)
Held Onto Property	22% (1,210)	78% (4,225)	3% (5,435)
Other Self-Protective Measure	21% (4,231)	80% (16,428)	10% (20,659)

[a]Subcategories may not sum to total because of rounding.

[b]Multiple response question: Victims may have reported more than one form of self-protective measure and thus subcategories may sum to more than 100 percent.

[c]Row percent.

[d]Percent of "total" victimizations.

victim injury is also of considerable interest. For purposes of this comparison, offenders were categorized as "strangers" if the victim reported that the offenders were unknown, were known by sight only, or if the victim did not know whether or not they were strangers. "Nonstrangers" include relatives, persons who were well known but not related to the victim, and casual acquaintances. Overall in these eight cities, in 80 percent of the personal victimizations, the offender was a stranger to the victim. Of those who were victimized by strangers, 23 percent received some physical injury, whereas among those who were victimized by nonstrangers, 35 percent received some injury. Therefore, *the victim was more likely to be injured in a personal crime when the victim and the offender were nonstrangers than when they were strangers.*

Offender Characteristics and
Victim Injury

All victims of personal crimes uncovered in the survey were asked several questions pertaining to characteristics of the offenders. Unfortunately, the validity of victims' perceptions regarding offenders' characteristics such as age and race is not known as no systematic developmental research has been done in the area.[19] It would seem, a priori, that problems regarding valid perceptions may be most serious in connection with estimates of the ages of offenders, and hence only broad categories of offenders' estimated ages will be discussed here.

Using the dichotomy for age of offender of "under twenty-one" and "twenty-one or older," the age of offenders is not substantially related to victim injury; 26 percent of the victims attacked by offenders under twenty-one years of age and 27 percent of those attacked by offenders twenty-one or older were injured in the course of the victimization.[20] Those victims attacked by female offenders were about as likely to be injured as those attacked by male offenders (30 percent versus 26 percent).

Similarly, those attacked by white offenders and those attacked by black/other offenders had comparable rates of injury (30 percent and 25 percent, respectively). Finally, neither the number of offenders nor the number of victims was related to injury. Of those victims attacked by only one offender, 26 percent were injured, while 28 percent of the victims attacked by more than one offender were injured; although 25 percent of the lone victims reported some injury, 26 percent of the victims who were not alone when victimized reported some injury.

By way of summary, a number of offense characteristics have been found to relate to whether or not the victim was injured as a result of the victimization. The place of occurrence was found to be important, in that *victimizations taking place within the victim's own home were most likely to result in injury. Nighttime victimizations,* especially those occurring between midnight and 6 A.M., *resulted in greater proportions of injured victims than did daytime victimizations. Victimizations in which weapons, especially "other" weapons, were used, those in which the victim used a physical force self-protective measure, and those in which the victim and offender were nonstrangers were more likely to result in injury.* On the other hand characteristics of the offender (such as sex, race, and age) and the number of victims and offenders involved in the victimization were not closely associated with an injurious outcome as defined here.

SERIOUS INJURY

The analyses presented so far, although isolating some important and informative correlates of physical injury, are limited in at least two important respects: (1) injury has been treated as a homogeneous outcome, in which differences in seriousness (and possible concomitant differences in correlates) have not been taken into account; and (2) the correlates of injury that have been examined cannot be assumed to be independent of each other. For example, the place of occurrence and victim-offender relationship can be assumed to be correlated; those attacked inside the home are probably more likely to be attacked by nonstrangers than are those who are attacked on the street.

Clearly, there are a variety of ways in which personal injury may be defined for analytical purposes. The previous section relied on the injury–no injury distinction, in which any reported physical injury to the victim was classified as injury. Given the distribution of particular types of injury noted above, this definition of injury necessarily gives greater weight to the more numerous, less serious forms of injury. It may be important to analyze the correlates of those victimizations that involve *serious* injury to victims, because such victimizations may have characteristics, other than the nature of the injury itself, that are qualitatively different from less serious injury victimizations. One unique and valuable feature of victimization survey data of the type relied upon in this study is that such analyses are feasible.

Attempts to analyze the seriousness of criminal incidents have received widespread interest in the criminological literature in recent years (Sellin and Wolfgang, 1964; Akman, Figlio, and Normandeau, 1967; Christiansen, 1970; Wellford and Wiatrowski, 1975; Figlio, 1975; Riedel, 1975). Most of these efforts have not focused exclusively upon physical injury, but rather have attempted to scale criminal events on a variety of dimensions such as property loss, property destruction, and injury.

With the victimization survey data, it is possible to construct a serious injury category by combining victimizations that resulted in such injuries as broken bones or teeth, gunshot wounds, and internal injuries and by classifying all other injuries as "not serious." The major defect in such a procedure, of course, is that even among those who reported suffering only bruises or cuts, many may be quite severely injured and even require extensive medical attention. An alternative procedure that may be preferable, but which by no means obviates all the problems inherent in classifications by seriousness, is to group together those forms of injury that *required* medical attention, regardless of the specific form of injury, and to consider such cases as "serious injury."[21]

It will be recalled that among all victims of personal crimes, 25 percent were injured; however, 10 percent reported that they required medical attention as a result of the injuries that they suffered.

Table 3-5 presents the *Uniform Crime Reports* categories of personal crimes and the percentage within each category that resulted in serious injury (i.e., those requiring medical attention) to the victims. Although each UCR class, with the exception of personal larceny, contains a proportion of serious injury victimizations, there

Table 3-5. Serious Injury by *Uniform Crime Reports* Categories, Eight-City Aggregate, 1972[a]

Uniform Crime Reports Category	Serious Injury		
	Yes	*No*	*Total*
Rape	19%[b]	81%	100%
	6%[c]	3%	3%
	(1,324)	(5,505)	(6,829)
Robbery	12%	88%	100%
	38%	31%	32%
	(7,901)	(58,249)	(66,150)
Aggravated Assault	18%	82%	100%
	43%	22%	24%
	(8,863)	(40,738)	(49,601)
Simple Assault	5%	96%	100%
	12%	28%	27%
	(2,527)	(53,499)	(56,025)
Larceny from the Person	0%	100%	100%
	0%	16%	14%
	(0)	(30,113)	(30,113)
Total	10%	90%	100%
	100%	100%	100%
	(20,615)	(188,104)	(208,719)

[a]Subcategories may not sum to total because of rounding.
[b]Row percent.
[c]Column percent.

is substantial variation among the categories in the extent of serious injury. For rape, which had the highest rate of injury, nearly one out of five victimizations resulted in serious injury. Aggravated assault (18 percent) had a higher proportion of seriously injured victims than did either robbery (12 percent) or simple assault (5 percent). By comparing these results for serious injury with those reported for serious and minor injuries combined, it is apparent that the ranking of the index crimes is the same for both indicators of injury. However, when serious injury is used as the criterion, the respective rates of injury for rape and aggravated assault are nearly identical, whereas when any injury was used as the criterion, the respective injury rates for these two offenses were much more disparate (48 percent versus 35 percent).

An interesting question is whether or not the various correlates of injury that were examined in the previous section are similarly related to serious injury. The answer to this question can be summarized briefly. Victimizations occurring in the victim's own home, at night, in which weapons were used and in which the victim used or tried to use physical force as a self-protective measure were found to have relatively high rates of serious injury. *Thus, in general, the correlates of injury found in the previous section hold when serious injury is the focus of concern.*

HOSPITAL TREATMENT

The definition of serious injury as an injury requiring medical attention is not without shortcomings. The interpretation of what constitutes injury requiring medical care may vary among victims to an unknown extent. It may be, for example, that variations in types of crimes are associated with victim characteristics that, in turn, are related to differential interpretations of the need for medical attention. In addition, the need for medical attention itself can be quite variable, ranging from very minor attention given to cuts, to extensive hospital care. Therefore, in order to refine further the definition of injury, a measure of the extent of medical care given to injured victims was used. For the purpose of this discussion, all victims reporting either that they received emergency room treatment at a hospital or that they stayed in a hospital overnight or longer were classified as having suffered "hospital injuries."[22]

Eight percent of the victimizations in these eight cities resulted in injury to the extent that some hospital treatment was administered. Although the relevant data are not displayed here, overall the patterns exhibited by undifferentiated injury and serious injury as defined by the need for medical attention are also in evidence for hospital injury. Thus, for all three measures of injury used herein, the correlates are found to be similar. *This provides us with some confidence that the correlates examined are not related to injury merely as an artifactual result of having operationally defined injury in a particular way.*

As was pointed out earlier, a discussion of the correlates of physical injury that attends only to bivariate relationships is limited because the various attributes cannot be assumed to be independent. Thus, it is imperative that the joint effects of the correlates be examined. As we discussed in Chapter 2, the function-specific analytic approach may be a useful strategy to accomplish this aim.

INJURY FUNCTION-SPECIFIC OFFENSE ANALYSIS

The preliminary analyses presented above support the notion that there are important differences in the characteristics of criminal victimizations that result in injury to the victim and those that do not. The purpose of this section is to organize the attributes of criminal victimization in such a way as to take the fullest possible advantage of these differences and to define certain subgroups of criminal victimizations that differ in terms of the likelihood of resulting in injury to the victim. The aim here is to classify victimizations on the basis of the offense attributes available from the NCS so that the classes differ as much as possible among themselves in injury rates. Thus, the classificatory principle is criterion-based, because a specific dependent variable—injury—is used.

The desired classification of offenses should have a number of qualities in addition to maximizing group differences in injury rates. The analysis must be reliable if it is to be useful. That is, once subgroups that differ in injury rates are isolated, they must consistently do so from sample to sample if confidence is to be placed in the results. Thus, the subgroups should not be artifacts of the sample studied, but the classification should have utility for other samples from the population. Additionally, a simple classification is to be preferred to a complex one, other things being equal.

As discussed in Chapter 2, the ultimate property that our injury-based analytic solution must achieve is that it must be heuristic. The elements that describe the subgroups of victimization must help us to understand variability among the groups in rates of injury. Optimally, this analysis will allow careful inferences about the nature of injurious criminal victimizations.

Method

Because this analysis is to be criterion based—that is, victimizations will be segmented according to how various attributes relate to injury—it is analogous to a predictive classification. In predictive classifications, the aim is to organize the attributes in such a way as to form subgroups that have differing probabilities of manifesting a given criterion. Thus, in this case, injury may be thought of as the criterion to be predicted, and the aim is to form subgroups of offenses that have differing probabilities of resulting in injury to the victims involved. As was discussed in Chapter 2, a numerical taxonomic technique well suited to this problem is predictive attribute analysis (PAA).

As with any classification tool, rules must be adopted to guide the formation of the subgroups. For PAA the rules should increase the discriminatory ability of the scheme while at the same time ensuring maximum reliability of the resulting system. These rules include the measure of association to be employed, the minimum value of the measure of association for which a split will be permitted, the minimum number of cases in any subgroup for which a further subdivision will be permitted, and the minimum number of cases that result in the subgroups after a split has been made. If the statistic measuring the degree of association is too small, the discrimination provided by the split may not be large enough to warrant the division. If the number of cases in the subgroup is too small, the solution may not be reliable. Of central importance, then, are the rules to be adopted for guiding the formation of the hierarchical classifications. The following rules were adopted: (1) the value of the statistic—in this case Somers' d, an asymmetric measure of association (Somers, 1962)[23]—will be greater than or equal to $\pm$ 0.10; (2) no subgroup that contains fewer than 900 weighted cases will be further divided; (3) no split will be made if the resulting subgroups contain fewer than 450 weighted cases; and (4) no subdivision will proceed if the division results in a subgroup containing fewer than 5 percent of the cases in the parent group. This latter rule was adopted to preclude divisions that may be based on high discriminatory ability yet which produce numerically trivial subgroups.

Results

All variables in the analysis were coded as dichotomous attributes (see Appendix C). The criterion for the injury analysis consists of the attribute "injury versus no injury"; all victimizations in which the victims reported to the survey interviewers that they suffered *any* injury were classified as "injury" and all others as "no injury."

Figure 3-1 presents the hierarchical classification diagram, or dendrogram, resulting from the predictive attribute analysis of injury in
the *construction* sample, a random half sample of the eight city
victimizations. All attributes in the data set were allowed to enter
the analysis, with two exceptions: (1) attributes that are logically
or necessarily correlated with the criterion, such as type of injury
and number of days hospitalized; and (2) characteristics of victims,
because our focus here is on the characteristics of the event associated
with injury. Figure 3-1 shows the number of victimizations falling
into each cell, the percentage of victimizations in each cell resulting
in injury, and a brief description of the variable used to make each
split. Because the results shown in this figure are cumbersome to
discuss, the diagram should be studied and continually referred to
in reading the text below.

As foreshadowed by earlier analysis, the attribute most highly
associated with injury (Somers' d = 0.36) is whether or not the
victim resisted the offender with physical force. Therefore, two
groups are formed, one consisting of all victimizations in which the
victim did not use physical force, in which 20 percent of the victimizations resulted in injury, and the other consisting of all victimizations in which the victim did use physical force, in which 56
percent resulted in injury.

Within the subgroup not using physical force in resistance, the
attribute most highly associated with injury is whether the offender
used an "other" weapon (such as a club, bottle, or chain). When the
victim did *not* use physical force in resistance, and an "other"
weapon *was not* used 17 percent of the victims were injured—
somewhat below the overall injury rate for the sample. However,
when the victim did *not* use physical force but an "other" weapon
was used, the percentage of injured victims (47 percent) is considerably greater than that for the construction sample as a whole
(26 percent).

An advantage of using predictive attribute analysis as an analytical tool for this problem may be seen by examining the attributes
that further subdivides the part of the sample in which the victim did
use a physical force self-protective measure. Although among the
victimizations in which the victim did not use physical force, the
attribute "other" weapon was found to be the next most predictive
attribute, among the class in which the victims did use physical
force, the most predictive attribute turns out to be a loss category.
Among those victimizations in which the victim used physical
resistance and the total financial loss (due to property loss or damage
and monetary loss) was not between $10 and $49, the percentage

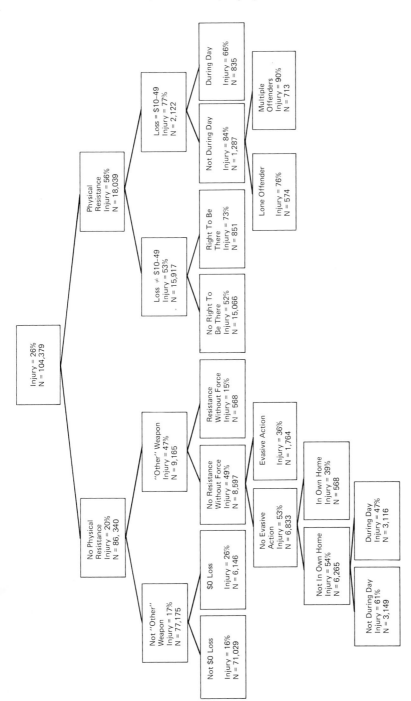

Figure 3-1. Predictive Attribute Analysis of Injury, Random Half Sample of Eight-City Aggregate, 1972[a]

[a]Subcategories may not sum to total because of rounding. See Appendix C for definitions of attributes.

injured is 53. On the other hand, of victimizations in which the victim used physical force and lost between $10 and $49, the injury rate was 77 percent. By considering just three attributes thus far in the analysis, the percentage of injured victims falling into each class ranges from a low of 17 percent to a high of 77 percent.

By referring to Figure 3-1, it can be seen that most of the sub-categories, having met one of the stopping rules, terminate after the third step, while two categories are subject to further subdivision. Each terminal branch of the network is then considered a class, and as shown in Table 3-6, twelve classes were defined. This table presents in summary fashion the elements defining each class, the number and percentage of all victimizations falling into each class, and the percentage of victimizations in each class that resulted in injury. The percentage of injured victims ranges from a low of 15 percent in Class 1 to a high of 90 percent in Class 12. Thus, one of the criteria we set forth as necessary for a useful analytic solution, that the classes be heterogeneous in relation to injury, is met with this solution. However, two issues, which are not totally independent, immediately arise. First, the reliability of this solution has not been assessed. This is particularly important because several classes contain small numbers of victimizations. Second, if one examines the proportion of all cases that fall into the various classes, it can be seen that one class contains 68 percent of the cases. This problem arises when one or both of two conditions are met: (1) the predictor attributes are highly skewed and intercorrelated, and (2) the associations of the available predictors with the criterion are not strong.

That the great bulk of personal victimizations do not involve injury is reflected in the rather low percentage of injury (16 percent) in Class 2, the terminal class containing by far the most victimizations. Every other class, with the exception of one, has an injury rate considerably higher than the rate of this most populous class. The attributes available for study simply cannot further subdivide Class 2 in a meaningful fashion. Recalling however that the principal purpose for this classification effort is heuristic, the classes that result in higher injury rates, although containing only 32 percent of the sample, may provide valuable insights into the nature of injurious criminal victimization.

The Stability of the PAA Solution
The issue of the reliability of the classification has been addressed in two ways. The first is reflected in Table 3-6. It will be recalled that the total sample was randomly split to form two subsamples.

The first was used to construct the analytic solution shown in Figure 3-1 and the "construction" portion of Table 3-6. The second, or "validation" sample, was used to assess the reliability of this solution.

Following traditional cross-validation procedures, all victimizations in the validation sample were sorted into the classes that resulted from the construction sample PAA. That is, all victimizations in the validation sample were "forced" into the terminal group solution that had been achieved with the construction sample. The percentage of victimizations resulting in injury to the victims was then computed for each of the twelve terminal groups in the validation sample and compared to those in the construction sample.

The purpose of this form of reliability study is to assess the extent to which the construction sample capitalized on chance variations. As noted earlier, predictive attribute analysis proceeds from vectors of measures of associations. However, these measures are actually sample statistics; they are *estimates* of the population parameters. Because they are only estimates, they are not error-free, but rather, some of these statistics will be overestimates and some will be underestimates. But it will be recalled that the technique calls for selection of the highest association measure upon which to split the entire sample. Thus, the procedure may be expected to capitalize on overestimated statistics when splitting the sample. The result is that the analytic solution will overestimate the heterogeneity in injury rates among the terminal classes. It is the degree of this overestimation that needs to be addressed by means of cross-validation.

Table 3-6 presents both the construction and validation injury results—the number and percentage of cases within each sample falling into the various classes and the percentage of victimizations within each class that resulted in injury. For example, Class 2, which contains 68 percent of the construction sample and had an injury rate of 16 percent in the construction sample, also contains 68 percent of the validation sample cases, again with an injury rate of 16 percent. By examining the classes and their respective injury rates between the construction and validation samples it can be seen that, in general, where the classes contain a large number of cases, the corresponding injury percentages are very similar. In Class 7, which contains 14 percent of the construction sample cases and 15 percent of the validation sample cases, the respective injury rates are 52 percent and 49 percent. It should be noted, however, that the vast majority of injury rates regress back toward the mean of the total sample—that is, the majority of classes have

Table 3-6.   Summary of Terminal Groups for Predictive Attribute Analysis of Injury, Eight-City Aggregate, 1972

Class	Constituent Elements[a]	Construction Terminal Group Size	Construction Percent Injured	Validation Terminal Group Size	Validation Percent Injured	Total Terminal Group Size	Total Percent Injured
1	SPM[b] resist without force, weapon-other, not SPM physical force.	1%[c] (568)	15	1% (650)	22	1% (1,218)	19
2	Loss, not weapon-other, not SPM physical force.	68% (71,029)	16	68% (71,032)	16	68% (142,061)	16
3	No loss, not weapon-other, not SPM physical force.	6% (6,146)	27	5% (5,551)	19	6% (11,697)	23
4	SPM evasive action, not SPM resist without force, weapon-other, not SPM physical force.	2% (1,764)	36	2% (2,089)	30	2% (3,853)	33
5	In own home, not SPM evasive action, not SPM resist without force, weapon-other, not SPM physical force.	1% (568)	39	(d) (398)	33	(d) (966)	37
6	During day, not in own home, not SPM evasive action, not SPM resist without force, weapon-other, not SPM physical force.	3% (3,116)	47	2% (2,453)	49	3% (5,569)	48
7	No right to be there, loss ≠ $10–49, SPM physical force.	14% (15,066)	52	15% (16,030)	49	15% (31,096)	50

8	Not during day, not in own home, not SPM evasive action, not SPM resist without force weapon-other, not SPM physical force.	3% (3,149)	61	3% (3,372)	53	3% (6,521)	57
9	During day, loss = $10–49, SPM physical force	1% (835)	66	1% (583)	44	1% (1,418)	57
10	Right to be there, loss ≠ $10–49, SPM physical force.	1% (851)	73	1% (876)	67	1% (1,727)	70
11	One offender, not during the day, loss = $10–49, SPM physical force.	1% (574)	76	1% (566)	71	1% (1,140)	73
12	More than one offender, not during day, loss = $10–49, SPM physical force.	1% (713)	90	1% (740)	74	1% (1,453)	82
Total		100% (104,379)	26%	100% (104,340)	25%	100% (208,719)	25%

a Subcategories may not sum to total because of rounding. See Appendix C for definitions of the constituent elements.
b SPM is an abbreviation for self-protective measure.
c Column percent.
d Less than 1 percent.

higher than average injury rates, and upon validation they move down somewhat. Where the number of cases is relatively small, as in Classes 9 and 12, the shrinkage is substantial.

Because the aim here is to construct a stable hierarchical classification system in which the various classes are heterogeneous in relation to injury, there is considerable interest in the extent to which the two solutions produce similar injury rates for the terminal classes. This is assessed in three ways: with Spearman's *rho* to determine the extent to which the classes are similarly *ranked* according to their injury rates in the construction and validation samples; with Pearson's *r* to determine whether the *magnitude* of the differences in injury rates among classes is similar in the construction and validation samples; and with the mean absolute difference between injury rates for classes in the construction and validation samples, where the absolute difference for each pair of classes is weighted by the validation sample class size. This last measure provides an assessment of difference between construction and validation injury rates that is sensitive to the size of the class for which the absolute difference is computed.

For the results shown in Table 3-6, Spearman's *rho* is 0.94, Pearson's *r* is 0.96, and the weighted mean absolute difference between construction and validation terminal class injury rates is 1.69. By all of these criteria, the construction to validation sample stability is very good. Hence, some confidence can be placed in the solution.

In order to determine how general this solution is, we also used data from the five largest cities for "validation" purposes. Although identical survey instruments and procedures were used in both the eight-city and five-city surveys, the latter differ in at least two important respects: (1) the sizes of the cities from which the samples were drawn are considerably larger (the cities are New York, Los Angeles, Philadelphia, Chicago, and Detroit); and (2) the interviews were conducted approximately six months later (in the early months of 1973).

For this portion of the reliability study, the original eight-city construction sample, as classified in Table 3-6, was again used as a construction sample, the entire five-city sample (estimated number of personal victimizations = 768,906) was treated as the validation sample. All cases in the validation sample were "forced" into the solution developed from the construction sample. Table 3-7 presents the summary information useful in comparing the results for the two groups.[24] It can be seen that the injury rates in the five-city validation sample ranged from a low of 14 percent in Class 2 to a

Table 3-7. Five-City (1973) Validation of the Eight-City (1972) Predictive Attribute Analysis of Injury[a]

Class [b]	Construction (Eight-City Sample)		Validation (Five-City Sample)	
	Terminal Group Size	Percent Injured	Terminal Group Size	Percent Injured
1	1%[c] (568)	15	1%[c] (3,528)	25
2	68% (71,029)	16	72% (546,840)	14
3	6% (6,146)	27	7% (50,927)	19
4	2% (1,764)	36	1% (10,976)	29
5	1% (568)	39	1% (4,578)	41
6	3% (3,116)	47	3% (21,354)	40
7	14% (15,066)	52	12% (93,368)	49
8	3% (3,149)	61	2% (18,806)	46
9	1% (835)	66	1% (5,652)	71
10	1% (851)	73	1% (3,869)	64
11	1% (574)	76	1% (4,217)	57
12	1% (713)	90	1% (4,792)	88
Total	100% (104,379)	26	100% (768,906)	22

[a]Subcategories may not sum to total because of rounding.
[b]For the constituent elements of each class, see Table 3-6.
[c]Column percent.

high of 88 percent in Class 12. The percentages of cases that fall into each class in the validation sample are similar to those found for the construction sample. For example, the largest class in the construction sample, Class 2, contains 68 percent of the cases and had an injury rate of 16 percent, whereas the same class in the validation sample contains 72 percent of the victimizations and had an injury rate of 14 percent. Class 7, which contains 14 percent of the construction cases with an injury rate of 52 percent, contains 12 percent of the five-city sample cases with an injury rate of 49 percent. In some of the smaller classes, the differences in injury rates are more substantial; for example, Class 10 contains 1 percent of the construction cases, with an injury rate of 73 percent, and accounts for 1 percent of the validation cases, with an injury rate of 64 percent.

Clearly, the classes vary somewhat in their respective rates of injury between the construction and validation groups; the weighted mean absolute difference between injury rates for classes in the construction and validation samples was 3.23. Spearman's *rho* was 0.94 as was Pearson's *r*, suggesting simultaneously that these results are not simply an artifact of capitalization on chance variation and that the solution generalizes to an independent sample from other cities.[25]

DISCUSSION OF INJURY ANALYSIS

As was pointed out in Chapter 2, the utility of the derived analytic solution can be addressed in numerous ways. One major way, and one for which evidence has already been provided, relates to whether the solution can reliably serve as a mechanism for organizing empirical knowledge concerning injury. Another measure of utility is whether or not the analysis is suggestive of the processes that culminate in injury to the victim.

The bivariate and PAA results presented indicate that victimizations resulting in injury to the victim differ in important respects from those not resulting in injury to the victim. *Perhaps the two most important correlates of injury to the victim are the victim's use of physical force as a self-protective measure and the offender's use of an "other" weapon.* In addition, victimizations in which the offender is known to the victim and victimizations occurring during nighttime hours have relatively high rates of injury. One of the reasons that victims of nonstrangers suffer higher rates of injury than victims of strangers is that the former are more likely than the latter to take self-protective measures, especially physical force self-protective measures (Hindelang, 1976:230). The greater tendency to take self-protective measures when the offender is a nonstranger may be due to the victim's belief that he or she can predict the offender's probable reaction if a self-protective measure is taken, something that persons who are victimized by strangers may be less likely to believe. Further, it is possible that when the victim and the offender are known to each other, "victim-precipitation" (Wolfgang, 1958), which in retrospect may become defined as a self-protective measure, disproportionately occurs. The ways in which the victim-offender interchange may affect the outcome of the event will be discussed further below.

The finding that nighttime victimizations have higher rates of injury than daytime victimizations may be linked to several factors. Victims who are confronted at night may be more vulnerable to injury because fewer bystanders may be available to take notice of, and possibly intervene in, a victim-offender confrontation. Further, because alcohol has been found to be a factor in assaultive crimes (Wolfgang, 1958; Pittman and Handy, 1964; Amir, 1971), and because the consumption of alcoholic beverages occurs disproportionately at night, the association between injury to victims and time of occurrence may be accounted for, in part, by the presence of alcohol in the offender and/or in the victim.

The consequences of the victim-offender interaction are dependent upon which of a sequence of alternative courses of action the participants in victimization events—both victims and offenders—choose to follow. For example, when an offender initiates a robbery, he may do so either by threatening a victim or by actually using force against the victim. When the victim is confronted with a threat or actual violence, he may choose to submit to the offender or to resist. In turn, an offender faced by a resisting victim may desist or may escalate the level of force. How this pattern of moves and countermoves evolves determines whether the victim sustains injuries.

The alternative moves available to victims and offenders when various weapons are used in the victimization may help explain the relationship between type of weapon and extent of injury. Recall the relatively low rate of injury when a gun was present, in comparison to the relatively high rate of injury when an "other" weapon was used (17 percent versus 52 percent). An offender with a gun may rely primarily on the threat of using it rather than on any actual attack with the weapon to convince the victim to cooperate. On the other hand, an offender with a club or bottle (i.e., an "other" weapon) may feel the need to establish the credibility of his weapon by actually attacking the victim. In addition, an offender with a gun may be much more reluctant to actually use it than an offender who has a less lethal weapon. From the victim's perspective, the use of a self-protective measure may appear to be more of a viable option when faced with an "other" weapon than when faced with a gun. As Figure 3-1 shows, however, even among those not using a physical force self-protective measure, being confronted by an offender with an "other" weapon is closely related to bodily injury.

In some instances, the victim may be faced with the dilemma of risking physical injury in order to avoid property loss. As noted above, whether or not the victim uses a physical force self-protective measure is the attribute most strongly associated with injury. The PAA results (Figure 3-1) indicate that the injury rate for those who used a physical force self-protective measure (56 percent) was nearly three times greater than for victims who did not use such self-protective measures (20 percent). Among victims who did not offer physical resistance to the offender, those faced with an "other" weapon also had injury rates nearly three times greater than similarly situated victims not faced with "other" weapons (47 percent versus 17 percent). *Thus, it is apparent that both type of weapon and the nature of victim resistance to the offender are critical elements in relation to the probability of injury.*

Separate analyses of the phenomenon of property loss (presented in the next chapter) indicate that when self-protective measures are used, in theft-related victimizations, the likelihood of property loss is reduced. When a self-protective measure was taken, 15 percent of the victimizations resulted in loss, compared to 51 percent when no self-protective measure was taken. Thus, both injury and loss of property are related to self-protective measures taken by the victim. It was noted earlier that the important question of whether the victim's use of self-protective measures preceded or followed his or her injuries cannot be resolved with the data at hand. There is simply no way, with the data available, of disentangling the time sequence of the unfolding event.[26] Thus, while many injuries may be stimulated by the victim's use of physical force self-protective measures, many thefts may be thwarted by the victim's use of a self-protective measure. It therefore appears that victims are trading bodily injury in return for retaining possession of their property. For the victim who is most concerned with reducing his or her risk of injury in theft-related victimizations, the optimal strategy is clear: *give up the property and refrain from attacking the offender.*

THE INTERSECTION OF EVENTS
AND PERSONS

Another measure of the utility of our analytical work with injury is whether the resulting solution can be useful in conjunction with characteristics of persons who suffer criminal victimization. The NCS victimization surveys systematically collect a great deal of information about the personal characteristics of respondents (see Appendix A). These characteristics can serve as a basis for determining how characteristics of persons are related to characteristics of victimizations.

One way of examining the victim correlates of the injury offense classes is to ask the question, How representative of the population being studied are the victims of these specific crimes? By seeking answers to this question, we will be able to determine whether some characteristics of persons are disproportionately represented among victims of very specific forms of criminal victimization. In one sense, then, this analytic method seeks to find whether there are "types of persons" associated with types of crimes. Of course, this analysis is limited to those demographic variables that are collected by the survey interviewers. Other forms of victim typologies may look for variation in entirely different sets of variables, and thus the validity of alternative approaches is not in question here.

Method and Result

In order to construct baseline figures against which to compare the distribution of personal characteristics of victims in the PAA terminal subgroups, population estimates for the demographic characteristics of these cities were derived from the NCS samples.

All victims in the sample were categorized according to the specific type of crime they experienced (as defined by the PAA solution), and the distribution of personal characteristics (marital status, race, sex, family income, and age) was computed for each class. These data, along with the distribution of the characteristic in the populations of these eight cities, the proportion injured in each class, and the number of victimizations in each class, are shown in Table 3-8.

The bottom row on Table 3-8 indicates that 60 percent of the persons in the population studied (eight-city aggregate) were married or widowed, 65 percent were white, 45 percent were male, 13 percent had family incomes under $3,000 per year, and so forth. Although the table is rather complex and cumbersome, careful study demonstrates some striking findings.

The class with the highest injury rate, Class 12 (82 percent injured), which is comprised of offenses in which the victim used physical resistance when attacked by multiple offenders during the night and lost $10-49, is disproportionately comprised of victims who are single, divorced, or separated (61 percent); nearly proportionate in terms of race; disproportionately male (77 percent); disproportionately from low income groups (59 percent under $7,500); and disproportionately between the ages of twenty to twenty-four. With the exception of the overrepresentation of males and of twenty to twenty-four year olds, Class 11 (73 percent injured) has nearly identical victim characteristics. Class 11 differs in offense elements from Class 12 only in that there is only one offender in the former, while there are multiple offenders in the latter.

These offense and victim patterns clearly involve nighttime theft

Table 3-8. Victim Characteristics for Injury Offense Classes, Compared to Characteristics of General Population, Eight-City Aggregate, 1972[a]

Class[c]	Percent Injured	Number of Cases	Marital Status (percent)		Race (percent)		Sex (percent)		Family Income[b] (percent)						Age (percent)						
			Married or Widowed[d]	Single, Separated, Divorced	White	Black/ Other	Male	Female	Under $3,000	$3,000 7,499	$7,500 9,999	$10,000 14,999	$15,000 24,999	$25,000 Or More	12-15	16-19	20-24	25-34	35-49	50-64	65 or Older
1	19	(1,219)	51[d]	49	83	17	72	28	12	14	17	31	17	5	12	13	21	24	14	8	8
2	16	(142,061)	42	58	64	36	54	46	17	31	11	19	10	3	14	16	16	17	15	14	8
3	23	(11,697)	47	53	50	50	51	49	23	31	11	14	8	3	6	12	15	17	22	18	10
4	33	(3,853)	34	66	79	21	70	30	17	27	10	23	10	7	22	32	18	11	9	7	1
5	37	(967)	43	57	65	35	37	63	32	30	5	19	5	1	5	19	12	12	25	15	13
6	48	(5,569)	23	72	70	30	57	43	15	30	13	19	8	8	34	21	20	12	12	8	3
7	50	(31,096)	29	71	68	32	67	33	15	30	10	22	11	3	20	28	20	15	10	6	2
8	57	(6,521)	36	64	65	35	77	23	10	37	12	20	10	2	11	25	17	19	17	9	3
9	57	(1,415)	33	67	61	39	57	43	17	35	13	15	9	9	23	25	13	22	9	2	7
10	70	(1,727)	20	80	58	42	27	73	30	30	5	21	2	3	4	18	27	32	11	4	4
11	73	(1,140)	31	69	61	39	41	59	20	37	11	15	9	0	2	10	51	17	13	5	2
12	82	(1,453)	39	61	62	38	77	23	20	39	12	12	4	6	4	16	25	22	22	8	3
Percent in Population	60		40		65	35	45	55	13	28	13	20	12	4	10	11	18	20	19	14	14

[a]Subcategories may not sum to total because of rounding.
[b]Persons whose family income was not ascertained are not included in this table.
[c]Class numbers refer to the classes shown on Table 3-6.
[d]Row percent

(with losses between $10 and $49) victimizations in which the victim resorts to physical force in resistance. The fact that the victims of these crimes are low income single persons in young adulthood is informative. These persons may be expected, moreso than married older persons or single younger persons, to frequent public places at night, perhaps for entertainment (including the consumption of alcoholic beverages), where there is a high *opportunity* for violent theft incidents. The fact that these theft-related incidents turn into injurious encounters may be explained in part by the victim's use of physical resistance. Generally, what these patterns indicate is that these personal characteristics may be associated with lifestyle differences among persons, which in turn are associated with placing the victim in situations at times during which the opportunity for victimization is high. It may be that what the victim does during the actual victim-offender encounter is then determinative of an injurious outcome. Much more will be said of these notions about "lifestyle/ exposure" in later chapters.

There are striking patterns of association in other classes as well. Class 10, which has an injury rate of 70 percent and which is comprised of offenses in which the victim used physical resistance, there was not a loss of $10-49, and "the offender had a right to be there,"[27] contains victims who are disproportionately single, divorced, or separated (80 percent), female (73 percent), lower income (30 percent under $3,000), and between the ages of twenty and thirty four (59 percent). These combinations of offense and victim attributes suggest a very high injury rate for single females who are primarily of low income and in their young adult years who are victimized by persons known to them within their own homes. These interpersonal conflicts may be accentuated by the victim's use of physical force in resistance. Again, it may be that the personal characteristics of victims are associated with certain lifestyles that increase the opportunities for victimization. And, there are again clear indications that victim behavior during the event may have dramatic consequences for the outcome.

Some interesting patterns of victim characteristics are also associated with Class 6 (48 percent injured), in which the offenses are comprised of daytime events involving "other" weapons, not taking place within the victim's own home, and in which the self-protective measures of physical resistance, resistance without force, and evasive action are not used. Table 3-8 shows that victims in this category are disproportionately single, divorced, or separated (72 percent), disproportionately male (57 percent), proportionately representative of race and income groups, and disproportionately young (55 percent twelve to nineteen years old).

In sharp contrast to the victim characteristics found to occur disproportionately in these high injury classes are those found in the classes with relatively low injury rates. In some of these latter classes, the victim characteristics tend to be more representative of the characteristics of the population as a whole. Thus, in the class containing the largest proportion of victimizations, Class 2 (16 percent injured—loss, not "other" weapon, and no physical resistance), most of the victim characteristics parallel those found in the general population. Only sex (54 percent male) and marital status (58 percent single, divorced, or separated) are slightly disproportionate. Other low injury classes, however, show some marked variation in victim characteristics. For example, Class 1 (19 percent injured) is comprised of victims who are disproportionately white (83 percent), male (72 percent), and of high income groups (53 percent $10,000 or more). The lack of either physical resistance or "other" weapons in this offense category indicates that these higher income males may be selected by offenders as likely targets for theft, and the low rate of personal injury may imply a reluctance on the part of these victims to attempt to protect their property by self-protective measures. It is interesting to note that those offense classes in which physical resistance was used *and* in which the victim suffered injury involve disproportionate numbers of victims from lower income groups.

Summary
Clearly there are many informative patterns in the relationships between the victim characteristics and the specific offense types represented in Table 3-8. Many of these findings, along with those discussed above, will be integrated into later chapters. What this section has served to demonstrate, however, is that the analytical method of linking types of crimes with types of persons leads to the discovery of some meaningful and informative patterns that could not be suggested a priori. The method of function-specific analysis employed in this chapter has therefore been successful in several important respects. It has demonstrated that high discrimination in rates of a phenomenon of central criminological interest can be reliably achieved using numerical taxonomic methods. These methods are empirical and objective in that classes are formed solely on the basis of observable similarities and differences. The solution has served to organize the data in a way that not only furthers our knowledge concerning the nature of bodily injury but also stimulates ideas concerning the nature of the derived classes. High reliability for the solution was demonstrated. Further, the system appears to have utility for organizing our understanding of the victims of

criminal behavior in an objective fashion and of the ways that they may differ from the general population in the cities surveyed. Based on these encouraging results, the application of these methods to another type of harm, property loss, seems appropriate.

NOTES

1. Some of these data were presented and discussed in Gottfredson and Hindelang (1976).
2. We will explore some of these issues in Chapter 8, where the relationships between attitudes and victimization will be analyzed.
3. For example, the definition of aggravated assault used by the UCR is "an unlawful attack by one person upon another for the purpose of inflicting severe or aggravated bodily injury. This type of assault usually is accompanied by the use of a weapon or by means likely to produce death or great bodily harm" (Kelley, 1974b:85). Assaults that do not meet these criteria are classified as "other assaults."
4. The fact that studies cited here used official statistics for data concerning injury may indicate that the extent and nature of injuries within UCR categories is even more variable than reported in these studies. Evidence suggests that the extent of injury is correlated with the decision to report crimes to the police. See Hindelang and Gottfredson (1976).
5. Seriously wounded was defined as being incapacitated to the extent that the victim required hospitalization (Pittman and Handy, 1964: Table 3-8).
6. Interviewers were instructed to record only *physical* (bodily) injuries that the victim received from the attack, such as bruises, broken bones, gunshot wounds, internal injuries, etc. Mental anguish was not considered as injury.
7. This question is a multiple response item to which victims may have given several answers. Thus, not all victims who received these minor injuries *only* received minor injuries.
Rape and attempted rape injuries are injuries, in addition to the rape or attempted rape itself, suffered during crime. Not all victime of rape or attempted rape suffered such injuries. Because this is a multiple response question, if other injuries were sustained, they would also be tallied (see Table 3-2). Unfortunately, Bureau of the Census documentation does not further define or explain "rape or attempted rape injuries."
8. See the rules in *Uniform Crime Reporting Handbook* (Kelley, 1974b).
9. The classification problem was addressed in the *San Jose Methods Test of Known Crime Victims.* In this study, overall, 84 percent of the victimizations were classified the same as the police classification. For a discussion of the various sources of error in such classification procedures, see LEAA (1972:10).
10. Larceny from the person includes such crimes as purse snatching and pocket picking in which no force or threat of force is directed at the victim.
11. Of interest is that aggravated assaults appear to result in a greater proportion of physical injuries to victims than do robberies, although robberies are considered more serious for UCR index purposes; see Kelley (1974a:35).
12. By variation within a UCR category we mean that some victims are

injured while others are not. The within category variation is at its maximum when the proportion of victims within that category who are injured equals 0.5.

13. Except for rape, in which the most common injuries were rape or attempted rape injuries. See footnote 7.

14. Characteristics of victims that are associated with injury will be examined later in this chapter.

15. It should be noted that although the 6 A.M. to 6 P.M. category contains 48 percent of the cases, it is twice as long as each of the nighttime categories.

16. Excluding those cases in which weapon use was not ascertained.

17. The analyses of Sellin and Wolfgang were restricted to crimes involving juvenile offenders.

18. It should be stressed that injury here refers to *any* physical injury reported by the victim, without regard to the gravity of the injury. Thus, while the proportion of victims injured by weapon type varies considerably, so too may the nature of those injuries.

19. Therefore, characteristics of offenders should be regarded as *perceived* characteristics of offenders. It should be noted that a similar problem is germane to studies that analyze offender characteristics from police offense reports. If the offender is not apprehended, such data derive mostly from victim reports.

20. The offender characteristic relationships exclude cases in which the relevant offender attribute (e.g., age or sex) was unknown. In multiple offender incidents, if any offender was twenty-one or older, all were classified as twenty-one or older.

21. Note that such a definition might not be as acceptable if the classification principle was injury that *actually resulted in medical attention*, as factors other than injury could come into play—for example, the victim's access to medical care.

22. The objection may be raised that this classification may be confounded by the victim's prior physical condition or by his or her ability to pay for or proclivity to use hospital treatment; this may in turn have important implications for the correlates of serious injury. This is a difficult problem and part of the reason that the alternative definition of *serious* injury was used above.

23. In a 2×2 situation, Somers' d is equivalent to the percentage difference on the dependent variable between the two categories of the predictive attribute.

24. The injury base rate in the five-city sample is somewhat lower than that found for the eight-city sample, 22 percent versus 25 percent.

25. In addition to the cross-validation procedure, we also performed replication analyses for all of the predictive attribute analyses reported in this book. By replication we mean that we undertook a separate PAA on the validation sample using identical criteria and decision rules and compared the results to that obtained for our "construction" sample. Perhaps because of the relatively large samples available to us for such analyses, the results of these replication studies were fairly encouraging. Although the final solutions for the replication analyses differed somewhat from those obtained via the construction samples, the central attributes (i.e., those that serve as the basis for the first few breaks) were always the same.

26. Because the lack of time sequencing elements introduces such ambiguity into interpretations of injury victimizations, we performed another PAA that excluded from the list of independent variables the self-protective measure attributes. The criterion and decision rules remained the same. Although the overall predictability of the criterion was less with this PAA, the sample was first partitioned on the attribute "other weapon" and, similar to the PAA reported in this chapter, attributes relating to the loss of property, the time of occurrence, and the place of occurrence were important.

27. If the victimization occurred within the victim's own home, the victim was asked whether the offender lived there or had a right to be there (see source code item 115 in Appendix A). If the answer was no, or if the question was not applicable (i.e., the victimization did not occur in the victim's home), then the event is coded as involving an offender who did not have a right to be there.

※ *Chapter 4*

The Loss of Property in Personal Crimes

Crimes of personal theft have long been a focus of concern not only to the criminologist but to the general public as well. Within its crime index, the *Uniform Crime Reports* defines two major categories of personal theft-related victimizations, robbery and larceny. Among the various forms of crime, these two categories annually account for an extremely large proportion of the FBI's crime index; for example, in 1975, the crimes of robbery and larceny accounted for nearly 60 percent of the index crimes known to the police (Kelley, 1976).[1] Perhaps because of the dual threat of property loss and personal injury, the crime of personal robbery has been suggested as a major contributor to the public's fear of crime (President's Commission, 1967:4).

The major classificatory principle differentiating robbery and larceny in the UCR scheme is the dimension of force or threat of force. The UCR definition of robbery is: "the taking or attempting to take anything of value from the care, custody, or control of a person or persons by force or threat of force or violence and/or by putting the victim in fear." The UCR definition of larceny is: "the unlawful taking, carrying, leading, or riding away of property from the possession or constructive possession of another" (Kelley, 1974b:26). Both personal larceny and robbery involve face-to-face confrontations between the victim and offender, but, by definition, the latter involves force or threat of force directed at the victim.

As pointed out in Chapter 2, a systematic study of theft-related victimizations would appear to be needed. It is essential to know, for example, what characteristics of personal crimes are most closely

71

associated with the element of property or monetary loss. Such elements as the time and place in which these victimizations occur, the role of weapons in theft-related crimes, and the apparent influence of victim self-protective measures are important concerns for a more complete understanding of the nature of criminal victimization. Additionally, it is important to know if such factors as the use or threat of force have an appreciable interaction with victim behavior during a theft-related incident. Because the use of some forms of self-protective measures were found to be important in injury-related victimizations, the question of their relation to theft needs to be addressed.

Our strategy for analyzing these data, as with that for injury, includes an examination of both the bivariate and multivariate correlates of theft victimizations. The ways in which elements of offenses combine in relation to theft may stimulate hypotheses about how the various constellations of elements arise. And, in order for theoretical work to have some empirical grounding, a numerical analysis that could reliably discriminate probabilities of personal loss would appear to have utility. As shown in Chapter 2, the elements of theft and bodily injury are found to have occurred jointly in only 6 percent of all personal victimizations. Therefore, the question of whether empirical correlates of these outcomes are dissimilar arises. Throughout this chapter, the correlates of theft will be compared with those discovered for injury. Similarly, the numerical taxonomy will be compared systematically to that obtained for injury.

PRIOR THEFT-RELATED RESEARCH

To a large extent, the component of theft is obscured when common classification systems are employed in studies of the correlates of victimizations. Although theft is a major classification dimension in the UCR scheme for defining the crimes of robbery and larceny, it is an element not routinely reported for other crimes in which it may be involved. Thus crimes such as homicide and rape may also involve the loss of property, but the loss is not typically systematically tabulated. Additionally, even within the UCR categories that attend to loss, there may be extraordinary diversity in the elements comprising a theft-related victimization. For example, incidents that differ with regard to the use of weapons, physical force, and the extent of monetary loss are grouped under the single category of robbery. Such a practice may severely limit the utility of the classification for scientific purposes.

Several major studies of robbery in the United States were conducted utilizing police offense reports in the late 1960s and the 1970s. These studies constitute a valuable source of information concerning the present state of knowledge about personal theft victimizations. The President's Commission on Crime in the District of Columbia (1966) studied the nature of robbery in the District of Columbia, utilizing the annual reports of the metropolitan police department in conjunction with a detailed analysis of 297 robberies reported in December of 1965. Reiss (1967) performed a similar analysis of the 14,888 police robbery reports for the city of Chicago for the year 1965, supplemented by a sample of detailed police reports. Perhaps the most comprehensive analysis of robbery undertaken from police offense reports is the study by Normandeau (1968), who selected a yearly 10 percent random sample of all crimes of robbery listed by the police in Philadelphia for the years 1960 through 1966. His total sample consisted of 1,722 police robbery reports. A similar descriptive study is provided by Conklin (1972), who selected all robbery incidents known to the Boston police in the first six months of the years 1964 and 1968, resulting in 396 and 847 cases, respectively. Finally, Mulvihill, Tumin, and Curtis (1969), in an examination of violent crimes for the National Commission on the Causes and Prevention of Violence, were concerned with the crime of robbery as one of the violent crimes in their study. They took a 10 percent random sample of the 1967 offense and arrest reports from seventeen large American cities, which resulted in a total sample of 2,385 robberies available for analysis.

The amount of loss incurred by victims of robbery has been found to be quite variable by both Normandeau (1968:116) and Conklin (1972:81). Both found the distribution of loss values to be highly skewed toward lower values; the majority of robbery incidents resulted in a loss of less than $50 to the victim in both studies (63 percent and 58 percent, respectively). Normandeau found that 10 percent of the victims he studied lost more than $250, while Conklin reported that 24 percent lost more than $99. Indications are, then, that within the UCR category of robbery, the value of loss in individual cases may be quite variable. Additionally, because loss is substantially related to whether or not the victim notifies the police of the victimization—i.e., the greater the loss the more likely the incident will be reported to the police (Hindelang and Gottfredson, 1976)—these official data on robbery probably underestimate the heterogeneity of loss values in robbery victimizations.

As described in Chapter 3, the extent and nature of injuries suffered by victims of robbery are variable. Similarly, the research studies described here have found weapon use and methods of intimidation to differ substantially among individual cases of robbery. Normandeau (1968:204) found that 33 percent of the robbery offenses involved the use of guns, 9 percent knives, 9 percent blunt instruments, and 39 percent physical intimidation. The corresponding figures cited by the President's Commission on Crime in the District of Columbia (1966) are 29 percent, 5 percent, 6 percent, and 23 percent.

In contrast to other crimes of violence, the robbery studies reviewed here have consistently found that strangers account for the vast majority of robbery incidents. For both armed and unarmed robbery (Mulvihill, Tumin, and Curtis, 1969: 220) and across time (Normandeau, 1968:130), about 85 percent of robbery incidents have involved persons who were strangers to the victim.[2]

The place of occurrence has been found to be an important factor in robbery incidents. Consistently, the most frequent place of occurrence for personal robberies has been on the street. Reiss (1967:22) found that 56 percent of the incidents he studied occurred on the street; Mulvihill, Tumin, and Curtis (1969:221) determined that 42 percent of the armed and 62 percent of the unarmed robberies took place on the street; and Normandeau (1968:244) found that 56 percent of the robbery incidents he studied took place on the street.[3]

One major limitation inherent in attempts to assess correlates of personal theft victimizations by using the UCR offense categories is that the definitions of the categories themselves may limit the types of variables that may be considered. For example, all robbery victimizations (whether or not they involve a loss of property) must necessarily include the component of force or threat of force. Larceny, whether or not a loss occurs, must not involve either force or threat of force. Thus, the relation between the offenders' use of force in a personal confrontation and whether or not the victim actually suffers loss may be obscured by this classification rule. Some elements of theft-related victimizations may be common to theft incidents regardless of whether the incident is classified as robbery or personal larceny. For example, the place of occurrence may be an important correlate of loss, regardless of whether robbery or personal larceny is the focus of study. Thus, by considering how the elements of all personal victimizations, regardless of statutory classification, are associated with loss, some important differences between loss and no loss victimizations may be uncovered.

THE NATURE OF LOSS IN THE
NCS SAMPLE

The criterion of loss may be defined several ways according to the offense elements available from the victimization survey data. Monetary loss, property loss, and property destruction could each serve as the focus of concern; or, alternatively, some combination of the elements of loss or destruction could be employed. In keeping with the focus on observable and measurable personal harm, the exclusive element of interest for this analysis will be completed thefts—that is, crimes in which the victim in a personal confrontation had money or property taken from his or her person. Regardless of whether the crime would be classified according to UCR rules as rape, attempted rape, robbery, or personal larceny, if a completed theft occurred, it will be considered a theft for our purposes. Our aim in this chapter is to develop an analytical classification of elements of personal victimizations designed to create subgroups of offenses that differ as much as possible in the probability of resulting in loss to the victim.

All victimizations studied in this chapter include the element of personal confrontation; the pool of victims of theft is limited to cases in which there is a direct confrontation between the victim and offender. Thus, the criterion variable is defined by two items: (1) the element of *personal* confrontation between the victim and offender, and (2) response to the question about loss of property. Table 4-1 presents the estimated number of personal victimizations in the eight-city sample in which there was some loss, and among those in which there was some loss, the victim's estimate of the value of the stolen property. As can be seen, 32 percent of the personal victimizations in these eight cities resulted in some loss to the victim. Most losses (57 percent) fell into categories of less than $50; when "not ascertained" losses are excluded, 63 percent of the losses were under $50.[4] Losses of great value were extremely rare in these personal victimizations; losses of between $250 and $999 comprised only 5 percent of all victimizations that involved loss, and losses of $1,000 or more comprised only 1 percent.

In order to examine the distribution of theft according to the *Uniform Crime Reports* categories, as was done in Chapter 3 for injury, all personal victimizations in the sample were classified as they would be under the UCR system. As shown in Table 4-2, with the exception of aggravated and simple assault, which, by UCR definition, cannot involve the element of theft, each category con-

Table 4-1.   Value of Loss in Personal Victimizations, Eight-City Aggregate, 1972[a]

Total Personal Victimizations	Victimizations Without Something Stolen	Victimizations With Something Stolen	Value of Loss							
			None	$1-9	$10-49	$50-99	$100-249	$250-999	$1,000 Or More	Not Ascertained
100% (208,719)	68%[b] (141,058)	32%[b] (67,650)	1%[c] (720)	21% (14,470)	35% (23,250)	15% (10,370)	11% (7,590)	5% (3,260)	1% (950)	10% (6,940)

[a]Subcategories may not sum to total because of rounding.
[b]Percent of total personal victimizations.
[c]Percent of personal victimizations in which something was stolen.

Table 4-2.   Loss by *Uniform Crime Reports* Categories, Eight-City Aggregate, 1972[a]

	Loss		
	Yes	No	Total
Rape	15%[b]	85%	100%
	1%[c]	4%	3%
	(1,006)	(5,823)	(6,829)
Robbery	62%	38%	100%
	60%	18%	32%
	(40,891)	(25,259)	(66,150)
Aggravated	0%	100%	100%
Assault	0%	35%	24%
	(0)	(49,601)	(49,601)
Simple	0%	100%	100%
Assault	0%	40%	27%
	(0)	(56,025)	(56,025)
Larceny from	86%	14%	100%
the Person	38%	3%	14%
	(25,764)	(4,350)	(30,114)
Total	32%	68%	100%
	100%	100%	100%
	(67,661)	(141,058)	(208,719)

[a]Subcategories may not sum to total because of rounding.
[b]Row percent.
[c]Column percent.

tains a proportion of victimizations in which there was some actual loss of property. Thus, 15 percent of the rape victimizations, 62 percent of the robbery victimizations, and 86 percent of the personal larceny victimizations resulted in property loss to the victim.

CORRELATES OF PROPERTY LOSS

Prior to embarking on our analytic classification of offense elements around the dimension of loss, it may be valuable to examine the associations between some of the offense attributes available from the victimization survey and loss. This analysis will focus on the categorical variable "loss" versus "no loss," as defined above.

Place and Time of Occurrence

There is some variation in the proportion of victimizations resulting in loss according to the place of occurrence. Victimizations that took place inside offices (9 percent), inside schools (20 percent), and inside the victim's home (25 percent) had the lowest rates of loss, whereas those that took place near the victim's home[5] (31 percent), on the street (34 percent), and inside commercial buildings or public conveyances (43 percent) had higher rates of personal loss. It is interesting to note that the place of occurrence categories that contained the highest proportion of victimizations resulting in loss, such as inside commercial buildings, were found in the injury analysis to have low rates of injury. Conversely, at-home victimizations, which had fairly low loss rates, were found to have the highest injury rates. That such places as public conveyances, commercial buildings, and public streets had relatively high loss rates should not be particularly surprising because these places are where strangers come into contact with each other.

Although the rates of injury according to the time of occurrence categories were found to be highest in the midnight to 6 A.M. category and lowest in the 6 A.M. to 6 P.M. category, the rates of loss demonstrate the opposite trend. Victimizations that occurred between 6 A.M. and 6 P.M. had the highest loss rate (35 percent), followed by victimizations that took place between 6 P.M. and midnight (31 percent), and those in the midnight to 6 A.M. category had the lowest loss rate (28 percent). It should be noted that these differences were small and were less marked than those found for injury.

Prior Relationship Between the Victim and the Offender

The victim-offender relationship, whether the offender was known to the victim or was a stranger, was found to be substantially related to whether or not the victim received injury, and somewhat related to the probability of serious bodily injury. The higher risk of injury was associated with being attacked by a nonstranger. For theft victimizations the association is reversed; persons victimized by strangers were over three times more likely to incur a loss of property than were persons victimized by nonstrangers. Whereas 11 percent of the nonstranger victimizations resulted in some theft of property, 39 percent of the stranger victimizations resulted in some theft. Such a substantial association between the victim-offender relationship and theft should not be surprising, because it may simply reflect the fact that offenders who attack nonstrangers disproportionately have assault, rather than theft, as their motive. After all, for an offender whose primary motivation involves the successful theft of property, the probability of not being apprehended increases if he or she is unknown to the victim.

Offender Characteristics

Whether the offender was a male or a female was associated with theft in personal victimizations. Table 4-3, which presents the distribution of perceived offender characteristics according to whether the victim suffered any loss, shows that 16 percent of the victimizations involving female offenders resulted in loss compared to 31 percent in which the offender was a male. The distribution of loss in personal victimizations according to the perceived age of the offenders is informative when read in conjunction with the injury findings. Whereas the offender's age was not found to be associated with bodily injury, there is a slight association between the loss of property and the offender's age, with victimizations perpetrated by

Table 4-3. Loss By Offender Characteristics, Eight-City Aggregate, 1972[a]

	Loss		
	Yes	*No*	*Total*
Age of Offender(s)[b]			
All Under 21	31%[c] (26,733)	69% (60,125)	100% (86,858)
Any 21 or Older	22% (16,607)	78% (58,457)	100% (75,064)
Sex of Offender(s)			
Male	31% (51,762)	69% (116,579)	100% (168,341)
Female	16% (2,643)	84% (13,378)	100% (16,021)
Number of Offender(s)			
One	21% (22,495)	79% (82,583)	100% (105,078)
More Than One	39% (35,228)	61% (54,434)	100% (89,663)
Race of Offender(s)			
White	13% (8,590)	87% (59,993)	100% (68,583)
Black/Other	39% (45,676)	61% (71,426)	100% (117,102

[a]Subcategories may not sum to total because of rounding.
[b]Only cases in which relevant offender characteristics were ascertained are included. Victimizations that involved multiple offenders of mixed sexes or races have been excluded from this table.
[c]Row percent.

younger offenders more often resulting in the loss of property. Thirty-one percent of the victimizations involving offenders perceived to be under twenty-one years of age resulted in loss compared to 22 percent of those involving offenders twenty-one years of age or older.

Among the offender characteristics available for study, the largest relation to loss in personal victimizations was found for the perceived race of the offender. Nearly four out of ten personal victimizations involving offenders perceived to be black/other resulted in loss, but only 13 percent of those involving offenders perceived to be white resulted in loss. Thus, although injurious victimizations were virtually unrelated to the race of the offender, victimizations involving black/other offenders were substantially more likely to result in loss than were victimizations involving white offenders. If column percentages were to be computed in Table 4-3, it would be seen that when the victimization resulted in loss to the victim, more than four out of five offenders were black/others, whereas in no-loss victimizations, slightly more than one-half of the offenders were black/others.

Both the number of offenders and the number of victims present in a victimization are related to the theft of property. In victimizations in which there was only one offender involved, 21 percent resulted in loss, and in those in which more than one offender was involved, 39 percent resulted in loss. The ability of multiple offenders to dominate a victim-offender encounter is a possible explanation for the high loss rate in such victimizations. On the other hand, and perhaps surprisingly, the number of victims present during the incident is positively related to loss; in situations in which only one victim was present, 15 percent resulted in loss, while the corresponding figure for cases involving more than one victim is 40 percent.

Weapon Use and Intimidation

The presence of particular types of weapons on the part of the offender was found to be closely associated with bodily injury to the victim. The use of "other" weapons was indicative of a high probability of victim injury and of serious injury as well. Guns, on the other hand, were found to be somewhat predictive of lower than average injury rates. In Chapter 3 it was argued that these patterns of weapon use can be attributed largely to the influence that the nature of the weapon exerts over the victim-offender interaction. Because of their potentially lethal nature, or at least their potential for very serious injury, it was reasoned that strong inhibitions surround the use of guns on the part of offenders and that victims faced with such weapons are less likely to use provocative self-protective measures. When the offender faces the victim with an "other" weapon, however, similar inhibitions may not be present on the part of either the victim or the offender, a situation more likely to result in bodily injury. Additionally, as was pointed out, an offender using an "other" weapon may need to establish the credibility of the weapon to the victim by an actual attack, a demonstration that is little needed when a gun is employed. Finally, it can be argued that the use of "other" weapons may be more common in heated confrontations in which the spontaneity of the moment induces one participant to select the most readily available object to use against the other.

When theft is a component of the victimization, an entirely different constellation of weapon use relations may be expected to emerge. The actual use of weapons may be a last resort in such confrontations, with the purpose of displaying a weapon on the part of the offender being designed to induce fear or to intimidate the victim. Several studies of robbery offenders would support the "inducement of fear" rather than the "infliction of injury" purpose of weapon use on the part of offenders in theft-related victimizations. For example, Letkemann (1973:114) writes that "the establishment of authority is no doubt enhanced by the display and use of weapons. . . . [M]uch of the robber's activity during a robbery is necessitated only because he does not want to use his gun. He is, therefore, rightly dismayed at the condescension of those who fail to appreciate that his technique revolves around the nonuse, rather than the use of guns."

These arguments suggest, then, that the patterns of weapon involvement by offenders in theft-related victimizations will differ substantially from those in injury-related events. Specifically, they suggest that weapons with a fairly high intimidation value, such as guns, are more likely to produce victimizations with loss than are weapons of lower intimidation value. Table 4-4, which presents the percentage of all personal victimizations that resulted in loss according to the nature of the weapon involved, largely supports these arguments.

There is no substantial relation between the presence or absence of a weapon and whether the victimization resulted in loss. Weapon-present victimizations resulted in loss 28 percent of the time, and weapon-absent victimizations resulted in loss 30 percent of the time. There is, however, considerable variation in loss rates depending upon the type of weapon employed. When the offender had a gun, 36 percent of all personal victimizations resulted in loss; when the offender was armed with a knife, 27 percent resulted in loss; and

Table 4-4. Loss By Offender's Weapon Use, Eight-City Aggregate, 1972[a]

| | *Loss* | | |
	Yes	*No*	*Total*
Weapon[b]	28%[c]	72%[c]	47%[d]
	(23,277)	(61,143)	(84,421)
No Weapon	30%	70%	53%[d]
	(28,793)	(66,599)	(95,392)
Total	29%	71%	100%[d]
	(52,070)	(127,742)	(179,812)
Gun	36%	64%	44%[e]
	(13,404)	(23,548)	(36,952)
Knife	27%	73%	28%
	(6,338)	(17,430)	(23,769)
Other	16%	84%	30%
	(4,083)	(21,214)	(25,298)

[a]Subcategories may not sum to total because of rounding. Includes only cases in which weapon use was ascertained.
[b]Multiple response question: Victims may have reported more than one type of weapon, and thus subcategories may sum to more than 100 percent.
[c]Row percent.
[d]Percent of "total" victimizations.
[e]Percent of victimizations in which weapons were used.

when the offender was armed with an "other" weapon, 16 percent of the victimizations resulted in loss. Therefore, although those victimizations in which guns were involved were least likely to result in bodily injury to the victim, they were the most likely to result in the loss of property. Similarly, those victimizations that involved "other" weapons had an extremely high rate of injury, yet were the least likely to involve property loss.

Assault and Bodily Injury

Those victimizations in which the victim was physically attacked were less likely than victimizations in which the victim was not physically attacked to result in property loss to the victim. Although 26 percent of the victimizations involving a physical attack resulted in loss, 37 percent of those not involving a physical attack resulted in loss. Among the various forms of attack, victimizations in which the offender grabbed, held, or pushed the victim were most likely (31 percent), and victimizations in which the victim was hit by a thrown object were least likely (8 percent), to result in property loss. Of all personal victimizations resulting in loss, 5 percent involved shooting at or knifing the victim; 20 percent involved hitting, slapping, or knocking down the victim; 14 percent, grabbing, holding, or pushing; and 3 percent, some other form of attack.

Bodily injury to victims of personal crime is inversely associated with having something stolen during the incident. Twenty-five percent of those incidents resulting in injury to the victim also resulted in loss, whereas 35 percent of the noninjury victimizations resulted in loss. Considering only those victimizations in which there was something stolen from the victim, one in five also resulted in injury to the victim. Thus, *four out of five actual theft victimizations resulted in no injury to the victim.*

As might be expected, there is some degree of variability in loss rates according to the specific type of injury suffered. For example, among those receiving bruises or black eyes (78 percent of all injured victims), 26 percent also had something stolen, whereas 35 percent of those with broken bones or teeth and 39 percent of those receiving internal injuries had something stolen.

Self-Protective Measures and the Victim-Offender Relationship

The use of some form of self-protection during the victimization was explored at length in the discussion of bodily injury. It was found that the use of specific self-protective measures, in particular physical resistance, was highly correlated with an injurious outcome. However, it was pointed out that the exact role that victim resistance plays in terms of injury is problematic due to our lack of knowledge about the sequence of events; whether injury preceded or followed the victim's physical resistance is unknown. Any relation between the victim's use of self-protective measures and loss would seem to be less ambiguous. That is, an offender who is resisted may be more inclined (than he was before the victim resisted) to attack the victim, but there is less reason to believe that an offender who is resisted will be more inclined (than he was before the victim resisted) to demand or take the victim's property.

That many victims perceive some utility in taking self-protective measures is evidenced by the fact that over one-half of all victims of personal crime took some form of defensive action. Of those who took a self-protective measure, only 15 percent had something stolen, while 51 percent of those not taking a self-protective measure had something stolen. As Table 4-5 indicates, the percentage of victimizations resulting in theft varied substantially by the specific form of self-protective measure taken. When the victim used or brandished a weapon in a personal victimization, only 8 percent of

Table 4-5. Loss By Victim's Use of Self-Protective Measures, Eight-City Aggregate, 1972[a]

	Loss		
	Yes	No	Total
No Self-Protective Measure Taken, Not Ascertained	51%[c] (51,929)	49%[c] (49,811)	49%[d] (101,739)
Some Self-Protective Measure Taken[b]	15% (15,732)	85% (91,247)	51% (106,979)
Total	32% (67,661)	68% (141,058)	100% (208,719)
Physical Force (Hit, Kicked)	16% (5,901)	84% (30,931)	18% (36,833)
Evasive Action (Left Scene)	7% (2,108)	93% (26,197)	14% (28,305)
Try to Get Help (Yelled, Screamed)	29% (4,154)	71% (10,105)	7% (14,259)
Resist Without Force (Argued, Threatened, Reasoned)	12% (1,475)	88% (11,189)	6% (12,665)
Weapon	8% (628)	92% (7,475)	4% (8,103)
Held Onto Property	29% (1,578)	71% (3,857)	3% (5,435)
Other Self-Protective Measure	14% (3,001)	86% (17,658)	10% (20,659)

[a]Subcategories may not sum to total because of rounding.
[b]Multiple response question: Victims may have reported more than one self-protection measure and thus subcategories may sum to more than 100 percent.
[c]Row percent.
[d]Percent of "total" victimizations.

the time was a theft completed in the event. In victimizations in which the victim used physical resistance, 16 percent resulted in loss; when the victim argued, threatened, or reasoned with the offender, 12 percent; when the victim tried to get help, 29 percent; and when the victim tried to hold onto his or her property, 29 percent resulted in loss. It is clear, then, that victim behavior during the confrontation is closely associated with whether or not there is a loss of property.

In connection with our last three topics of discussion—the use of weapons, assault and bodily injury, and self-protective measures—it seems particularly appropriate to explore how these variables are related to loss when only those victimizations in which there was an apparent theft motive are included. That is, to appreciate the effectiveness of weapons and attacks in completing thefts, and the effectiveness of self-protective measures in thwarting thefts, we should focus on victimizations in which theft was attempted or actually completed. For example, many self-protective measures may be most frequently employed by victims during assaultive encounters that do not involve either theft or attempted theft. Thus, the strong relations between these self-protective measures and theft may simply reflect the fact that when self-protective measures are used, the principal component of the crimes is assault without theft and thus an artificial relation is necessarily obtained. For example, the use of a weapon as a self-protective measure may not be indicative of thwarting a loss of property (as the 8 percent theft rate in Table 4-5 would imply) but may rather be indicative of the fact that the use of a weapon by the victim occurs primarily during crimes in which theft is not a motive.

In the absence of knowledge about the offender's motivation, there is no entirely satisfactory manner in which these various explanations about the role of self-protective measures in theft victimizations can be addressed. However, some indication may be gained by examining the percentages of attempted and completed thefts by type of weapon, attack, and type of self-protective measure for victimizations in which there was an apparent theft motive—that is, for victimizations in which there was an attempted or completed theft.

In our discussion of the relationship between loss and use of weapons when all personal victimizations were included (Table 4-4), it was noted that no substantial relationship between the presence or absence of a weapon and loss was found. In Table 4-6 it can be seen that in those personal victimizations in which there was an apparent theft motive, weapon-present victimizations were slightly *less* likely to be completed than were weapon-absent victimizations (66 percent versus 68 percent). In these theft-motivated victimizations in which the offender was armed with a gun, 77 percent were completed, compared with 59 percent when the offender had a knife and 54 percent when the offender had an "other" weapon. These findings parallel those reported above when all personal victimizations were included (Table 4-4).

As noted in our discussion of the relationship between physical attack and loss when all personal victimizations were considered, victimizations in which the victim was physically attacked were

Table 4–6. Loss by Offender's Weapon Use (Theft-Motivated Victimizations Only), Eight-City Aggregate, 1972[a]

| | Theft-Motivated Victimizations Only | | |
| | Loss | | |
	Yes	No	Total
Weapon[b]	66%[c]	34%[c]	36%[d]
	(23,277)	(12,268)	(35,545)
No weapon	72%	28%	64%[d]
	(28,793)	(13,422)	(42,214)
Total	69%	31%	100%[d]
	(52,070)	(25,690)	(77,759)
Gun	77%	23%	49%[e]
	(13,404)	(4,082)	(17,485)
Knife	59%	41%	30%
	(6,338)	(4,475)	(10,814)
Other	54%	46%	22%
	(4,083)	(3,524)	(7,607)

[a]Subcategories may not sum to total because of rounding. Includes only those victimizations in which there was a completed or attempted theft.
[b]Multiple response question: Victims may have reported more than one type of weapon and thus subcategories may sum to more than 100 percent.
[c]Row percent.
[d]Percent of "total" victimizations.
[e]Percent of victimizations in which weapons were used.

less likely to result in loss than those in which there was no physical attack (26 percent versus 37 percent). The finding is similar, though the difference is smaller, when only theft-motivated victimizations are considered; when there was an actual physical attack, 66 percent were completed, compared to 71 percent when there was not an attack.

By excluding victimizations in which there was no theft or attempted theft, some indication of the extent and utility of victim self-protective measures may be gained. As shown in Table 4–7, there were an estimated 97,353 personal victimizations involving theft or attempted theft in these eight cities; of these, 31 percent involved an attempt to steal something and 69 percent involved an actual theft. In 38 percent of these events, the victim took some form of self-protective measure. Of interest is the finding that in theft-motivated victimizations in which a self-protective measure was used, 42 percent were completed, whereas in those in which no self-protective measure was used, 86 percent were completed. Table

4-7 also shows that for each type of self-protective measure, the theft was considerably less likely to be completed than when no self-protective measure was used. These results suggest that a relatively high proportion of victims employ self-protective measures in theft-related incidents and that such measures apparently are effective in thwarting property loss. It is especially noteworthy that physical resistance, the self-protective measure most closely associated with bodily injury, is among the three *least* likely forms of self-protective

Table 4-7. Loss by Victim's Use of Self-Protective Measures (Theft-Motivated Victimizations Only), Eight-City Aggregate, 1972[a]

	Theft-Motivated Victimizations Only		
	Loss		
	Yes	*No*	*Total*
No Self-Protective Measure	86%[c] (51,929)	14%[c] (8,147)	62%[d] (60,076)
Self-Protective Measure[b]	42% (15,732)	58% (21,545)	38% (37,277)
Total	69% (67,661)	31% (29,692)	100% (97,353)
Physical Force (Hit, Kicked)	45% (5,901)	55% (7,229)	35%[e] (13,131)
Evasive Action (Left Scene)	30% (2,108)	70% (4,906)	19% (7,013)
Try to Get Help (Yelled, Screamed)	57% (4,154)	43% (3,096)	19% (7,250)
Resist Without Force (Argued, Threatened, Reasoned)	41% (1,475)	59% (2,129)	10% (3,604)
Weapon	26% (628)	74% (1,760)	6% (2,388)
Hold Onto Property	30% (1,578)	70% (3,596)	14% (5,174)
Other Self-Protective Measure	48% (3,001)	52% (3,305)	17% (6,306)

[a]Subcategories may not sum to total because of rounding. Includes only those victimizations in which there was a completed or attempted theft.

[b]Multiple response question: Victims may have reported more than one type of weapon and thus subcategories may sum to more than 100 percent.

[c]Row percent.

[d]Percent of "total" victimizations.

[e]Percent of victimizations in which self-protective measures were used.

measures to thwart a theft. When these findings are read in conjunction with what was learned about the use of self-protective
measures in connection with injury, they lend support to the inference that *a major tradeoff for victims in theft-related incidents
may be retaining their property at the risk of increasing their likelihood of injury.*

Summary of Loss Correlates

That injury and loss, at the bivariate level, are differentially
related to the elements of personal victimization examined lends
substantial support to the approach taken here, in which separate
analyses are undertaken for loss and injury. Both loss rates and
injury rates were found to vary according to the place in which the
event occurred; however, the greatest risk of loss during personal
victimizations was for "on the street" and "inside commercial
buildings or public conveyances," while the greatest risk of personal
injury was "inside the home."

Variation in loss rates was found to be slightly associated with
the various time of occurrence categories, with daytime victimizations more likely to result in loss to the victim than nighttime
victimizations. The distribution of loss rates by the presence of
specific types of weapons used by offenders was found to be substantially different from the relations found for bodily injury.
Victimizations in which a gun was present had relatively high loss
rates (yet low injury rates), whereas when an "other" weapon was
involved, there was a corresponding low loss rate and a high injury
rate. The conscious selection of high intimidation value weapons by
offenders in loss-motivated events and the victims' differential
propensity to resist according to the types of weapons with which
they are confronted were suggested as possible explanations for
these relationships.

Both the specific forms of self-protective measures and the victim-
offender relationship were found to be associated with the theft of
property. Additionally, of the offender variables, only race was
strongly related to differential loss rates.

Our bivariate analyses have demonstrated that informative differences in rates of loss for personal victimizations may be uncovered
by considering the various elements of the events. It is now time to
investigate how these various aspects of the victimization experience
are related to loss when they are considered simultaneously.

LOSS FUNCTION-SPECIFIC
OFFENSE ANALYSIS

Predictive attribute analysis again served as our analytic tool. Decision rules employed were identical to those used for the analysis of injury. Again, the random split-half cross-validation technique was used to assess the reliability of the solution. The dichotomous attribute "something stolen" versus "nothing stolen" served as the criterion, with all offense elements coded as attributes (see Appendix C). Variables that were necessarily associated with theft, such as the amount of loss or the type of property stolen, were excluded from the analysis.

Figure 4-1 presents the dendrogram of the PAA solution performed on the first random half sample of the eight-city victimizations. Of the estimated 104,340 personal victimizations in this half sample, 32 percent resulted in something being stolen from the victim. Among those attributes available for analysis, whether or not the victim took *any* self-protective measure is most highly associated with loss. Among those victimizations in which the victim took a self-protective measure, 14 percent resulted in loss, whereas when no self-protective measure was taken, 51 percent resulted in loss. Thus, as was the case for physical injury, it appears that what the victim does during the victim-offender encounter is relatively strongly related to the outcome of the event. When injury was the criterion variable, the use of physical resistance was the most highly associated attribute, with the use of physical force being associated with a greater injury rate. In this analysis of loss, the most predictive attribute is the use of *any* self-protective measure, with the use of a self-protective measure being associated with a lower loss rate.[6]

Moving to the second level of the dendrogram, among those who did not use a self-protective measure during the event, the race of the offender is the most predictive attribute. In those victimizations in which the offender's race was perceived to be white, 22 percent incurred some loss, whereas in those events in which the offender's race was perceived to be black/other, 58 percent incurred some loss. On the other side of the diagram, it can be seen that among those using a self-protective measure, the specific self-protective measure of "tried to get help" is most highly associated with loss. Those trying to get help incurred a loss rate of 12 percent, while those not employing this measure had a loss rate of 28 percent.

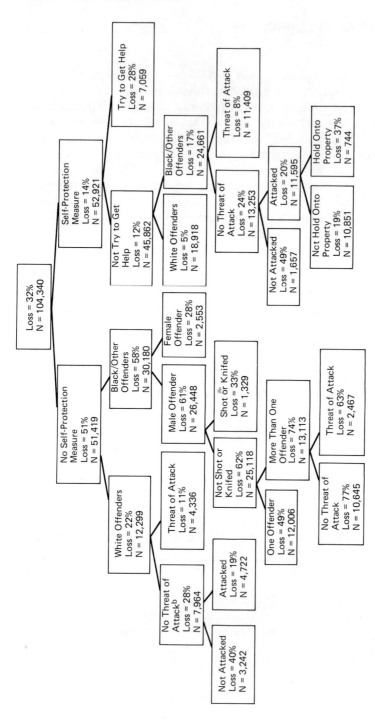

Figure 4-1. Predictive Attribute Analysis of Loss, Random Half Sample of Eight-City Aggregate, 1972[a]

[a]Subcategories may not sum to total because of rounding and missing data. See Appendix C for definitions of attributes
[b]Persons who were actually attacked are included. See Appendix C.

Thus, by the second level of the analysis, four subgroups of victimizations have been defined on the basis of objective characteristics of the victimization; they have rates of loss ranging from a low of 12 percent to a high of 58 percent.

Each of these categories was further subdivided, as shown in Figure 4-1, and further discrimination was achieved. The category defined as "no self-protective measure" and "white offenders' was found to break next according to whether or not the offenders made a threat to attack the victim in any way (but did not actually attack the victim).[7] Among those who were so threatened, 28 percent suffered some loss, but only 11 percent of those not so threatened had a loss. Within the group characterized by "not taking self-protective measures" and "black/other offenders," the sex of the offender(s) was the splitting attribute. When the offender was a male, the loss rate was extremely high (61 percent), whereas when the offender was a female, the loss rate (28 percent) was somewhat below the mean for the entire sample.

On the other side of the diagram, when self-protective measures were used *and* the victim did not try to get help, the race of the offender is most highly associated with loss. Victimizations of this type in which the offender was white resulted in loss 5 percent of the time, and those in which the offender was black/other resulted in loss 17 percent of the time.

The PAA solution proceeded for six levels in some branches, resulting in fourteen terminal groups. Whether or not the victim was actually physically attacked by the offender, the use of threats and intimidation by the offender, and several offender characteristics were found to enter the solution. The terminal categories have been summarized, along with the loss rates and the percentage of the sample falling into each category, in Table 4-8. The loss rates for this construction sample ranged from a low of 5 percent (for victimizations in which the offender(s) was white and the victim did not try to get help but some self-protective measure was used) to a high of 77 percent (for victimizations in which there was no threat of attack, there was more than one offender, the victim was not shot or knifed, the offender(s) was male and black/other, and no self-protective measure was taken). An examination of Table 4-8 shows that, unlike the injury PAA, this loss PAA results in no single terminal group containing a majority of the victimizations. Whereas the construction sample for injury contained one group with 68 percent of the sample cases, the largest terminal category for loss contains 18 percent of the cases (Class 14); this class had the lowest loss rate (5 percent). Thus, this PAA was able to achieve considerable

Table 4-8. Summary of Terminal Groups for Predictive Attribute Analysis of Loss, Eight-City Aggregate, 1972

Class	Constituent Elements[a]	Construction		Validation		Total	
		Terminal Group Size	Percent Loss	Terminal Group Size	Percent Loss	Terminal Group Size	Percent Loss
1	No threat of attack, more than one offender, not shot or knifed, male offenders, black/other offenders, no SPM.[b]	10%[c] (10,645)	77	10% (9,981)	74	10% (20,626)	76
2	Threat of attack, more than one offender, not shot or knifed, male offenders, black/other offenders, no SPM.	2% (2,467)	63	3% (2,765)	51	3% (5,232)	57
3	One offender, not shot or knifed, male offenders, black/other offenders, no SPM.	12% (12,006)	49	11% (10,497)	53	11% (22,503)	51
4	No attack, no threat, black/other offenders, not try to get help, SPM.	2% (1,657)	49	2% (1,578)	54	2% (3,235)	52
5	Not attacked, no threat of attack, white offenders, no SPM.	3% (3,242)	40	3% (3,252)	42	3% (6,494)	41
6	Hold onto property, attack, no threat, black/other offenders, not try to get help, SPM.	1% (744)	37	1% (789)	37	1% (1,533)	37
7	Shot or knifed, male offenders, black/other offenders, no SPM.	1% (1,329)	33	2% (1,789)	41	1% (3,118)	38
8	Female offender, black/other offenders, no SPM.	2% (2,553)	28	2% (2,442)	24	2% (4,995)	26

9	Try to get help, SPM.	7% (7,059)	28	7% (7,171)	30	7% (14,230)	29
10	Not hold onto property, attack, no threat, black/other offenders, not try to get help, SPM.	10% (10,851)	19	11% (11,047)	18	10% (21,898)	18
11	Attacked, no threat of attack, white offenders, no SPM.	4% (4,722)	19	5% (5,433)	18	5% (10,155)	18
12	Threat of attack, white offenders, no SPM.	4% (4,336)	11	3% (3,122)	10	4% (7,458)	11
13	Threat, black/other offenders, not try to get help, SPM.	11% (11,409)	8	11% (11,367)	12	11% (22,776)	10
14	White offender, not try to get help, SPM.	18% (18,918)	5	19% (19,867)	7	19% (38,785)	6
Total		(104,340)d	32%	(104,379)d	32%	(208,719)d	32%

[a]Subcategories may not sum to total because of rounding and missing data. See Appendix C for definitions of the constituent elements.

[b]SPM is an abbreviation for self-protective measures.

[c]Column percent.

[d]Included in this total, but not reflected in separate classes, are cases for which offender characteristics were not ascertained.

discrimination among the subgroups in rates of loss, without a concentration of victimizations in any single subgroup.

The Stability of the PAA

Before considering this classification in detail, the requisite cross-validation process needs to be examined. The results of a forced validation on the alternate random half of the eight-city sample are also presented in Table 4-8. Of the 104,379 victimizations in this cross-validation sample, 32 percent resulted in some loss to the victim. In comparing the respective loss rates for categories between the construction and validation samples, it can be seen that most categories are very consistent; the most substantial incomparability exists for Class 2, one of the smallest terminal subgroups, in which the construction sample had a loss rate of 63 percent and the validation sample had a loss rate of 51 percent. Some indication of the relative comparability of the construction and validation samples is given by the weighted mean absolute difference between construction and validation sample loss rates, 2.52. In addition, the Spearman *rho* for the construction and validation class ranks was 0.97 and the Pearson's *r* was also 0.97.[8]

DISCUSSION OF LOSS ANALYSIS

The results of the loss analysis, when read in conjunction with the injury analysis, substantially support our initial decision to analyze the harms of injury and loss separately. These results suggest that quite dissimilar offense elements are important in accounting for variation in rates of injury and loss. This, in turn, suggests that analytic solutions that do not differentiate between these harms may mask important information about the nature of personal victimization. Before discussing several specific subcategories of the loss system in detail, some general observations are in order.

The attribute most highly correlated with loss in these eight cities was whether or not the victim used some form of self-protective measure. Thus, as was true for injury, it appears that what the victim does during the event is highly related to the outcome. It will be recalled that a specific type of self-protective measure (physical force) was most predictive of bodily injury. Of central importance, however, are the directions of the relationships obtained: *for injury, the use of physical resistance was associated with increased probabilities of bodily harm, while for loss, the use of any self-protective measure was associated with decreased probabilities of loss. As*

Table 4-5 shows, every type of self-protective measure was associated with a lower than average loss probability.

Whereas offender characteristics were not important in the injury analytic solution, a number of offender characteristics are central to explaining variation in loss probabilities. The race of the offender was found to have a substantial bivariate association with loss, and the offender's race enters the classification system at two points. In both instances, as foreshadowed by the bivariate analysis, victims who were confronted by black/other offenders had higher loss rates than did victims confronted by white offenders. At one point in the classification structure, sex interacts with race and self-protective measures to produce a loss rate of more than 60 percent for victimizations involving male, black/other offenders and no self-protective measure.

The type of weapon used by the offender, which was found to be so important in accounting for variation in injury, is not important in the loss PAA solution.[9] What appears to be of more importance in this structure is whether or not the victim was threatened with harm. At each point in the PAA at which the attribute of threat enters the solution there is a negative association with loss—that is, when there was no threat, the loss rate is higher than when a threat was made.

Another set of attributes that is notable for its absence from the loss PAA solution is the place of occurrence categories. It will be recalled that place of occurrence was an important dimension in the injury analysis, and the absence of any place of occurrence categories in the loss analytic solution is of interest. The bivariate relationships discussed earlier indicated only moderate variation in loss rates according to the place in which the victimization occurred, and evidently these relationships are accounted for by attributes entering early in the PAA.

The category in the loss classification with the highest overall probability of loss is defined by no self-protective measure, multiple black/other male offenders, not shot or knifed, and no threat of attack. These offense elements clearly suggest victimizations in which the victim was confronted by a group of offenders with a demand for money or property. This class differs from Class 2 (also with a high rate of loss) only in that in Class 2 there was some form of verbal threat. Class 3, which also had a high loss rate (49 percent), had offense elements similar to those in Classes 1 and 2, but differed in that only one offender was involved in the incident. These findings may indicate that intimidation by multiple male offenders may reduce the likelihood that victims will take self-protective measures and increase the likelihood of loss. It is worth noting that Class 3, in which *lone* offenders were involved, had a substantially smaller loss rate than either Class 1 or Class 2, in which multiple offenders were involved.

At the other extreme in loss rates are victimizations in which a self-protective measure was used that did not consist of "trying to get help." In such situations in which the offender was white, the loss rate was only 5 percent, and in such situations further character- ized by black/other offenders who gave no threat of attack, the loss rate was only 8 percent. Most probably these victimizations reflect interpersonal encounters in which, unlike the group offender situa- tions discussed above, theft is not a primary motive.

In general, the loss analysis demonstrates that a number of em- pirically derived and reliable classes of offense elements may be constructed that substantially differentiate victimizations according to probabilities of loss. The crucial role that victim behavior during the event plays is clearly indicated by the resulting structure. The fact that identifiable offender characteristics are important in account- ing for variation in loss but not injury, suggests that, for the most part, the two forms of harm may not be closely linked. Our attention now turns to the manner in which victim characteristics are related to these classes.

THE INTERSECTION OF EVENTS
AND PERSONS

The procedure for studying the associations among victim character- istics and the various function-specific offense classes that was adopted for the injury analysis will be followed in this discussion of loss. Table 4-9 presents the distribution of selected victim character- istics for each terminal class derived from the loss analysis, the number of victimizations falling into each class, the rate of loss for each class, and the overall distribution of selected personal character- istics in the eight-city population. The description corresponding to the class numbers in Table 4-9 can be found in Table 4-8.

Several striking patterns emerge from Table 4-9. Class 8, which consists of the elements no self-protective measures, black/other offenders, and female offenders, was almost exclusively comprised of female victims (89 percent). These victims were also primarily single, divorced or separated (70 percent), and under twenty years of age (50 percent). The corresponding proportions of these character- istics, as they are estimated to occur in the eight cities studied, are 55 percent, 40 percent, and 20 percent. The victims in this class were

Table 4-9. Victim Characteristics for Loss Offense Classes Compared to Characteristics of General Population, Eight-City Aggregate, 1972[a]

Class[c]	Percent Loss	Number of Cases	Marital Status (percent) Married or Widowed	Single, Separated, Divorced	Race (percent) White	Black/ Other	Sex (percent) Male	Female	Family Income[b] (percent) Under $3,000	$3,000- 7,499	$7,500- 9,999	$10,000- 14,999	$15,000- 24,999	$25,000 Or More	Age (percent) 12-15	16-19	20-24	25-34	35-49	50-64	65 or Older
1	76	(20,626)	44[d]	56	46	54	63	37	21	36	12	13	6	2	11	13	11	11	20	22	13
2	57	(5,232)	30	70	47	53	78	22	15	30	12	20	13	2	26	24	11	14	12	11	1
3	51	(22,503)	40	60	41	59	44	56	21	34	9	17	9	2	15	13	14	16	15	16	11
4	52	(3,235)	49	51	60	40	16	84	22	39	8	18	8	0	9	11	8	10	21	25	16
5	41	(6,494)	48	52	91	9	60	40	16	27	10	21	10	6	8	14	16	17	17	16	12
6	37	(1,533)	39	61	61	39	44	56	20	21	14	30	11	1	24	14	6	7	14	27	8
7	38	(3,118)	35	65	25	75	81	19	23	33	13	13	5	1	15	15	10	15	26	14	6
8	26	(4,995)	30	70	54	46	11	89	15	31	8	20	13	5	30	20	11	11	10	10	8
9	29	(14,230)	43	57	69	31	19	81	20	31	12	18	7	3	12	14	20	16	11	14	9
10	18	(21,898)	27	73	46	54	65	35	17	35	10	18	10	3	22	25	16	11	16	7	3
11	18	(10,155)	32	68	93	7	59	41	19	31	8	21	10	3	20	22	15	14	11	10	4
12	11	(7,458)	38	62	96	4	71	29	12	26	11	24	13	5	15	21	23	20	12	7	3
13	10	(22,776)	40	60	57	43	65	35	14	30	13	20	13	4	15	21	18	20	20	10	3
14	6	(38,785)	40	60	94	6	66	34	13	26	11	25	17	4	13	20	24	21	13	7	3
Percent in Population	60		60	40	65	35	45	55	13	28	13	20	12	4	10	10	11	16	20	19	14

[a]Subcategories may not sum to total because of rounding.
[b]Persons whose family income was not ascertained are not included in this table.
[c]Class numbers refer to numbers shown in Table 4-8.
[d]Row percent.

97

also slightly more likely (in terms of their representation in the population) to be black/other (46 percent). Although this grouping makes up a small proportion of the personal victimizations in the eight cities (2 percent), there are clearly close associations between the victim characteristics and the offense elements. Given that the loss rate for this offense class was 26 percent, it may be that these victimizations were primarily assaultive crimes. If this is true, it is interesting that both the victims and the offenders were female.

Another loss class in which the victims were almost exclusively female is Class 9, which is comprised of the offense elements "self-protective measure" and "try to get help." The loss rate for Class 9 was 29 percent, and the victims were disproportionately female (81 percent) and somewhat disproportionately from families with low annual incomes (20 percent under $3,000). It may be that the offense element "try to get help" is important in segregating females into this class. The category is composed of victimizations in which the victim attempted to attract attention, screamed, yelled, called for help, and so forth. Data not presented here demonstrate that female victims were more likely than male victims to report using such forms of self-protection during a victimization. It is of interest to note in this regard that the bivariate analysis of self-protective measures and loss suggests that this form of self-protective measure was the least effective in preventing property loss. This analysis may indicate, then, that for this specific type of victimization in which women were involved, the use of attention-attracting measures may not be effective in preventing the loss of property.

A third offense class, Class 4, which is comprised of the offense elements not attacked, no threat of attack, black/other offenders, not try to get help, and self-protective measure, also involved almost exclusively female victims (84 percent). Of further interest is that this class, which had a high loss rate (52 percent), disproportionately contained lower income persons (61 percent under $7,500 per year) and older persons (41 percent over fifty years old). This class is one of the few that contained a greater proportional representation of older persons than that found in the general population. The fact that these victimizations involved neither threats nor physical attacks and that females were the primary victims suggests that a major component of these events may be "grab and flee" purse snatches. It is noteworthy that whereas older females may be the most appropriate targets for such events from the offender's point of view, due perhaps to a lessened ability to resist or pursue the offender, these victims might also be expected to carry fewer valuables, as indicated by the relatively low total family incomes. This may suggest, then, that the certainty of completing the crime may be of more concern to the offenders involved in Class 4 victimizations than the amount of personal gain from any one event. Also, lower income female victims are likely to reside in lower income areas in these cities and hence to be convenient targets for offenders who also disproportionately reside in lower income areas.

This reasoning may also be germane to Class 1, which had the extremely high loss rate of 76 percent and is comprised of the offense elements no threat of attack, more than one offender, not shot or knifed, male offenders, black/other offenders, and no self-protective measures. Earlier it was suggested that the lack of self-protective measures may be accounted for in this class by the fact that multiple offenders were involved, presenting a disparity too great to overcome by the use of some form of self-protection. The victim characteristics that predominate in this class lend support to this notion, as well as to the argument that certainty of completion may be more important to some offenders than the amount of gain. The victim characteristics in Class 1 indicate an overrepresentation of black/others (54 percent), males (63 percent), and persons of low family income (57 percent under $7,500). The age distribution of persons in this category indicates a proportional representation to persons in the general population. It is again interesting to note the marked association between personal characteristics and specific elements of the offense. Males were the primary victims in these events, suggesting that offending in groups may be seen by the offenders themselves as a strategy for ensuring compliance with the demand for money or property.

Class 2 (57 percent loss rate), which differs from the foregoing class only in that there was a threat of attack, is again comprised disproportionately of male victims (78 percent), who are proportionately representative in terms of family income but, importantly, who are disproportionately young (50 percent under nineteen years of age). To a large extent, the demographic characteristics of the victims in this class may explain why threats were used in these victimizations but not in the otherwise identical victimizations in Class 1. These younger male victims may be expected to offer more resistance than the older victims found in Class 1, and thus a verbal threat of physical harm by the offender may be thought necessary to overcome resistance.

Class 7 (38 percent loss rate) is comprised of victimizations in which the victim was shot or knifed, the offenders were male and black/other, and no self-protective measures were used. Because the victims here were disproportionately black/others (75 percent), the offense class is largely intraracial. In addition, these victims were disproportionately single, separated or divorced (65 percent), males (81 percent), young (30 percent under twenty years old), and from families with lower incomes (56 percent under $7,500 per year).

Racial disproportionality among victims is found to exist in many of the specific offense categories. Three of the offense categories with the lowest loss rates were almost exclusively made up of white victims. In Class 14, which had a loss rate of 6 percent, 94 percent of the victims were white. Similarly, Class 12 had a loss rate of only 11 percent, with 96 percent white victims, and Class 11 had a loss rate of 18 percent, with 93 percent white victims. In each of these classes the victims were disproportionately male and young (under twenty-five years of age). Importantly, one offense element that defines each of these classes is that the offenders were white. Thus, the intraracial nature of these victimizations with a very low loss rate is apparent; the low loss rate suggests that these events are primarily assaultive crimes in which theft was not the motive.

Classes 11 and 12 differ from each other only in that in the latter there was some threat of physical attack (but no actual attack), while in the former there was an actual physical attack. In neither case did the victim use a self-protective measure. It is of some interest to note that females made up a greater proportion of the victims in Class 11, in which there was an actual attack, than in Class 12, in which there was not. Class 5 differs from Class 11 only in that the victim was not attacked, although the loss rate in the former was considerably higher (40 percent versus 19 percent). The victims in Class 5 had characteristics similar to those in Class 11, with the exception that the former tended to be somewhat older than the latter and were more likely to be married or widowed.

Clearly, the amount of information presented in Table 4-9 is extensive and could serve as the basis for a great deal of discussion. This method of analysis has, however, demonstrated that the notion of linking specific elements of offenses with specific characteristics of persons appears to be a valuable analytical tool. Many personal characteristics have been found to be highly associated with specific forms of offenses that differ not only in their constituent elements, but also in the probabilities of a loss outcome. Some of these associations indicate that some offenders may be more concerned with the certainty of completing a victimization than with the potential gain. The data also suggest an intraracial nature for many specific forms of personal victimization, and many of the victims in classes evidencing high rates of loss are disproportionately of lower family incomes.

Much more will be said about personal characteristics associated with victimization in later chapters, in which some of the implications of these results will be drawn. The function-specific analysis of victimizations presented in this chapter has indicated that it can be an extremely valuable technique, not only for a more complete understanding of criminal offenses, but as a tool to aid in the comprehension of characteristics of persons victimized. A great deal has been learned about personal loss and physical injury to victims of crime in this and the preceding chapter. The relative success with the method supports the notion that it may also have utility in helping us to isolate characteristics of respondents that are associated with risks of personal victimization. This is the subject of the next chapter.

NOTES

1. Unfortunately, the UCR does not differentiate between larceny from the person and larceny of property not in the possession of the person such as larcenies from the household and from commercial establishments. Undoubtedly, a large proportion of UCR larcenies do not involve a confrontation between the victim and the offender. All of the larcenies discussed here involve some form of personal contact between the victim and the offender. Further, the UCR does not differentiate between personal and commercial robbery. All commercial robberies have been excluded from the robberies discussed here.

2. The marked difference in the proportion of strangers involved in theft versus assaultive crimes lends some support to the distinction made in the present research between injury and theft.

3. All three of these studies, however, included business robberies, which are more likely than personal robberies to occur indoors. Thus, these percentages probably underestimate the proportion of personal robberies that occur on the street.

4. The category "none" under value of loss refers to the theft of valueless items (such as a letter) as well as stolen checks or credit cards.

5. Near the victim's home includes the yard, driveway, and sidewalk.

6. In a separate analysis not presented here, when only theft-motivated victimizations were included, the first break was also on self-protective measures. For those not using self-protective measures, 86 percent incurred loss, and for those using self-protective measures, 42 percent incurred loss.

7. As the skip pattern for the detailed incident questionnaire in Appendix A indicates, only those victims who were not attacked were asked whether the offender threatened them in any way.

8. Our replication analysis (see Chapter 3, footnote 25) produced a similar solution, particularly with regard to the first partitioning attributes.

9. As Table 4-4 shows, however, type of weapon was related to probabilities of loss at the bivariate level.

The Risk of Personal Victimization

In Part I, our principal focus was on the consequences of personal victimization in terms of bodily injury and property loss suffered by victims of personal crimes, and we gave only peripheral attention to the characteristics of victims. In Part II our focus shifts to the victims themselves. Chapter 5 asks the general question of what personal characteristics differentiate victims from nonvictims. More specifically it attempts to discover differences between (1) persons who suffer victimization with bodily injury, and (2) persons who suffer either no personal victimization or no personal victimization involving bodily injury. Parallel differences between persons who suffer property loss victimizations and persons who do not are also sought. In Chapter 5 these contrasts between certain types of victims and nonvictims are again accomplished using predictive attribute analysis as an analytic classification method.

In Chapter 6 our concern is also on victimization risk characteristics. In this chapter, however, we are primarily concerned with multiple victimization. Multiple victimization, in our narrowest use of the term, is defined as two or more victimizations reported by the same person within the twelve-month reference period. These victimizations need not be of the same specific type (e.g., robbery) in order to be counted as multiple victimizations. More broadly, multiple victimization also encompasses victimization of two or more persons from the same household within the twelve-month reference period. Within Chapter 6, the context will make clear how the concept of multiple victimizations is being used.

The analysis of multiple victimization is important because it provides additional clues about victimization experiences that are of considerable theoretical and empirical import. In Chapter 6 our analytic method is primarily tabular in nature, because it is useful to view many of the results as conditional probabilities. How does the unconditional likelihood of being an assault victim within the reference period compare to the likelihood of being an assault victim *given* that the respondent has also been a victim of robbery within the reference period? Similarly, is the likelihood of being the victim of a personal crime greater for individuals from households that contain another respondent who has been victimized than for individuals from households that do not contain any other person who has been victimized? The answers to these and similar questions are suggestive of mechanisms that may help to explain variations in risks of personal victimization.

✳ *Chapter 5*

Personal Characteristics and the
Probability of Personal Victimization

Most previous work in what may be termed the "victimization risk" area may be broadly categorized into three
approaches. First, a number of theoretical victim typologies
have been developed (Fattah, 1967; Lamborn, 1968; Silverman,
1974; von Hentig, 1948).[1] Although some of these theoretical
works include components that suggest factors associated with the
probability of becoming a victim of crime (e.g., von Hentig, 1948),
most have been concerned primarily with differentiating among
types of victims. For example, a major dimension along which
victims are classified in many of these theoretical works is the degree
of culpability of the victim in the crime (e.g., Lamborn, 1968).
And, importantly, most of these positions have not been grounded in
empirical research.

Second, empirical studies have examined demographic characteristics of victims using official data (e.g., Wolfgang, 1958; Amir,
1971; Normandeau, 1968). Unfortunately, studies relying on official
data may be limited for this purpose in three important respects:
(1) It is not known how representative "official victims" are of the
population of victims in general. (2) Official statistics are not generally
geared for collecting large numbers of victim characteristics, and as
a result these studies have been limited to only a few victim characteristics. (3) Such studies have not given central attention to the
question of how those victim characteristics that are available relate
to the characteristics of the general population. Before statements
concerning differential victimization risk can be made, it is necessary
to answer the question of whether or not selected characteristics of

105

victimized persons—such as age, race, marital status, employment status, and income—are disproportional in relation to the distribution of these characteristics in the general population.

Third, the demographic correlates of victimization have been studied by using victimization survey data (e.g. Ennis, 1967; Hindelang, 1976). These studies have examined characteristics of persons that are differentially associated with rates of personal victimization by means of traditional tabular procedures. Typically, such approaches have involved analyses of variations in rates of victimization when one, two, or at most three personal characteristics are considered. For example, variability in rates of personal victimization have been examined when victimization survey respondents are subdivided by race and family income, or by age, sex, and race. These approaches have been limited to a simultaneous consideration of only two or three variables because, as the survey respondents are categorized into finer and finer subgroups, the number of respondents in each cell decreases and the estimated rates of victimization become less and less reliable. Furthermore, because of the intercorrelation of many demographic variables—such as age, income, race, and marital status—the traditional tabular approach leaves us uncertain about whether the apparent relationship between a given demographic variable and victimization would remain if other relevant demographic variables were simultaneously considered. It therefore is clear that in order to shed additional light on victimization risk characteristics, it is necessary to move beyond these traditional procedures.

There are numerous analytic procedures that might be used in the construction of a victim probability classification. For example, persons could be categorized along dimensions that have been shown to be related to personal victimization—such as age, sex, and marital status—or along dimensions suggested from theoretical perspectives about victimization. Alternatively, a criterion-based classification approach similar to that used in Chapters 3 and 4 could be used.

In this chapter, several function-specific victim probability analyses will be reported. One such analysis has as a criterion whether or not the respondent was a victim of a personal crime during the reference period. Characteristics of respondents are systematically examined in order to determine which characteristics, and in what combinations, are most highly predictive of suffering *any* personal victimization. Optimally, the characteristics should be combined in such a way as to maximize their potential for explaining variation in rates of personal victimization. If the subgroups that emerge from such an analysis have substantially different probabilities of victimization, then these subgroups may serve as the basis for speculation about the sources of differential probabilities of victimization. In addition, and consistent with the focus in the preceding part of this book on objective and observable harm in personal victimization, separate analytic solutions are developed using bodily injury and property loss as criteria. For example, whether or not a respondent suffered physical injury from a personal victimization serves as one of our criteria, and personal attributes are used as predictors to separate respondents into "injury-risk" categories. It is important to stress that such victim classifications may have utility not only for organizing and ordering empirical observations concerning victimization, but may also lead to meaningful hypotheses about the nature of victimization risks.

CHARACTERISTICS OF VICTIMS OF PERSONAL CRIMES

As shown in Appendix A, the NCS victimization studies collect a variety of detailed information about interviewees. Until the advent of victimization surveys, very little systematic data concerning victims of common theft and assault were available. Researchers interested in the characteristics of victims of crime were, by and large, forced to rely on limited victim data collected for other purposes, particularly in police offense reports. With the relatively new technique of victimization surveying, valuable detailed data concerning characteristics of the victims of crime—and equally important, characteristics of the general population—can be obtained.

The correlates of personal victimization in these eight-city surveys have been examined in an earlier work (Hindelang, 1976). A brief review of these findings was presented in Chapter 1. This prior work suggests that there are demographic characteristics that are associated with variations in rates of victimization. The fact that substantial differences in personal victimization rates are found to be associated with the personal characteristics indicates that there may be some advantage in constructing a numerical taxonomy that attempts to maximize the power of these attributes in discriminating risks. The question that is posed is: How can these personal characteristics best be combined so as to account for the greatest proportion of variance in risks of personal victimization? Similar questions can be posed about differentiating personal characteristics to account for risks of bodily injury and loss. As was the case with our analytic work in

Chapters 3 and 4, predictive attribute analysis serves as the tool for addressing these questions.

Predictor Attributes

Each respondent in the survey was asked a number of questions regarding personal characteristics. For each respondent, age, sex, race, marital status, educational attainment, and employment status were ascertained whenever possible. In addition, the person designated as the household respondent (see Appendix B) was asked to give the total family income for the previous year; this information was then attached to the record of each person living in the household.

Because the analytic technique, predictive attribute analysis, requires the use of data in the form of attributes, each personal characteristic was recoded to reflect a dichotomous attribute. Whenever possible, personal characteristics were dichotomized according to natural cutting points (male versus female). Race was recoded into the categories "white" and "black/other." Both age and family income were "dummy coded" as several variables. Family income was categorized as "less than $3,000" versus "not less than $3,000," "$3,000 to $7,499" versus "not $3,000 to $7,499," and so forth up to "$25,000 or more" versus "not $25,000 or more." Similarly, age was dummy coded, as for example "sixteen to nineteen years old" versus "not sixteen to nineteen years old." See Appendix C for the complete recoding scheme.

The Criteria

The criteria for our analyses are whether or not (1) the respondent reported being the victim of a personal crime during the twelve month reference period, (2) the respondent reported being the victim of an injury, and (3) the respondent reported being the victim of a loss victimization. Regardless of the number of times the respondent reported being the victim of a crime, that person was counted as a "victim," whereas a person not reporting any victimizations was classified as a "nonvictim."[2] These criteria, then, will permit the classification of persons (based on the attributes available for study) into groups that differ in the probability of suffering *at least one* personal victimization, *at least one* injury victimization, and *at least one* loss victimization during the reference period.[3]

It is important to emphasize that rates of victimization as discussed in Chapter 1 and in Hindelang (1976) are defined as the ratio of the number of *victimizations* to the number of persons at risk. Thus, persons suffering more than one victimization during the reference period have each of their victimizations represented in the numerator.

This contrasts with the procedure used in this chapter in the sense that the focus here is on the number of distinct persons who were victimized *at least once.* That is, our "likelihood of victimization" per 1,000 persons at risk is the equivalent of ten times the percentage of persons in the risk category that were victimized at least once.

VICTIM-NONVICTIM ANALYSIS

One problem in using a multivariate technique for analyzing likelihoods of victimization is that the likelihood of personal victimization in the eight-city sample is, from a purely statistical point of view, low—51 per 1,000 persons twelve years old or older. This low base rate implies that, when standard measures of association are used to subdivide the sample, any obtained coefficients are likely to be small. In light of this, criteria must be established for our PAA that do not obscure subdivisions that would produce meaningful differences in likelihoods of victimization.

By a process of observing measures of association and the corresponding subgroup differences in likelihoods of victimization, the following criteria were established for our victim versus nonvictim predictive attribute analysis: (1) The value of the association statistic (Somers' *d*) had to be greater than ± 0.015. (2) No subgroup containing fewer than 20,000 weighted cases was further divided. (3) No split was made if the resulting subgroup would contain fewer than 10,000 cases. These rules were modified for our likelihood analyses of loss and injury. Because of the lower base likelihoods, the criterion for the value of the association statistic was changed to ± 0.010. In establishing these procedural rules, it is necessary to strike a balance between the ability to identify subgroups that are heterogeneous in their likelihoods of victimization and the danger of subdividing the data so finely that unreliable results are produced. The minimum cell size requirement is designed to ensure adequate bases for the likelihoods, and the minimum Somers' *d* value to ensure that subdivisions resulting in trivial likelihood differences are not made. These criteria are to some extent arbitrary and were evolved in the process of extensive predictive attribute analyses using the victimization data.

Figure 5-1 presents the dendrogram of the PAA solution, with "victim-nonvictim" as the criterion. It can be seen that the overall likelihood of personal victimization in these eight cities was 51 per 1,000 persons twelve years of age or older. *Among the personal characteristics available for study, age (sixteen to nineteen years*

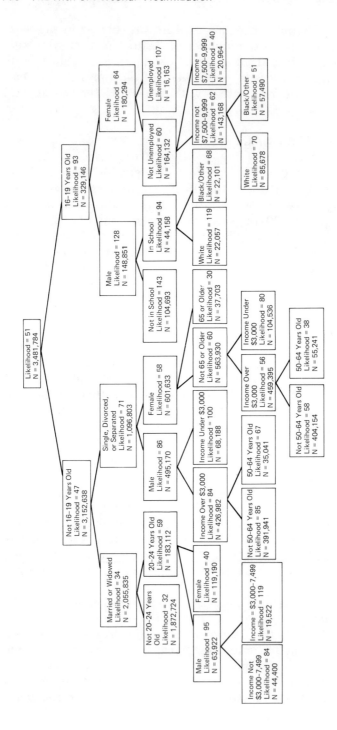

Figure 5-1. Predictive Attribute Analysis of Victimization, Eight-City Aggregate, 1972[a]

[a]Subcategories may not sum to total because of rounding. See Appendix C for definitions of attributes.

*old versus not sixteen to nineteen years old) was most closely asso-
ciated with being the victim of a personal crime during the reference
period.* The likelihood of victimization for those not sixteen to
nineteen years old was 47 per 1,000 persons, while the likelihood for
those sixteen to nineteen years old was nearly twice that figure:
93 per 1,000 persons. The first split is reflective of the correlates
discussed earlier, where it was shown that in these data the peak
age for personal victimization was sixteen to nineteen years old.

Among those who were not sixteen to nineteen years old, the
attribute that further subdivided the sample was marital status.
Those persons not sixteen to nineteen years old who were either
married or widowed were substantially less likely to be victims of
personal crimes than were those persons who were single, divorced,
or separated. The likelihood for the latter was more than twice
that of the former (71 versus 34).

For persons sixteen to nineteen years old, the sex of the respondent produced the most discriminating subgroups. For sixteen to
nineteen year old males the likelihood (128) was twice that of
sixteen to nineteen year old females (64). Thus, after two subdivisions, the likelihoods of personal victimization ranged from a
low of 34 per 1,000 married or widowed persons who were not
sixteen to nineteen years old, to a high of 128 per 1,000 sixteen to
nineteen year old males.

At the third level of the dendrogram, the category comprised of
respondents who were married or widowed and not sixteen to
nineteen years old is subdivided according to whether the respondents were twenty to twenty-four years old. Those persons who
were married or widowed, but who were neither sixteen to nineteen
years old nor twenty to twenty-four years old, had a personal victimization likelihood (32 per 1,000) considerably below the base
likelihood of the sample as a whole (51 per 1,000). Because these
persons were or had been married, it is probably correct to assume
that very few twelve to fifteen year olds were included in this sub-
category. Hence, this terminal category may be described generally
as consisting of married or widowed persons over the age of twenty-
four.

As shown in Figure 5-1, the sex of the respondent was again
found to be an important discriminator, this time for persons not
sixteen to nineteen years old who were either single, divorced, or
separated. Males with these characteristics had a personal victimization likelihood of 86 per 1,000, whereas females had a personal
victimization likelihood of 58 per 1,000.

Whether or not the person's major activity was defined as "in school" is the classification attribute that further subdivides that part of the sample characterized by sixteen to nineteen year old males.[4] Although both persons in school and not in school had very high personal victimization likelihoods, the likelihood for persons not in school (143) was 50 percent larger than the corresponding likelihood for persons in school (94). The classification attribute for sixteen to nineteen year old females on which the next subdivision occurred was an employment status attribute. Persons classified as unemployed had a substantially higher likelihood of personal victimization (107) than did persons classified as "not unemployed" (60).

As may be seen by inspection of Figure 5-1, the predictive attribute analysis proceeded for six levels of the dendrogram, at which point stopping rules were met for each branching network. The solution resulted in eighteen terminal groups, with considerable discrimination among the groups in risks of personal victimization. As shown in Table 5-1, the likelihoods of personal victimiza-

Table 5-1. Summary of Predictive Attribute Analysis on Victim-nonvictim, Eight-City Aggregate, 1972[a]

Class	Constituent Elements	Terminal Group Size	Likelihood of Victimization (Per 1,000)
1	65 years or older, female, single or divorced or separated, not 16–19 years old.	1%[b] (37,703)	30
2	Not 20–24 years old, married or widowed, not 16–19 years old.	54% (1,872,724)	32
3	50–64 years old, family income not less than $3,000, not 65 or older, female, single or divorced or separated, not 16–19 years old.	2% (55,241)	38
4	Female, 20–24 years old, married or widowed, not 16–19 years old.	3% (119,190)	40
5	Family income $7,500–$9,999, employment status: not unemployed, female, 16–19 years old.	1% (20,964)	40
6	Black/other, family income not $7,500–9,999, employment status: not unemployed, female, 16–19 years old.	2% (57,490)	51
7	Not 50–64 years old, family income more than $3,000, not 65 or older, female, single or divorced or separated, not 16–19 years old.	12% (404,154)	58

Table 5-1 continued

Class	Constituent Elements	Terminal Group Size	Likelihood of Victimization (Per 1,000)
8	50-64 years old, family income $3,000 or more, male, single or divorced or separated, not 16-19 years old.	1% (35,041)	67
9	Black/other, employment status: school, male, 16-19 years old	1% (22,101)	68
10	White, family income not $7,500-9,999, employment status: not unemployed, female, 16-19 years old.	2% (85,678)	70
11	Family income less than $3,000, not 65 or older, female, single or divorced or separated, not 16-19 years old.	3% (104,536)	80
12	Family income not $3,000-7,499, male, 20-24 years old, married or widowed, not 16-19 years old.	1% (44,400)	84
13	Not 50-64 years old, family income $3,000 or more, male, single or divorced or separated, not 16-19 years old.	11% (391,941)	85
14	Family income less than $3,000, male single or divorced or separated, not 16-19.	2% (68,188)	100
15	Employment status: unemployed, female, 16-19 years old.	(c) (16,163)	107
16	White, employment status: school, male, 16-19 years old.	1% (22,057)	119
17	Family income $3,000-7,499, male, 20-24 years old, married or widowed, not 16-19 years old.	1% (19,522)	119
18	Employment status: not school, male, 16-19 years old.	3% (104,693)	143
Total		100% (3,481,784)	51

[a]Subcategories may not sum to total because of rounding.
[b]Column percent.
[c]Less than 1 percent.

tion for these classes ranged from a low of 30 per 1,000 in Class 1 to a high of nearly five times that—143 per 1,000 in Class 18.

As would be expected, many of the subgroups defined by the classification structure contain small proportions of the total number of respondents. The largest proportion of persons is found in Class

2, in which 54 percent of the sample—defined as married or widowed and over twenty-four years old—had a personal victimization likelihood of 32 per 1,000, considerably below that for the sample as a whole. Nearly 12 percent of the cases fall into Class 7—defined as being neither sixteen to nineteen years old nor over fifty years old; female; single, divorced, or separated; and with a family income of less than $3,000—which had a personal victimization likelihood of 58.

Class 13, with the high likelihood of 85 persons victimized per 1,000 persons, comprises 11 percent of the sample and is composed of persons who were neither sixteen to nineteen years old nor fifty to sixty-four years old; male; single, divorced, or separated; and with family incomes of $3,000 or more.[5]

Injury-Noninjury Analysis

Before we explore the victim-nonvictim analytic solution in more detail, it is of interest to study the ways in which personal characteristics are related to the probability of injurious and loss-related victimization. Of central importance is the extent to which the analytical solutions of the harms of loss and injury will differ.

We therefore constructed a predictive attribute analysis with injury—defined as victimizations in which the victim reported receiving *any* injury—as the criterion. All respondents not reporting a personal victimization and those victims not reporting having received injury as a result of the victimization were classified as "not injured" for this analysis. The PAA dendrogram is presented in Figure 5-2.

As defined here, the likelihood of injury in the eight-city population was estimated to be 15 per 1,000. As was the case for our "victim-nonvictim" PAA, the attribute sixteen to nineteen years old was the attribute among those available in the NCS that best discriminated the likelihoods of injurious personal victimization. *Those persons sixteen to nineteen years old had an injury likelihood that was more than twice as great as those eight-city residents not sixteen to nineteen years old (31 per 1,000 versus 13 per 1,000).*

Among those not sixteen to nineteen years old, Figure 5-2 shows that the attribute twelve to fifteen years old was the most predictive of the risk of injury from a personal crime. The dendrogram shows that those persons in the eight cities who were over nineteen years of age (i.e., not twelve to fifteen and not sixteen to nineteen) had an injury likelihood (12 per 1,000) that was half that of those twelve to fifteen years old (26 per 1,000) and slightly over one-third that of those sixteen to nineteen years old (31 per 1,000). Clearly, then, age was an important factor in the likelihood of injury from personal crimes.

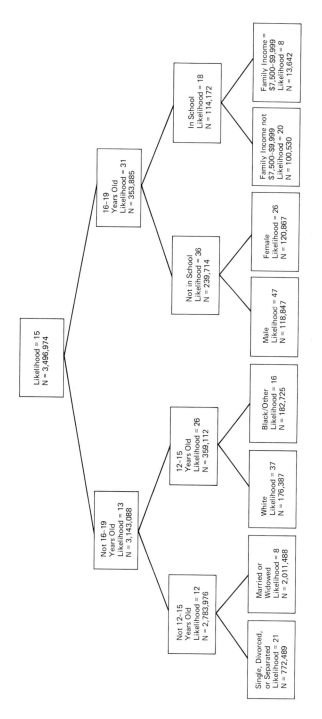

Figure 5-2. Predictive Attribute Analysis of Injury (Likelihood per 1,000 Persons Twelve Years of Age or Older), Eight-City Aggregate, 1972[a]

[a]Subcategories may not sum to total because of rounding. See Appendix C for definitions of attributes.

Among sixteen to nineteen year olds, whether or not the person was in school was closely associated with injury-producing victimizations. Those sixteen to nineteen year olds who were not attending school had a likelihood of injury in personal crimes that was twice as high as the likelihood for those sixteen to nineteen year olds who were attending school (36 per 1,000 versus 18 per 1,000). Thus, as was found in our earlier victim classifications, the daily activities of the eight-city residents appear to be related to their risk of criminal victimization.

At the lowest level of the dendrogram presented in Figure 5-2, it can be seen that among the eight-city residents who were over nineteen years old, marital status was the attribute among those available that was most predictive of bodily injury from a personal victimization. The likelihood of injury for those over nineteen who were married was 8 per 1,000, whereas the corresponding likelihood for those who were single, divorced, or separated was 21 per 1,000.

As shown in Table 5-2, the highest likelihood of injury among the classes in the PAA was for sixteen to nineteen year old males who were not in school (47 per 1,000). The likelihood for females in this age group who were not attending school was also high (26 per 1,000). The lowest injury likelihoods were found for married or widowed persons over nineteen years old (8 per 1,000) and for sixteen to nineteen year old persons who were attending school and whose total family income was between $7,500 and $9,999 per year (8 per 1,000).

These results for injury likelihoods are generally consistent with the results of the victim-nonvictim PAA described earlier. However, it is informative that the likelihoods of victimizations actually resulting in injury to the victim can be differentiated to such a degree (from 8 to 47 per 1,000) using so few personal characteristics. Before discussing explanations for these findings in detail, it is important to see how personal characteristics may be classified so as to explain variation in the likelihood of a loss victimization.[6]

Loss-Nonloss Analysis

Using the same decision rules as in the injury PAA and defining loss as in Chapter 4, we constructed a PAA of victim characteristics around the likelihood of a loss victimization. Figure 5-3 presents the dendrogram showing that the overall likelihood of loss victimization for the eight-city residents was 19 per 1,000. *The attribute among those available that was most predictive of suffering a loss from a personal crime was whether or not the individual's total family income was less than $3,000 per year.* The likelihood of

Table 5-2.   Five-City (1973) Validation of the Eight-City (1972) Predictive Attribute Analysis of Injury Likelihoods[a]

Class	Constituent Elements	Construction (Eight-City)		Validation (Five-City)	
		Terminal Group Size	*Injury Likelihood (percent)*	*Terminal Group Size*	*Injury Likelihood (percent)*
1	Married or widowed, not 12–15 years old, not 16–19 years old.	58%[b] (2,011,488)	8	60%[b] (7,611,428)	8
2	Family income $7,500–9,999, in school, 16–19 years old.	(c) (13,642)	8	(c) (44,097)	10
3	Black/other, 12–15 years old, not 16–19 years old.	5% (182,725)	16	3% (411,172)	25
4	Family income not $7,500–9,999, in school, 16–19 years old.	3% (100,530)	20	3% (424,491)	20
5	Single, divorced or separated, not 12–15 years old, not 16–19 years old.	22% (772,489)	21	24% (3,018,376)	17
6	Female, not in school, 16–19 years old.	3% (120,867)	26	2% (250,917)	33
7	White, 12–15 years old, not 16–19 years old.	5% (176,387)	37	5% (631,751)	26
8	Male, not in school, 16–19 years old.	3% (118,847)	47	2% (260,088)	51
	Total	100% (3,496,975)	15	100% (12,652,300)	13

[a]Subcategories may not sum to total because of rounding. See Appendix C for definitions of the constituent elements.
[b]Column percent.
[c]Less than 1 percent.

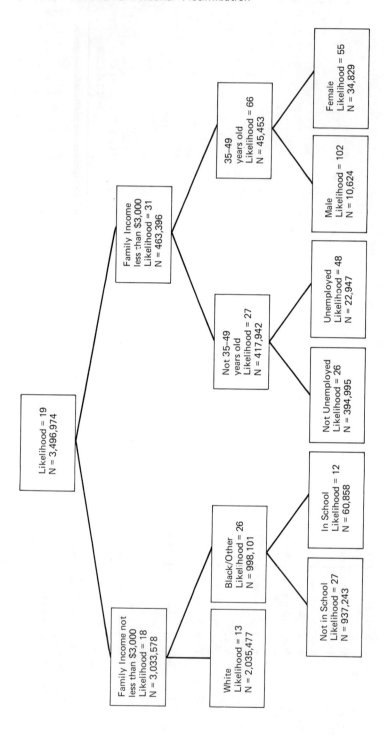

Figure 5-3. Predictive Attribute Analysis of Loss (Likelihoods per 1,000 Persons Twelve Years of Age or Older), Eight-City Aggregate, 1972[a]

[a]Subcategories may not sum to total because of rounding. See Appendix C for definitions of attributes.

suffering a personal victimization resulting in a loss was considerably higher for those whose annual family incomes were below $3,000 (31 per 1,000) than for those whose incomes were $3,000 or more (18 per 1,000).

Among those in the $3,000 or more income category, race was the next most predictive attribute; the likelihood of loss victimization for black/others in this income category was twice the rate for whites (26 versus 13 per 1,000). Black/others who did not have low family incomes exhibited a likelihood of loss that was more similar to the likelihood for low income respondents than to the likelihood for whites who did not have low family incomes. *This suggests that area of residence may have a great influence on the likelihood of loss through a personal crime.* Offenders disproportionately reside in low income areas of cities (Turner, 1969; Shaw and McKay, 1942; Boggs, 1965; Pope, 1975), and racially segregated housing patterns may force black/others of higher incomes to live in lower income areas. Residents of low income areas, whether or not they themselves have low total family incomes, may have greater exposure to theft-oriented offenders in the course of their daily activities than do others. If offenders were selecting their targets primarily on the basis of high reward from the crime, it would not be expected that such high likelihoods would be found for those with low family incomes. This suggests that easy access to potential victims may be important in accounting for loss risks in personal crimes.

Among those with total family incomes below $3,000 (shown on the right side of Figure 5-3), whether or not the person was thirty-five to forty-nine years old was the attribute most predictive of a personal property loss victimization. This side of the PAA is further subdivided on employment status and sex. In these eight cities, males between the ages of thirty-five and forty-nine with incomes under $3,000 had a loss likelihood of 102 per 1,000, and females in these age and income groups had a loss likelihood of 55 per 1,000.

Table 5-3 presents the classes derived from the PAA on loss, along with the personal attributes defining each class, the loss likelihood, and the proportion of the eight-city population falling into each class. The loss likelihoods ranged from a low of 12 per 1,000 to a high of 102 per 1,000. A major difference between this loss classification and those for injury and total personal victimizations is that low total family income and race are central classification attributes, whereas the age attribute sixteen to nineteen years old did not enter the system. The highest likelihoods of a personal victimization resulting in loss were found for males and females thirty-five to forty-nine years old with very low total family incomes.[7]

Table 5-3.   Five-City (1973) Validation of the Eight-City (1972) Predictive Attribute Analysis of Loss Likelihoods[a]

Class	Constituent Elements	Construction (Eight-City)		Validation (Five-City)	
		Terminal Group Size	Loss Likelihood (percent)	Terminal Group Size	Loss Likelihood (percent)
1	In school, black/other, family income not less than $3,000.	2%[b] (60,858)	12	2%[b] (230,668)	24
2	White, family income not less than $3,000.	58% (2,035,477)	13	67% (8,465,245)	23
3	Not unemployed, not 35–49 years old, family income less than $3,000.	11% (394,995)	26	7% (908,506)	40
4	Not in school, black/other, family income not less than $3,000.	27% (937,243)	27	23% (2,852,950)	35
5	Unemployed, not 35–49 years old, family income less than $3,000.	1% (22,947)	48	1% (66,100)	25
6	Female, 35–49 years old, family income less than $3,000.	1% (34,829)	55	1% (77,856)	49
7	Male, 35–49 years old, family income less than $3,000.	(c) (10,624)	102	(c) (50,944)	62
Total		100% (3,496,974)	19	100% (12,652,300)	27

[a]Subcategories may not sum to total because of rounding.
[b]Column percent.
[c]Less than 1 percent.

Discussion of Analytic Solutions

Clearly, complex and intricate analytic solutions have emerged from our numerical taxonomies of personal characteristics. In each analytical solution there is a large residue of persons with a fairly low likelihood of victimization that could not be finely sub-divided. The technique did, however, achieve relatively high levels of discrimination in likelihoods of victimization based on a few readily identifiable personal characteristics.

Four personal characteristics are central to the victim-nonvictim solution, on the basis of both the frequency and the primacy in which they occur: age, marital status, employment status, and sex. Each of these attributes had substantial bivariate associations with victimization, as shown in earlier research. When these variables are examined in a multivariate analysis of the type performed here, they, are in various combinations, predictive of the likelihood of personal victimization.

The question arises as to why these personal characteristics are associated with victimization. To a large extent, these variables and the patterns they exhibit in relation to victimization suggest a lifestyle-exposure hypothesis. It may be argued that the patterns of personal characteristics that combine to yield high likelihoods of suffering a personal victimization are characteristics that in-ferentially may be associated with differences in personal lifestyles. These lifestyles, in turn, may be related to being in places and situations with high *opportunities* for criminal victimization. The patterns of personal characteristics that combine to yield low prob-abilities of victimization may be associated with behavior patterns that do not as frequently place the person in high opportunity situations. Many of the patterns found in Figure 5-1 lend support to this interpretation. For example, it was found that among persons not sixteen to nineteen years old, the attribute of marital status defined subgroups that differed markedly in the likelihood of vic-timization. Married or widowed persons who are also over the age of twenty-four—persons whose lifestyles may reflect a relatively sedentary existence, in that they may less often frequent places or place themselves in situations with high opportunities for victimiza-tion—had low likelihoods of personal victimization. On the other hand, persons of similar ages who were single, divorced, or separated (and especially males in these categories) had considerably higher likelihoods of personal crimes. It might be expected that these persons would have higher victimization likelihoods as a consequence of having fewer at home responsibilities or commitments and, consequently, greater opportunity to frequent places of high victimization probability.

This lifestyle/exposure hypothesis may also help to account for variation in victimization likelihoods found on the right-hand side of Figure 5-1; that is, for persons sixteen to nineteen years old. For example, as the diagram shows, sixteen to nineteen year old males had exceedingly high likelihoods of personal victimization (128 per 1,000). It may be argued that persons in this age-sex-specific category are more likely to have lifestyles that afford opportunities for suffering personal crimes than are other persons; they are more likely than others to be out of the home in public places, often during the evening and nighttime hours. And, importantly, they are likely to be in situations that place them in contact with persons of similar ages and sexes. Both official statistics (Kelley, 1976) and victimization survey data (Hindelang, 1976) suggest that a disproportionate share of personal crimes are attributable to male offenders who are in the sixteen to nineteen year old group. Further, Hindelang (1976) has found that persons who are victimized are typically victimized by persons within their own age group. Persons who disproportionately come into contact with and/or associate with persons who have high rates of offending are likely to be disproportionately victimized.

Class 18 in the victim-nonvictim solution (composed of sixteen to nineteen year old males who were not in school) had the highest personal victimization likelihood of any of the classes in that solution. It can be argued that sixteen to nineteen year old males who were not in school were more likely than those in school to frequent places where the opportunity for victimization is high. Data presented in Figure 5-1 lend support to this notion. It can be seen that the victimization likelihood for those sixteen to nineteen year old males in school was substantially lower (94) than that for sixteen to nineteen year old males not in school (143). Further support is found in Class 15, which is composed of sixteen to nineteen year old unemployed (and not in school) females who had a personal victimization likelihood of 107 per 1,000. The rate for this group was considerably higher than the rate for sixteen to nineteen year old females who were not unemployed (60). Again, unemployed persons in this age-sex-specific group may be expected to have daily activities that are quite dissimilar from those who are not unemployed; such lifestyle differences may be expected to be associated with higher victimization opportunities.

At the other extreme of victimization likelihoods are classes of persons whose attributes are indicative of lifestyles that may expose them to fewer situations with a high potential for victimization. For example, older females who were not married had low likelihoods of personal victimization, as demonstrated by Classes 1 and 3 in the victim-nonvictim solution (30 and 38 per 1,000, respectively). Older females would certainly be expected to place themselves less often in common victimization opportunity situations. They would be expected to be less mobile and to spend a greater proportion of their time at home than males and younger persons.

Similar inferences can be drawn about the lifestyles of persons comprising Class 4, which had the relatively low victimization likelihood of 40 per 1,000. Married females twenty to twenty-four years old may spend a larger proportion of their time within their own home and are less likely to venture out of the home at night unaccompanied than are single persons and males. Similarly, persons in Class 2 (married persons over the age of twenty-four), whose victimization liklihood was 32 per 1,000, are more likely than single and younger persons to exhibit these behavior patterns.

Our loss analysis indicates that many of the lifestyle characteristics of the eight-city residents that are, inferentially, determined by their residential setting are closely related to victimization risks. Persons with low total family incomes and black/others, who are more likely to live in the poor sections of these eight cities, had, as a consequence, increased likelihoods of personal victimizations involving loss. Because these persons are forced to spend a disproportionate share of their lives in lower income neighborhoods, where offenders who engage in common theft are more likely to be found, their exposure to high victimization risk situations is substantially greater than that of higher income persons and, in general, of whites.

We recognize that concepts such as "exposure to risks of victimization" must ultimately be defined independently of empirically established likelihoods of victimization. In this chapter, our purpose has been primarily to lay the groundwork for analyses in subsequent chapters. In particular, the chapters on attitudes and our theoretical synthesis in the final chapter attempt to establish—independently of victimization likelihoods themselves—that personal characteristics such as age, sex, marital status, and major activity are indicative of lifestyles that, in turn, expose people to varying risks of victimization.

In the next chapter, we will continue our exploration of victimization likelihoods with an analysis of multiple victimization. The analysis will expand upon, and help to elucidate, some of the issues raised in this chapter.

NOTES

1. See Hindelang (1976: ch. 1) for a discussion of these typologists.

2. Because of the tremendous computer costs associated with analyses when all persons interviewed in the eight-city sample was the focus of analysis, sample files were constructed that consisted of all persons reporting a personal victimization and one out of fifteen persons who did not report a personal victimization. The "nonvictims" were then reweighted in order to reflect the total eight-city population. Because it was necessary to construct several of these files, the total estimated number of persons in the eight-city populations differs slightly from table to table in this chapter.

3. Series victimizations (see Appendix B) are excluded.

4. Respondents were asked: "What were you doing most of last week—working, keeping house, going to school, or something else?" (source code 048 in Appendix A). Responses to this item are referred to here as "major activity." See Appendix C for the categories of major activity.

5. For purposes of assessing the reliability of the analytic solution, the eight-city group was used as a construction sample and the five-city group was used as a validation sample. The five-city data were classified into the structure that emerged from the eight-city analysis. The likelihood of victimization for each subgroup was ranked. The resulting Spearman's *rho* was 0.71. Because of the relative rarity of victims in the eight-city sample, it was not feasible to divide it into random split halves as a cross-validation test.

6. The rank order correlation between the injury likelihoods in the terminal classes in the eight-city construction and the five-city validation samples was 0.81. The Pearson's *r* was 0.89, and the weighted mean absolute difference between the likelihoods in the eight-city and five-city samples was 2.02.

7. The rank order correlation between the loss likelihoods in the terminal classes in the eight-city construction and the five-city validation samples was 0.82, the Pearson's *r* was 0.85, and the weighted mean absolute difference between the likelihoods in the eight-city and five-city samples was 10.04.

Chapter 6

Multiple Victimization

Most of the published analyses of variations in rates of criminal victimization across characteristics of the population such as age, marital status, family income, and race have not examined the extent to which, or even whether, victimizations are concentrated among a small number of individuals (Hindelang, 1976; LEAA, 1976, 1975a, 1975b, 1975c, 1974). Rates of victimization have generally been defined as a function of the ratio of the number of victimizations reported during the reference period to the number of units (e.g., persons twelve years of age or older, or households) "at risk."[1] Computing rates in this way does not differentiate between five victimizations reported by a single respondent and five victimizations reported by separate respondents, though for some purposes it is clearly important to distinguish between these two situations. Defined in the conventional way, a victimization rate becomes less meaningful as an index of the likelihood that a randomly selected member of the population was victimized during the reference period as the ratio of the number of victimizations to the number of distinct persons victimized increases. By *likelihood* of victimization we mean the ratio of the number of *distinct* persons victimized to the number of persons at risk, thus, the likelihood of victimization per 1,000 persons is equal to ten times the percentage of persons victimized. In particular, the distinction between the rate of victimization and the likelihood of victimization is essential for analyzing victim "proneness"—the propensity of some persons to be repeatedly victimized.

Many theorists, in writing about criminal victimization, have suggested that personal characteristics affect the likelihood of victimization. Von Hentig (1948:404–38) has postulated not only that there are general classes of victims (the young, the female, the old, the mentally defective, etc.) but also "psychological types of victims" (the depressed, the wanton, and the tormentor). Similarly, Fattah (1967) has suggested "latent or predisposed victims," whose increased likelihood of becoming victims of crime arises from particular circumstantial factors or traits of character. Among circumstantial factors he includes occupation, physical or mental impairment, and way of life, and among character traits he cites greed, immorality, and credulity.[2] Finally, Wolfgang and Ferracuti (1967:188–89) have proposed that members of the "subculture of violence," who they argue are disproportionately young, male, black, lower class, and urban (1967:258–69), are more likely to be victims of violent crime because in many situations that involve confrontations between subcultural members, a violent response may be expected or even required.[3]

These diverse positions posit not only substantial variation in rates of victimization across characteristics of the population such as age, sex, race, and social class, but also a clustering of risks such that persons with particular characteristics are predisposed to repetitive victimization. The extent, nature, and correlates of multiple victimization are the topics to be examined in this chapter.

THE DATA

In Appendix B, series victimizations are defined as three or more similar victimizations that occur to the same person during the reference period and for which the victim cannot recall details of the individual events. For reasons discussed in Appendix B, and more fully in Hindelang (1976: Appendix F), serious problems attend to the analysis of series victimizations. Throughout this book, the emphasis is on nonseries victimizations, though series victimizations are discussed in this chapter.

Our earlier analyses confirmed that personal victimization is relatively rare. For all nonseries personal victimizations, the *rate* in the eight cities was 60 per 1,000 persons twelve years of age or older. Furthermore, the *likelihood* of victimization by nonseries personal crimes was 51 per 1,000. Therefore the number of persons who would be expected to suffer two or more nonseries personal crimes during the reference period is very small indeed. In order to have enough repetitive victims to produce reliable results, the analyses in this chapter are based on victimization survey data not only from the eight Impact Cities, but also from eighteen additional cities. As noted in Appendix B, NCS victimization surveys were conducted in the eight Impact Cities in 1972 and in the nation's five largest cities (Chicago, Detroit, Los Angeles, New York, and Philadelphia) in 1973. Surveys were also conducted in thirteeen additional cities (Boston, Buffalo, Cincinnati, Houston, Miami, Milwaukee, Minneapolis, New Orleans, Oakland, Pittsburgh, San Diego, San Francisco, and Washington, D.C.) during 1974. In each of these twenty-six cities, interviews were conducted with about 22,000 persons in 10,000 households. The basic survey design, sampling techniques, and procedures used in the eight Impact Cities were used in the remaining eighteen cities as well.[4]

The use of data from all twenty-six cities more than triples the number of cases available; nearly 600,000 persons in more than a quarter of a million households were interviewed in the twenty-six cities. But even with this huge pool of respondents, the rarity of repetitive personal victimization imposes stringent constraints on the analyses, as will be clear as we proceed.

REPETITIVE VICTIMIZATION IN PERSONAL CRIMES

In the twenty-six cities, 94 percent of those interviewed reported that they were victims of neither a series nor a nonseries personal victimization during the twelve-month reference period. Of the remaining 6 percent, the vast majority (93 percent) were victims of one nonseries personal crime; only four-tenths of 1 percent of those interviewed were victims of a series personal crime, but not victims of a nonseries personal crime.

Table 6-1 displays the observed distributions of the number of personal victimizations reported for series and nonseries crimes and indicates the extreme rarity of repetitive personal victimization. Only an estimated seven-tenths of 1 percent of the population suffered two or more nonseries personal victimizations, and only one-half of 1 percent suffered one or more series crimes. By definition, each series crime consists of at least three similar victimizations. Multiple victims of personal crimes are defined here as those who reported at least one series victimization or more than one nonseries victimization. Accordingly, an estimated 1.2 percent of the population in the twenty-six cities were multiple victims of personal crimes within the twelve-month reference period.[5]

In contemplating the "effects" of victimization on subsequent victimization, three general competing hypotheses are available. The

Table 6-1. Distribution of Observed and Poisson-Expected Frequencies of Personal Nonseries and Series Crimes, Twenty-six-City Aggregate, 1972-1974[a]

| | Number of Times Victimized by Personal Crimes | | | | | |
	None	*One*	*Two*	*Three*	*Four*	*Total*
Nonseries						
Observed	94.65% (20,713,000)	4.69% (1,026,000)	0.54% (118,000)	0.09% (20,000)	0.03% (6,000)	100% (21,884,000)
Poisson-Expected	94.04% (20,578,685)	5.78% (1,265,595)	0.18% (38,910)	0.00% (788)	0.00% (22)	100% (21,884,000)
Series						
Observed	99.46% (21,766,000)	0.50% (109,000)	0.03% (7,000)	0.00% (1,000)	0.00% (0)	100% (21,884,000)
Poisson-Expected	99.43% (21,758,517)	0.57% (125,111)	0.00% (350)	0.00% (0)	0.00% (0)	100% (21,884,000)

[a]Subcategories may not sum to total because of rounding.

first, as suggested by the victim typologists, is that criminal victimization depends in part on victim proneness—some disposition or characteristic of the victim that enhances the likelihood of victimization. If this is true, the pool of persons who are victimized contains a disproportionate number of victimization-prone persons, and hence the probability that these persons will be victimized again is, *because* of their victimization proneness, greater than that for persons selected from the general population. The second hypothesis might be termed the "once bitten, twice shy" or fear of crime hypothesis. It suggests that persons who are victimized modify their future behavior (e.g., by staying at home at night or by going out only in the company of others) in order to avoid high risk situations. By doing so, these persons have a smaller likelihood than those in the general population of subsequently becoming victims within a specified period of time.[6] Biderman (1975:1) has drawn an analogy between this phenomenon and "natural immunization" as the concept is used in medicine. The third hypothesis is that of independence; it proposes that the probability of having been victimized once does not affect, one way or another, the probability of subsequent victimization. To test these hypotheses, it would be preferable in most respects to have panel data. The cross-sectional data at hand, however, can be useful in choosing among these competing hypotheses because they provide information regarding victimizations during a twelve-month reference period.

If we assume that personal victimizations are independent of each other, then the observed distribution of respondents across the categories of number of reported victimizations would be expected to approximate a Poisson distribution. The Poisson expected probabilities (e.g., Chou, 1969:206) for exactly k victimizations during the reference period can be written as

$$\frac{e^{-v}\,(v^k)}{k!}$$

where v is the victimization rate (total number of victimizations divided by the total number of units at risk); k is the reported number of victimizations occurring during the reference period; and e is the constant, approximately equal to 2.71828. By computing the Poisson probabilities for $k = 0, 1, 2, 3, 4$ and multiplying by the number of respondents, we can compute the distribution of respondents across the "number of reported victimization" categories expected under the assumption that victimization experiences are statistically independent of each other—that is, that risks of victimization do not cluster. The expected frequencies, derived from the Poisson model under the assumption of no clustering of risks, can be compared with the observed frequencies and evaluated by the X^2 criterion to determine whether the deviation of the expected from the observed frequencies is greater than would be anticipated on the basis of chance alone.[7]

For nonseries personal victimizations in the twenty-six cities, $v = 0.0615$, and for series personal victimization, $v = 0.0058$. The distribution of expected frequencies resulting from the Poisson expansion is shown in Table 6-1. By comparing the observed and the expected frequencies in this table, it is apparent that multiple personal nonseries victimizations were reported substantially more often than the independence model predicts. For example, under the Poisson distribution it is expected that about 39,000 respondents will report two nonseries personal victimizations, but 118,000 are reported in the twenty-six cities. For three or four nonseries personal victimizations, the discrepancy between the Poisson expected frequencies and the observed frequencies is even more pronounced. Clearly, these data suggest that risks of nonseries personal victimization cluster.

The same conclusion is reached by examining series personal victimizations in the lower half of Table 6-1. Using the X^2 ($p < .001$, 4 $d.f.$) criterion, neither the nonseries nor the series distribution of personal victimizations conforms to the Poisson model; rather victimizations are disproportionately concentrated among some segments of the population. If they were not, the distribution of expected victimizations under the Poisson model would more closely correspond to the observed distributions. *Apparently, for whatever reasons, some respondents are "victimization prone," at least within the confines of the reference period surveyed.*

In order to investigate more closely the conditional likelihoods of victimization, Table 6-2 has been constructed. The main diagonal of this table shows the number of persons per 1,000 who were victimized one or more times by the type of crime indicated.[8] For example, the entry for the robbery row and the robbery column (22) indicates that in the twenty-six cities, a person's unconditional likelihood of being the victim of a robbery at least once during the reference period was 22 out of 1,000. Also shown are the likelihoods of each type of victimization for respondents who were victims of the crimes specified by the columns. For example, among those who reported being victims of aggravated assault during the reference period, 95 out of 1,000 also reported being victims of robbery at least once during the reference period. A comparison of the proba-

Table 6-2. Estimated Likelihood (per 1,000 Persons Twelve Years of Age or Older) of Being a Victim of the Row Crime One or More Times During the Reference Period, Given That the Respondent Was a Victim of the Column Crime During the Reference Period, Twenty-six-City Aggregate, 1972–1974[a]

	Conditional Crime				
	Rape	*Robbery*	*Aggravated Assault*	*Simple Assault*	*Personal Larceny*
Rape	2	7	8	10*	6
Robbery	85	22	95*	72	54
Aggravated Assault	53	53	12	82*	27
Simple Assault	82	50	103*	15	26
Larceny from the Person	33*	28	25	26	11

[a]Unconditional likelihoods shown in main diagonal. The highest value in each row is indicated by an asterisk(*). The "Conditional Crime" is not necessarily temporally prior to the "Row Crime."

bility of being a robbery victim given that the person was an aggravated assault victim with the unconditional probability of being a robbery victim (95 versus 22) indicates that these two types of victimization are not independent. In fact, by reading across the robbery row it is apparent that for all columns, the conditional likelihood exceeds the unconditional likelihood. For robbery, the column condition that had the smallest effect on the probability of robbery victimization was personal larceny (purse snatching and pocket picking without force). But even this condition more than doubled the likelihood of robbery victimization (54 versus 22).

There is no type of crime row for which the condition specified by the column gave a likelihood less than the unconditional likelihood. *In general, for any given row, those meeting the condition specified by the column had a likelihood that was more than two times as great as the unconditional likelihood.* For some conditions, this excess over the unconditional likelihood was much more marked. For simple assault, the unconditional likelihood of victimization in the general population of the twenty-six cities was 15 per 1,000, but among victims of aggravated assault the likelihood was 103 per 1,000. Similarly, the unconditional likelihood of aggravated assault was 12, but among victims of simple assault it was nearly seven times as great (82).

In Table 6-2, the column conditions that are most closely associated with the greatest risk of victimization for each row crime are indicated with asterisks. The asymmetric nature of the relations shown in this table is apparent from the general lack of "reciprocity" in the table. That is, although aggravated assault was the condition that resulted in the greatest increase over the unconditional likelihood for the simple assault row and vice versa, this symmetry is nowhere else apparent.

Our analysis thus far has indicated a definite clustering of risks for personal crimes. By testing the actual distribution of number of personal victimizations against the distribution expected under an assumption of independence, it has been shown that risks of both series and nonseries personal victimization are clustered. Furthermore, the data presented in Table 6-2 indicate that this lack of independence holds for each type of personal crime. These data also demonstrate that for each type of victimization, the conditional effects of any other type of victimization are considerable. Whether this clustering of risks is due to personal attributes of the victim or some aspect(s) of his or her surroundings (or some combination of the two) has not yet been addressed. Before considering this question, it is important to introduce some data on household victimizations.

REPETITIVE VICTIMIZATION
IN HOUSEHOLD CRIMES[9]

Because household victimization is more common than personal victimization, it is not surprising that multiple victimization of households—two or more household victimizations suffered by the same household during the reference period—was more common than multiple victimization of individuals. As Table 6-3 indicates, 4 percent of the households in the twenty-six cities suffered more than one nonseries household victimization. This table also indicates that almost 2 percent of the households reported one or more series victimizations. If multiple household victims are defined as households that reported two or more nonseries household victimizations or one or more series household victimizations, then 6 percent of the households in the twenty-six cities were multiple victims.[10]

As with personal victimizations, it is possible to compare the actual distribution of household victimizations to the distribution expected under the Poisson model of independence. These data are shown in Table 6-3, again suggesting a lack of independence. For nonseries and series victimizations of households, the number of household victimizations reported does not conform to the Poisson distribution. *Rather, a clustering of risks of household victimization is indicated by the discrepancy, as measured by the* X^2 *(p < .001, 7 d.f.) criterion, between the observed and the Poisson-expected frequency distributions for both nonseries and series household victimizations*

The specific nature of the clustering of risks can be seen in Table 6-4, which parallels the data on personal victimization presented in Table 6-2. The unconditional likelihoods of a household's being victimized one or more times during the reference period by each specific type of household crime are shown in the main diagonal. Once again, the columns specify conditions (victimization by specific types of household crimes) that alter the unconditional likelihoods. *For each type of household victimization, the likelihood of victimization was substantially greater for households that reported having been victims of another household crime during the reference period.* The unconditional likelihood of being a victim of burglary was 106 per 1,000 households in the twenty-six cities; for households that were victims of at-home larcenies, however, 194 per 1,000 were victims of burglary. Similarly, the likelihood of at-home larceny was twice as great for household victims of vehicle theft (and vice versa) as in the general population of households. Once again, the asterisks in Table 6-4 indicate the column condition that is most

Table 6-3. Distribution of Observed and Poisson-Expected Frequencies of Household Nonseries and Series Crimes, Twenty-six-City Aggregate, 1972-1974[a]

| | Number of Times Victimized by Household Crimes | | | | | | | | |
	None	One	Two	Three	Four	Five	Six	Seven	Total
Nonseries									
Observed	81.47% (8,336,000)	14.25% (1,458,000)	3.31% (339,000)	0.75% (77,000)	0.15% (16,000)	0.04% (4,000)	0.01% (1,000)	0.01% (1,000)	100% (10,232,000)
Poisson-Expected	78.60% (8,042,260)	18.93% (1,936,652)	2.28% (233,187)	0.18% (18,714)	0.01% (1,126)	0.00% (51)	0.00% (0)	0.00% (0)	100% (10,232,000)
Series									
Observed	98.40% (10,068,000)	1.50% (154,000)	0.09% (9,000)	0.01% (1,000)	0.00% (0)	0.00% (0)	0.00% (0)	0.00% (0)	100% (10,232,000)
Poisson-Expected	98.30% (10,058,466)	1.68% (172,000)	0.01% (1,473)	0.00% (10)	0.00% (0)	0.00% (0)	0.00% (0)	0.00% (0)	100% (10,232,000)

[a]Subcategories may not sum to total because of rounding.

Table 6-4. Estimated Likelihood (per 1,000 Households) of Being a Victim of the Row Crime One or More Times During the Reference Period, Given That the Household Was a Victim of the Column Crime During the Reference Period, Twenty-six-City Aggregate, 1972-1974.[a]

	Conditional Crime		
	Burglary	At Home Larceny	Vehicle Theft
Burglalry	106	194*	175
At Home Larceny	149	81	168*
Vehicle Theft	56	70*	34

[a]Unconditional likelihoods shown in main diagonal. The highest value in each row is indicated by an asterisk (*). The "Conditional Crime" is not necessarily temporally prior to the "Row Crime."

closely associated with the risk of victimization for each row crime.

In contrasting Tables 6-2 and 6-4, the ratio of the highest likelihood in any given row to the main diagonal value for that row is greater for personal than for household crimes. For household crimes (e.g., vehicle theft—70:34), this ratio is never much greater than 2:1, but for personal crimes it is 3:1 for personal larceny, about 4.5:1 for rape and robbery, and nearly 7:1 for aggravated and simple assault.

How can these data be interpreted? As noted above, this clustering of risks may be due to attributes of the "target" (person or household) or to environmental conditions. It is not difficult to see how some persons could provoke victimization. Von Hentig (1948:419-38) discussed how persons who are "indifferent to peril and defense, unsuspecting, careless [and] fearless" increase their chances of victimization. Likewise, Fattah (1967) has suggested that some persons actually provoke victimization by creating situations likely to lead to crime. This is not unlike the victim precipitation that Wolfgang (1958), Normandeau (1968), and Amir (1971) have discussed in connection with the personal crimes of homicide, robbery, and rape, respectively. Thus, there has been considerable speculation about ways in which attributes of the victim may make victimization more likely. In addition to these "active" victim attributes, there are "passive" attributes such as apparent affluence that may make targets more attractive. Households may also have passive attributes such as apparent affluence or isolation that make them attractive targets and hence result in their being victimized more often than an independence model would suggest.

Not only the target attributes but also the environmental conditions in which the target is located must be taken into account. Particular persons and households may face disproportionate risks of victimization because the environments in which they reside or are located are frequented by offenders.[11] Such areas may be frequented by offenders in planned "forays" or incidentally because these areas are in proximity to areas in which offenders' residences are concentrated.

An interesting question that can be addressed with the data at hand is whether members of households that were victims of household crimes had a higher rate of *personal* victimization than members of households that were not victims of *household* crimes. Conversely, did households that contained at least one victim of a *personal* crime have higher rates of household victimization than *households* that contained no victims of personal crimes? With these two uses, our concept of multiple victimization is broadened, as is the potential for understanding the mechanisms linking various kinds of victimizations.

THE INTERSECTION OF PERSONAL AND HOUSEHOLD CRIMES

In the earlier analysis of victimization in the eight Impact Cities (Hindelang, 1976), age, marital status, and sex were among the strongest correlates of rates of personal victimization. The data in Table 6-5 show, per 1,000 persons twelve years of age or older, the number of persons who reported having experienced at least one nonseries or series personal victimization during the reference period. These data are displayed by age, marital status, and sex. Each of the twelve age–marital status–sex groups is further subdivided according to whether or not the respondent was a member of a household that was the victim of a nonseries or series household crime during the reference period. These data are consistent with our earlier findings that, *in general*, rates of personal victimization decreased with age, that those who were married had lower rates of victimization than those who were not married, and that males had higher rates of victimization than females. More important for our present purposes, however, is the finding that within each age–marital status–sex group, the likelihood of personal victimization was markedly affected by whether or not the respondent was a member of a household that was a victim of a household crime during the reference period. *Overall, regardless of the age, marital status, or sex of the respondent, the likelihood of having been a victim of at least one personal crime was about twice as great for members of house-*

Table 6-5. Estimated Likelihood (per 1,000 Persons) of Being a Victim of at Least One Personal Victimization During the Reference Period, by Respondent's Sex, Marital Status, and Age, and by Household Victimization Status, Twenty-six-City Aggregate, 1972-1974[a]

	Male						Female					
	Married			Not Married			Married			Not Married		
	12-19	20-34	35 or older	12-19	20-34	35 or older	12-19	20-34	35 or older	12-19	20-34	35 or older
Household not victimized by household crime	95 (27,000)	53 (1,127,000)	31 (3,187,000)	96 (1,264,000)	70 (1,082,000)	60 (996,000)	56 (78,000)	34 (1,451,000)	26 (2,902,000)	54 (1,308,000)	65 (1,180,000)	44 (2,491,000)
Household victimized by household crime	367[b] (6,000)	105 (406,000)	57 (764,000)	164 (535,000)	132 (373,000)	147 (179,000)	134 (28,000)	58 (480,000)	50 (654,000)	101 (485,000)	148 (348,000)	79 (424,000)

[a]Excludes 109,000 respondents for whom marital status was not ascertained. "Not married" includes never married, divorced or separated, and widowed. The bases on which the likelihoods were computed are shown in parentheses.

[b]Because of the small base, this estimated likelihood is less reliable than other likelihoods in this table.

holds that were victims of household crimes as for members of households that were not victims of household crimes. The range of likelihoods of victimization shown in Table 6-5 is very substantial. Although only 26 per 1,000 married females thirty-five years of age or older living in nonvictimized households reported a personal victimization, the comparable figure for unmarried males between twelve and nineteen years of age who reside in victimized households was 164, more than six times as great.

It is possible that the effect on the likelihood of personal victimization for persons residing in victimized households shown in Table 6-5 is spurious. It could be that factors associated with both household victimization and personal victimization, but which are not controlled in Table 6-5 (e.g., race and family income), account for the apparent effect of household victimization status.[12] In order to test this hypothesis, respondents were subdivided according to race and family income. In Table 6-6, of most interest to our present discussion is whether the effect of household victimization status maintains when two possible sources of spuriousness (family income and race) are controlled. *Within all six race and income groups, persons residing in victimized households had substantially greater likelihoods of personal victimization than those residing in nonvictimized households.* Among moderate income black/others, for instance, the likelihood of being personally victimized was 43 per 1,000 for those not living in victimized households and 79 per 1,000 for those living in victimized households.

It is interesting to note that for whites, the effect of household victimization status decreased as income increased. In the lowest income group, the likelihood of being personally victimized for persons living in victimized households was 2.45 times as great as for persons who were not living in victimized households; in the moderate and highest income groups these ratios were 1.95 and 1.78, respectively.

Although the data are not shown here in tabular form, when the respondents in Table 6-6 were further subdivided by sex and age, the effect of household victimization status on the likelihood of personal victimization maintained. For each of the forty-eight pairs of comparisons (two sex groups, two race groups, three age groups, four income groups), the likelihood of personal victimization was greater for those in victimized households than for those in nonvictimized households.

As expected on the basis of data presented in the two previous tables, Table 6-7 shows that the likelihood of household victimization was greater for households in which at least one household member was a victim of a personal crime than for households in

Table 6-6. Estimated Likelihood (per 1,000 Persons Twelve Years of Age or Older) of Being a Victim of at Least One Personal Victimization During the Reference Period, by Respondent's Race and Family Income, and by Household Victimization Status, Twenty-six-City Aggregate, 1972-1974[a]

		Family Income		
	Less than $7,500	*$7,500-$14,999*	*$15,000 or more*	*Not ascertained*
Household not victimized by household crime				
White	53 (3,930,000)	44 (4,366,000)	42 (2,736,000)	40 (1,360,000)
Black/other	60 (2,229,000)	43 (1,458,000)	40 (521,000)	43 (586,000)
Household victimized by household crime				
White	130 (830,000)	86 (1,172,000)	75 (926,000)	89 (285,000)
Black/other	127 (663,000)	79 (487,000)	80 (178,000)	99 (160,000)
Ratio[b]				
White	2.45	1.95	1.78	2.22
Black/Other	2.12	1.84	2.00	2.30

[a]The bases on which the likelihoods were computed are shown in parentheses.
[b]Ratio of the likelihood of being personally victimized for those in victimized households to the likelihood of being personally victimized for those not in victimized households.

Table 6-7. Estimated Likelihood (per 1,000 Households) of Being a Victim of at Least One Household Victimization During the Reference Period, by Race of Head and Family Income, and by Personal Victimization Status of Household Members, Twenty-six-City Aggregate, 1972-1974[a]

		Family Income					
		Less than $3,000	$3,000-$7,499	$7,500-$9,999	$10,000-$14,999	$15,000-$24,999	$25,000 or more
No household member victimized by a personal crime	White	134 (844,000)	140 (1,707,000)	181 (775,000)	184 (1,405,000)	210 (908,000)	223 (346,000)
	Black/Other	170 (487,000)	200 (773,000)	242 (290,000)	241 (359,000)	265 (199,000)	229 (38,000)
At least one household member victimized by a personal crime	White	316 (97,000)	333 (179,000)	291 (86,000)	366 (170,000)	343 (113,000)	297 (44,000)
	Black/Other	379 (70,000)	344 (117,000)	391 (39,000)	350 (54,000)	373 (31,000)	579[b] (6,000)
Ratio[c]	White	2.36	2.38	1.67	1.99	1.63	1.33
	Black/Other	2.23	1.72	1.62	1.45	1.41	2.53

[a]The bases on which the likelihoods were computed are shown in parentheses. Excluded from this table are households for which family income was not ascertained.

[b]Because of the small base, this estimated likelihood is less reliable than other likelihoods in this table.

[c]Ratio of the likelihood of a household's being victimized for households in which at least one household member was a victim of a personal crime to the likelihood of a household's being victimized for households in which no household members were victims of a personal crime.

which none of the household members was a victim of a personal crime. This effect is apparent for each race- and income-specific comparison. *Overall, the likelihood of household victimization was about twice as great for households in which a member was a victim of a personal crime than for households in which no member was the victim of a personal crime.* This effect tended to decrease as family income increased.

Establishing a link between the likelihood of personal victimization and the likelihood of household victimization is important on both methodological and theoretical grounds. From a methodological perspective, when either personal or household victimizations are analyzed separately, reports of multiple victimizations may simply reflect the propensity of a single respondent to be willing to spend the time reporting all victimizations to the interviewer, to recall more victimizations, to fabricate victimizations, etc. Because, except for proxy respondents, each respondent wàs interviewed personally about his or her personal victimizations (and a single household respondent was interviewed about the household's victimizations), the clustering of risks shown in Tables 6-1 through 6-4 could be attributable wholly to a reporting artifact generated by individual interviewees responding for themselves on personal crimes or for the household in the case of household crimes. However, because there was only one household respondent per household, most of the persons who were interviewed reported only on personal crimes.[13] Thus, there is substantial independence between the *reporting* of personal and household crimes, because only a minority of household members were designated as household respondents and were interviewed about both personal and household victimizations. For either personal crimes suffered by one individual or household crimes suffered by one household, however, no such independence in *reporting* exists. Although the household respondent and other household members may have similar *artifactual* reporting propensities—because they share the same socioeconomic status, race, and so on—the link between personal and household victimizations suggests that the clustering of risks discussed in this chapter probably cannot be attributed solely to the *reporting* behavior (as distinct from the victimization experiences) of respondents.

Fortunately, it is possible to subdivide the respondents in Table 6-5 according to whether or not the individual was the household respondent. If the link between the risk of household victimization and the risk of personal victimization is purely a reporting artifact attributable to the fact that about two out of five personal respondents were also household respondents, then among nonhousehold respondents the likelihood of personal victimization should be no greater for persons who were members of households that suffered a household victimization than for persons who were members of households that did not suffer a household victimization. *The data in Table 6-8 demonstrate that even among nonhousehold respondents, those persons who were members of households that reported a household victimization were about twice as likely to have reported at least one personal victimization as were persons who were members of households that did not report a household victimization.* This added risk of personal victimization held regardless of whether the personal respondent was also the household respondent and also held when age, sex, and marital status were controlled. Among twelve to nineteen year old unmarried females who were not household respondents, for example, those living in households that reported at least one household victimization had a likelihood of personal victimization of 94 per 1,000, while their counterparts living in households that did not report any household victimizations had a personal victimization likelihood of 52 per 1,000.

Before leaving Table 6-8, it is interesting to note that household respondents generally had a greater likelihood of personal victimization than did nonhousehold respondents, even when household victimization status, age, sex, and marital status were controlled. Household respondents answered screen questions designed to elicit household victimizations.[14] Dodge (1975) has reported that in the national sample for the 1974 data year, these household screen questions (asked only of household respondents) elicited 9.8 percent of the rapes, 7.6 percent of the robberies, 1.2 percent of the assaults, and 1.2 percent of the personal larcenies reported to survey interviewers as a result of all screen questions (household and personal) asked.[15] Because nonhousehold respondents were not asked the household screen questions, it is possible that they had a lower rate of personal victimization, at least in part, because they received fewer stimulus questions. There is some support for this hypothesis in findings reported by Murphy (1976) that indicate that a random half of respondents who were asked about attitudes toward crime *before* being asked about victimization experiences had significantly higher rates of victimization than respondents who were not first asked about attitudes toward crime. To the extent that the finding of lower rates of victimization among nonhousehold respondents was not an artifact of the screen questions, it may be contrary to the lifestyle/exposure hypothesis discussed in the previous chapter. This is because those found at home would appear to be less exposed to risks of victimization, which are substantially greater

Table 6-8. Estimated Likelihood (per 1,000 Persons) of Being a Victim of at Least One Personal Victimization During the Reference Period, by Respondent's Sex, Marital Status, Age, Whether Respondent Was Also the Household Respondent, and by Household Victimization Status, Twenty-six-City Aggregate, 1972-1974[a]

| | | Male | | | | | | Female | | | | |
| | | Married | | | Not Married | | | Married | | | Not Married | | |
		12-19	20-34	35 or older	12-19	20-34	35 or older	12-19	20-34	35 or older	12-19	20-34	35 or older
Nonhousehold Respondents	Household not victimized by household crime	98 (17,000)	44 (651,000)	30 (1,701,000)	92 (1,185,000)	62 (564,000)	46 (264,000)	59 (36,000)	33 (697,000)	24 (1,410,000)	52 (1,221,000)	45 (492,000)	28 (556,000)
	Household victimized by household crime	353[b] (5,000)	94 (234,000)	51 (467,000)	159 (502,000)	113 (215,000)	107 (65,000)	147 (13,000)	51 (199,000)	44 (327,000)	94 (450,000)	107 (140,000)	47 (126,000)
Household Respondents	Household not victimized by household crime	89 (10,000)	65 (476,000)	33 (1,486,000)	167 (79,000)	79 (518,000)	65 (732,000)	53 (42,000)	35 (753,000)	29 (1,493,000)	86 (87,000)	79 (688,000)	49 (1,935,000)
	Household victimized by household crime	410[b] (2,000)	119 (171,000)	67 (297,000)	238 (33,000)	159 (158,000)	169 (114,000)	123 (16,000)	63 (282,000)	56 (327,000)	186 (35,000)	175 (208,000)	92 (298,000)

[a]Excludes 109,000 respondents for whom marital status was not ascertained. The bases on which the likelihoods were computed are shown in parentheses.

[b]Because of the small base, this estimated likelihood is less reliable than other likelihoods in this table.

outside of the home. And, the person who was designated as the household respondent was likely to have been the first knowledgeable household member found at home by the interviewer. On the other hand, household respondents were virtually never interviewed by proxy about personal victimizations, whereas all twelve and thirteen year olds and some others who, for a variety of reasons, could not be interviewed personally were interviewed by proxy (see Appendix B). Prior research (LEAA, 1974) has shown that when individuals were personally interviewed (i.e., when the self-respondent method was used), substantially more victimizations were reported than when another household member responded for the subject. Thus, the use of proxy interviews for nonhousehold respondents, but not for household respondents, may account for some or all of the household respondent-nonhousehold respondent differences in Table 6-8.

Victimizations of Other
Household Members

Another means of exploring the environmental risk factor independently of reporting artifacts is by subdividing the respondents in Table 6-5 according to whether or not the respondent resided in a household in which at least one other household member reported having been the victim of a personal crime. If an individual who resided in a household in which another household member reported a personal victimization had a greater likelihood of reporting a personal victimization than did an individual who resided in a household in which no other household member reported a personal victimization, then this is additional evidence of an environmental effect. That is, members of the same household are exposed to the same environmental conditions for some proportion of the time. Of course they are also exposed to different conditions as well—school-aged children to one environment, adults working outside of the home to another, and adults keeping house to still another. Despite this differentiation, there is still the shared environment of the home and its surroundings to which all household members are generally exposed.

From Table 6-9, it is clear that the effect of household victimization on the likelihood of personal victimization generally maintained both for households in which no other household member (than the respondent) was the victim of a personal crime and for households in which at least one other household member was the victim of a personal crime. In addition, the personal victimization status of other household members was related to the personal victimization

Table 6-9. Estimated Likelihood (per 1,000 Persons) of Being a Victim of at Least One Personal Victimization During the Reference Period, by Respondent's Sex, Marital Status, Age, Whether Other Household Members Were Victims of a Personal Crime, and by Household Victimization Status, Twenty-six-City Aggregate, 1972–1974[a]

| | | Male | | | | | | Female | | | | | |
| | | Married | | | Not Married | | | Married | | | Not Married | | |
		12–19	20–34	35 or older	12–19	20–34	35 or older	12–19	20–34	35 or older	12–19	20–34	35 or older
No other household member victimized by a personal crime	Household not victimized by household crime	69 (25,000)	47 (1,077,000)	28 (2,999,000)	81 (1,056,000)	62 (987,000)	57 (952,000)	40 (73,000)	29 (1,366,000)	22 (2,708,000)	43 (1,134,000)	62 (1,109,000)	43 (2,366,000)
	Household victimized by household crime	283[b] (5,000)	96 (359,000)	51 (656,000)	131 (409,000)	119 (318,000)	144 (159,000)	95 (22,000)	49 (422,000)	46 (522,000)	75 (384,000)	138 (301,000)	75 (373,000)
At least one other household member victimized by a personal crime	Household not victimized by household crime	523[b] (2,000)	176 (50,000)	92 (189,000)	174 (208,000)	162 (95,000)	119 (44,000)	290[b] (5,000)	116 (84,000)	82 (194,000)	126 (174,000)	108 (72,000)	69 (125,000)
	Household victimized by household crime	736[b] (1,000)	175 (47,00)	93 (108,000)	269 (126,000)	213 (55,000)	167 (19,000)	286 (6,000)	127 (58,000)	67 (133,000)	199 (100,000)	209 (47,000)	111 (50,000)

[a] Excludes 109,000 respondents for whom marital status was not ascertained. The bases on which the likelihoods were computed are shown in parentheses.

[b] Because of the small base, this estimated likelihood is less reliable than other likelihoods in this table.

status of the respondent. For example, in households that did not report a household victimization, the likelihood of personal victimization for persons residing in households in which no other household member was personally victimized was 28 per 1,000 for married males who were thirty-five years of age or older; for their counterparts residing in households in which at least one other household member was personally victimized, the likelihood was 92 per 1,000. Among married females of the same age, the respective likelihoods were 22 and 82 per 1,000. It is notable that although age, sex, and marital status are among the strongest predictors of personal victimization, even when these variables were simultaneously controlled, household victimization status and the personal victimization status of other household members had substantial effects. *Within any given column of Table 6–9 (i.e, controlling for age, sex, and marital status), persons residing in households that reported a household victimization and in which at least one other household member reported a personal victimization had a likelihood of personal victimization that was generally three to four times greater than that for persons residing in households that did not report a household victimization and in which no other household member reported a personal victimization.* (Contrast the top and bottom rows in Table 6–9.)

These data lend additional weight to the hypothesis that environmental conditions are related to the probability of personal victimization. Those who reside in and therefore spend a large proportion of their time in environments in which victimized households are located are subjected to greater risks of personal victimization.

VICTIMIZATION BY NONSTRANGERS

To this point in the chapter, our attention has focused on likelihoods of victimization, to the exclusion of *characteristics* of victimization events. The finding that risks of personal victimization were "clustered" and that the personal victimization of one household member was associated with the personal victimization of another household member raises the possibility that some of this communality in the risk of personal victimization of members of the same household may be attributable to the environment inside of the home. It is possible, for example, that repetitive victimizations of a single individual disproportionately involved another family member as the offender. Or, to widen the network beyond the family, it may be that the victimizations of repetitive victims disproportionately involved an offender who was an acquaintance of the victim.

One means of gaining a perspective on this possibility is to examine the prior relationship between the victim and the offender for single and multiple victims. To accomplish this, we took each personal victimization reported to survey interviewers by an individual respondent and determined whether that respondent had reported any other personal victimizations to the interviewer. If not, the victimization was designated as having occurred to a "one-time" victim; otherwise the victimization was designated as having occurred to a repetitive victim. All series victimizations were coded as having occurred to repetitive victims.[16] Thus, in this section our unit of analysis is the victimization rather than the victim. In the case of repetitive victims, the characteristics of each victimization are treated separately. For repetitive victims, the prior relationship between the victim and the offender may be different on, say, the first and second victimizations suffered, and hence our analyses must use the victimization as the unit of count.

For personal victimization, the victim was asked whether or not the offender was known to him or her, and each victimization was categorized accordingly as having involved a stranger or a nonstranger. For our consideration here, strangers include those offenders whom the victim had never seen before, whom the victim knew by sight only,[17] or whom the victim could not identify as nonstrangers.[18] For victimizations in which more than one offender was involved, only if the victim did not know any of them or if the victim did not know whether any of them was known, were the offenders classified as strangers. Because detailed analyses of the victim's prior relationship to the offender have been presented elsewhere (Hindelang, 1976: ch. 7), our analysis here will focus on differences in the victim's prior relationship to the offender for one-time and repetitive victims.

The results in Table 6-10 indicate that the victimizations of repetitive victims were more likely than those of one-time victims to involve offenders who were not strangers to the victim. In robbery for example, 20 percent of the victimizations of repetitive victims and 7 percent of those of one-time victims involved offenders who were not strangers to the victim. The tendency was stronger for rape (41 percent versus 18 percent) and also held for assault (aggravated: 37 percent versus 26 percent; simple: 40 percent versus 26 percent).

These results indicate that one of the environmental risk factors that is tied to personal victimization is the associational network of the victims. Repetitive victims can be differentiated from one-time victims in that the former were more often victimized by nonstrangers

Table 6-10. Prior Relationship Between the Victim and Offender for One Time and Repetitive Victims, Twenty-six City Aggregate, 1972-1974[a]

	One-Time Victims		Repetitive Victims	
	Stranger	*Nonstranger*	*Stranger*	*Nonstranger*
Rape	82% (26,016)	18% (5,713)	59% (12,629)	41% (8,769)
Robbery	93% (91,044)	7% (6,554)	80% (73,137)	20% (17,994)
Aggravated Assault	74% (131,466)	26% (47,377)	63% (153,374)	37% (89,540)
Simple Assault	74% (165,711)	26% (57,868)	60% (244,833)	40% (163,343)
Larceny from the Person	98% (205,918)	2% (3,157)	94% (64,604)	6% (4,287)
Total	84% (620,155)	16% (120,669)	66% (548,577)	34% (283,933)

[a]Subcategories may not sum to total because of rounding.

than the latter. Therefore, part of the explanation for the clustering of risks of personal victimization is to be found among the personal relationships that some victims have. For some, the added environmental risk factor is to be found among the family and friends of the victim. However, it must be noted (Table 6-10) that this explanation does not help to account for the repetitive victim status of the two-thirds of the repetitive victims who were victimized by strangers.

From a theoretical perspective, the existence of a link between personal and household victimization—even when such known correlates of victimization as race, income, age, sex, and marital status were controlled—implies that an environmental factor is operative. Members of the same household spend a substantial amount of time in the area in which they reside. This area includes the home itself as well as the neighborhood in which it is located. The environmental characteristics of areas have consistently been shown to be closely linked to rates of crime (e.g., Shaw and McKay, 1942; Lander, 1954; Schmid, 1960a, 1960b; Schmid and Schmid, 1972; Boggs, 1965; Dunn, 1974). In the NCS city victimization survey data, no ecological characteristics are available. Just as it is problematic to make inferences about correlations on the individual level from ecological data, so too is it problematic to make inferences about ecological characteristics from data about individuals or households. Nonetheless, it seems reasonable (if not tautological) to assume that victimized households are located disproportionately in high property crime areas. When areas are used as the units of analysis, it has been found that those with high property crime rates also have high personal crime rates. In light of the relatively strong intercorrelations of index crimes when areas are used as the units of analysis (Schmid and Schmid, 1972; Hindelang, 1974a), victimization by one type of crime (e.g., against the person) is predictive of the likelihood of victimization by another type of crime (e.g., against the household) for targets in the same ecological area. Thus, in Table 6-6, for example, it seems reasonable to infer that persons of any race and income combination who were members of households that had been victimized were more likely to live in high crime areas (i.e., areas high in *both* personal and household crime) than their counterparts whose households had not been victimized. Household victimization status, because it is an *indicator* of whether the household is located in a high risk crime area (for households), also is a measure of whether individual household members are exposed to high victimization risk situations. Conversely, whether any household members have been victims of personal crimes becomes an indicator of the risk of household victimization.

To summarize, the data in this chapter have demonstrated that risks of victimization cluster in several senses. First, both once-victimized persons and once-victimized households were more likely to have suffered subsequent victimizations than were members of the population (persons or households, respectively) selected at random. For personal victims, this is accounted for—but only in part—by the finding that repetitive victims were more likely than one-time victims to be victimized by persons known to them. Second, persons living in households in which another household member had been personally victimized had a greater risk of personal victimization than persons living in households in which no other household member had been personally victimized.[19] Third, persons living in households that had been victimized by a household crime had a higher risk of personal victimization than persons living in households that had not been victimized by a household crime. All of these findings suggest that it is important to include ecological variables among the risk factors in a theoretical model designed to account for variations in victimization, a task to which we will turn our attention in the final chapter.

NOTES

1. Rates of crime as reported in the UCR share this shortcoming. Although, for example, the rate of aggravated assaults known to the police for any given time period is available, the percentage of the population that is victimized by aggravated assaults known to the police is not available. Only for homicide can rates per 100 be interpreted as the percentage of the population victimized by this crime.

2. Unfortunately, none of these traits is adequately defined.

3. Also see Curtis (1974, 1975).

4. See Appendix B for a detailed description of the eight-city design, sampling techniques, and procedures. Results from the five largest cities and the thirteen additional cities are reported in LEAA (1975a) and LEAA (1975c).

5. These data are not shown in tabular form. They are derived by cross-tabulating the number of nonseries personal victimizations by the number of series personal victimizations.

6. This proposition will also be examined in a subsequent chapter on attitudes and victimization.

7. Because of the extremely large Ns and the ease of rejecting the null hypothesis when N is large, the X^2 values were calculated on the unweighted number of cases, although weighted data are shown in the tables.

8. It should be reemphasized that this is not a rate of victimization in which multiple victimizations of the same person are counted more than once, but rather is ten times the percentage of persons who were victimized one or more times by series or nonseries personal crimes during the reference period.

9. Within this chapter household crimes include burglary, larceny from the household premises, and vehicle theft. Excluded are larcenies of the property of household members that occurred away from the household. These larcenies—referred to as larcenies without contact by LEAA (1975a, 1975b, 1975c) and household larcenies occurring elsewhere (i.e., not at home) by Hindelang (1976)—have been excluded here because in general they neither affect the entire household nor involve an intrusion of the household premises.

10. These data are not shown in tabular form. They are derived by cross-tabulating the number of nonseries and the number of series household victimizations.

11. Or, for personal targets, the environments that they frequent.

12. The relationship between race and rates of personal victimization interacts with age and type of crime. See Hindelang (1976: chs. 5 and 6).

13. In the course of these personal interviews, some household victimizations that were not reported by the household respondent were elicited. See Dodge (1975).

14. See questions 29-35 in Appendix A.

15. Undoubtedly, many of these victimizations would have been elicited by the personal victimization screen questions if they had preceded the household screen questions.

16. Series victimizations were weighted according to the number of incidents

in the series. This "proportional weighting method" is fully described in Hindelang (1976: Appendix F). One effect of this procedure is to increase substantially the number of weighted victimizations.

17. But to whom the offender had never said more than "hello."

18. This could occur, for example, if it was too dark to see the offender(s), if the victim was attacked from behind and did not see the attackers, etc.

19. This may be due to a small extent to the fact that when a single incident involved two or more victims, these victims were sometimes members of the same household. However, because more than 90 percent of the incidents involved lone victims, this effect could not have been very large.

 *Part III*

Attitudes About Crime and Victimization Experiences

In part III, our attention shifts somewhat away from the characteristics of victims and victimizations and toward the attitudes about, perceptions of, and behavioral reactions to crime among the residents of the eight cities, victims and nonvictims alike. In the consideration of criminal victimization, the role of attitudes, beliefs, and reactions in the general population would only be unimportant if victims were randomly selected by offenders from a population of people who had no influence on their own chances of being victimized. However, we have seen in Part II that victimization is far from randomly distributed across different subgroups of the population; proneness to victimization does appear to exist.

The question addressed in Chapter 7 is: Did respondents perceive crime as an imminent, threatening phenomenon in their immediate environments? The evidence presented in the chapter indicates that, at least for most people, the answer to this question is negative. Evidently, when people think about crime, they tend to conceptualize it as something that happens "out there" rather than nearby.

Chapter 8 deals with one specific attitude, the fear of crime. The analysis will explore whether the fear of crime expressed by respondents was related to demographic characteristics of the respondents, the risk of personal victimizations faced by particular subgroups of respondents, and the actual experiences of respondents with personal victimization.

In Chapter 9 we explore the issue of whether concern about crime had any influence on the behaviors of the eight-city residents.

A general indicator of behavioral change will be analyzed along with several measures of specific behaviors.

Finally, Chapter 10 is a methodological postscript that deals with analytic issues from Chapters 1 through 9. The postscript assesses the strengths and weaknesses of the analysis that has preceded it and serves as a convenient point to pause before we present a theoretical framework for the analysis of victimization in Chapter 11.

Chapter 7

Crime: A Nonlocal, Nonpersonal Issue

Up to this point, we have been concerned with variations in the risk of personal victimization and with the nature of those victimizations that do occur. However, actual experiences with personal victimizations, especially in their more serious forms, directly affect only a small proportion of the population annually. Yet almost everyone has a set of attitudes[1] about and behavioral reactions to "the crime problem." In this chapter and in Chapters 8 and 9, we will examine some of these attitudes and reactions and see how they are related both to respondent characteristics and to the victimization experiences reported by the respondents.

A random half of the households interviewed in the victimization portion of the NCS city surveys was selected for administration of the attitude questionnaire. Within the selected households, all members *sixteen years old or older* were eligible to be asked a set of individual attitude items. Because the attitude instrument was not administered to household members between the ages of twelve and fifteen, the population estimates presented in Chapters 7, 8, and 9 refer only to eight-city residents sixteen years of age or older, unlike the estimates in earlier chapters. In addition, the person designated as the household respondent was asked a set of household attitude questions. The attitude instrument appears in Appendix A, and further details of the procedures can be found in Appendix B.

As was done with the victimization data in preceding chapters, the attitude data are aggregated across the eight cities. Previous analysis (Garofalo, 1977) has shown not only that the *patterns* in the attitude data were similar across cities (e.g., fear of crime increased with age) but also that, with few exceptions, the *total distribution of responses* on each attitude item was similar from city to city.

There are a number of indications in the attitude data that, even though respondents expressed concern about crime, their concern stemmed less from some threat perceived as imminent or from actual experiences with crime than from a diffuse belief that "something is wrong." The eight-city respondents believed that crime was a problem, but the problem was viewed as being most serious and as having its greatest effects in places and on persons *outside* the immediate life boundaries of the respondents themselves.

CRIME TRENDS

In one pair of attitude questions, respondents were asked: "Within the past year or two, do you think that crime (in your neighborhood/in the United States) has increased, decreased, or remained about the same?" Table 7-1 shows that 86 percent of the respondents thought that crime in the United States had increased, which was almost twice as great as the proportion who said that crime in their own neighborhood[2] had increased (47 percent).

The different responses to these two crime trend questions are somewhat surprising; the respondents lived in large urban areas, yet they were more likely to believe that crime had increased nationally than in their own neighborhoods. Do these findings call into question the traditional assumptions that the fear of and actual occurrence of crime are predominantly urban phenomena? Where did the respondents believe crime had increased? In other neighborhoods within their own cities? In the two or three major metropolitan centers of the United States?

These questions are not answerable with the data at hand, but a possible explanation of the differences in perceptions of crime trends can be suggested. Note that, for both the United States and neighborhood crime trend questions, an extremely small proportion of respondents thought that crime had decreased (3 percent and 6 percent, respectively). On the other hand, there is a major difference between the proportions who said that crime had remained about the same (48 percent for the neighborhood and 11 percent for the United States). One possible explanation for these patterns can be based on differential probabilities of exposure to "sensational" crime news. The probability of reading or hearing about crimes, especially the most "sensational" crimes, that take

Table 7-1. Perceptions of United States and Neighborhood Crime Trends, Eight-City Aggregate, 1972[a]

	Perceptions of Crime Trends	
	United States	*Neighborhood*
Total persons sixteen years of age or older	2,969,770[b] 100%	2,691,210[c] 100%
Percent saying crime had:		
Decreased	3	6
Stayed the same	11	48
Increased	86	47
Total saying crime had increased	2,567,430 100%	1,259,880 100%
Percent with no specific type of crime in mind	34	22
Total mentioning the type(s) of crime that had increased	1,689,140 100%	981,880 100%
Percent mentioning:[d]		
Personal crimes[e]	61	34
Property crimes[f]	10	41
Both personal and property	15	14
Drugs	8	6
Other crimes	11	14

[a]For wording of attitude items, see source codes 345, 346, 348, and 349 in attitude questionnaire, Appendix A.
[b]Excludes respondents who gave no answer or who replied "don't know."
[c]Excludes respondents who gave no answer, who replied "don't know," or who said that they "haven't lived here long enough."
[d]Percentages may sum to more than 100 percent because respondents may have mentioned more than one crime.
[e]Personal crimes are defined here as attempted and completed murder, rape, robbery, and assault.
[f]Property crimes are defined here as attempted and completed burglary, larceny, and other forms of common theft.

place outside the neighborhood is much greater than hearing about such crimes occurring in one's own neighborhood because of the sheer size differentials of the populations involved. Yet perception may tend to pull all of these "outside" crimes together and attribute them to an undifferentiated place ("not neighborhood") that is then compared to the local neighborhood without regard to the difference in the sizes of the populations at risk.

This notion will receive support as it is shown that the difference between respondent perceptions of crime trends on the neighborhood and national levels is just one example of a general tendency that reappears in several other attitude items: *crime was perceived as being more serious (or extensive or fear-inducing) as the frame of reference moved farther away from the respondent personally.* Whether this tendency was produced by some sort of simple "distrust of the unfamiliar" or by some other mechanism, like the one discussed above, is open to question. In any case, if we assume that people more accurately estimate crime trends in settings with which they are very familiar (i.e., their own neighborhoods), then it appears that the eight-city residents, for some reason, may have been evaluating the national crime situation as more serious than it really has been.

Table 7-1 also reveals that there were qualitative as well as quantitative differences between respondents' attitudes about United States and neighborhood crime. Of those who said that crime had increased nationally, about one-third (34 percent) had no specific type of crime in mind; the same was true of only about one-fifth (22 percent) of the respondents who believed that neighborhood crime had increased. Farther down in Table 7-1, the distributions of persons who said that both United States and neighborhood crime had increased *and* who mentioned particular types of crime are shown. The responses of individuals who believed that specific types of crime in the United States had increased reflect a particular image of nonlocal crime: murder, rape, robbery, and assault were perceived as the primary components of the national "crime problem." In contrast, respondents who mentioned particular crimes that they believed were increasing in their neighborhoods tended to emphasize the property crimes of burglary, larceny, and other thefts, crimes that both the UCR and victimization surveys indicate have the highest incidence. Thus, indications from these two crime trend questions are that *local crime was perceived as being less violent and less sensational and, hence, less threatening than nonlocal crime.*

The discrepancy in Table 7-1 between the proportions of respondents who perceived increases in national and neighborhood crime possibly could be explained in terms of the actual distribution of crime rather than by images of crime. For example, if crime had been increasing in *most* areas of the nation but not *all* areas (i.e., not in the eight cities), and the net result was an increase in national crime, the 86 percent versus 47 percent differential in the top portion of Table 7-1 might be expected logically. However, the differences in the types of crimes that respondents were attributing to national and neighborhood crime increases cannot be explained so readily, nor can responses to some other attitude items in the survey, as will be shown below.

COMPARATIVE NEIGHBORHOOD DANGER

The eight-city respondents were asked to compare their own neighborhood with others in the same metropolitan area in terms of crime. The exact wording of the item was: "How do you think your neighborhood compares with others in this metropolitan area in terms of crime?" Because the samples were representative of each city, it might be expected that the proportion of respondents in the city thinking that their neighborhoods were relatively more dangerous than others would be roughly equal to the proportion rating their neighborhoods as less dangerous, with a sizable number of respondents perceiving their neighborhoods as about average. The actual distribution of responses, however, does not confirm this expectation. About half of the respondents felt that their own neighborhoods were either less or much less dangerous than other neighborhoods in the same metropolitan area. Almost as many rated their neighborhoods as average, but fewer than 10 percent said that their neighborhoods were either more or much more dangerous than others. This pronounced departure from an expected "normal distribution" of responses can be explained by a tendency to view the crime problem as more severe in unfamiliar locations than in one's immediate environment, regardless of objective circumstances. But several alternative explanations should be considered first.

1. It is possible that low crime areas were overrepresented in the results. Given the sophistication of the NCS sampling and weighting techniques, however, it seems unlikely that biased sampling could have produced such a skewed distribution. Furthermore, assuming that in a representative sample of residents, persons who report having been victimized are more likely than nonvictims to be residents of high crime areas, the tendency to view one's own neighborhood as relatively more safe than other neighborhoods should be less pronounced among victims than among nonvictims. However, the skewed response distribution is present among respondents who did and did not report to interviewers that they had suffered a victimization during the reference period, as will be shown later in Table 7-4.

2. The response pattern would be at least partially explainable if low crime rate neighborhoods within the cities had greater population concentrations than high crime rate neighborhoods. For example, if a city had six neighborhoods (three actually "less dangerous" and three actually "more dangerous") but 75 percent of the residents lived in the "less dangerous" neighborhoods, comparisons of neighborhood dangerousness from a representative sample of city residents would be expected to produce a skewed response distribu-

tion of the type found in the eight cities. The available evidence, however, indicates that crime rates show either a positive association with population density (Turner, 1969; Beasley and Antunes, 1974; Cho, 1974) or no significant association at all (Freedman, 1975; Spector, 1975).

3. The fact that the question referred to other neighborhoods "in this metropolitan area," rather than just to neighborhoods within the city where the interviews were conducted, may account for the distribution of responses. But this wording could only help to explain the pattern of replies if the respondents had a tendency to perceive suburban neighborhoods as having higher crime rates than neighborhoods within the city limits, which does not seem likely.

4. An apparently reasonable alternative explanation is that the respondents were using a point of reference other than the one intended in the question. Rather than comparing their neighborhoods with *all* the other neighborhoods in the metropolitan area, respondents might well have rated their neighborhoods against some one or two parts of the city that had "bad reputations" with respect to a variety of social ills, including crime. Very few people would rate their own neighborhood as more dangerous than those few parts of the city that "everyone knows" are high-crime areas.

This fourth "alternative explanation" is not really an alternative. It still assumes, as was first hypothesized, that the perception of places other than one's immediate environment as having the worst crime problems is not necessarily related to objective circumstances. From this perspective, the fourth "alternative" merely specifies a point of reference that might be operating within this perceptual phenomenon.

Unfortunately, respondent records from the NCS cannot be sorted according to geographic subareas within the cities; Bureau of the Census strict confidentiality rules prohibit that possibility. It is impossible, therefore, to determine how the residents of particular areas (e.g., census tracts) compared their neighborhoods with others. However, urban neighborhoods tend to be relatively homogeneous on race and family income (Taeuber and Taeuber, 1965; Clemence, 1967; Edwards, 1970), and the income and racial attributes of city areas are often found to be related to crime rates in ecological research (Boggs, 1965; Schmid and Schmid, 1972; Beasley and Antunes, 1974). So, by sorting respondents according to race and income, we are to some extent sorting them according to city areas that vary in rates of crime. This approach, of course, has limitations, because the correspondence between personal characteristics and the crime rates of areas of residence is far from perfect. Nevertheless, we can have some faith that, for example, people with incomes of less than $5,000 are more likely to live in high-crime areas than are people with incomes of $25,000 or more.

Table 7-2 shows the distribution of responses to the comparative neighborhood danger question within race and income categories. The independent effects of race and family income on perceptions of the relative dangerousness of one's neighborhood are apparent in Table 7-2. A higher proportion of whites than black/others in each income category viewed their neighborhood as less or much less dangerous than other neighborhoods. Likewise, within both racial groups, those with higher incomes were most likely to say that their neighborhoods were less or much less dangerous than others. But note the distribution of responses for black/others in families with less than $5,000 income. Only 10 percent of these respondents rated their neighborhoods as more or much more dangerous, while three times that many thought their neighborhoods were less or much less dangerous than other neighborhoods in the metropolitan area. *Evidently, even among respondents who might be thought to live in relatively high-crime neighborhoods, crime was still perceived as being more dangerous outside their immediate environment.*

LIMITING OF ACTIVITIES

The attitude questionnaire contained a set of three items designed to determine the generalized effect of crime on behavior. Respondents were asked whether the fear of crime had produced a limiting or changing of activities in the past few years. The three questions asked for the respondent's opinion about whether such effects had occurred to people in general, to people in the respondent's neighborhood, or to the respondent personally.[3] There was virtually unanimous agreement on the first of these items; 83 percent of the respondents said that people in general had limited or changed their activities because of crime. However, only 59 percent said that the same was true of people in their own neighborhoods, while only 46 percent said that they themselves had been affected similarly. *Thus, there is evidence that the impact of crime on behavior was perceived as being greater as frames of reference moved farther away from the respondent.*

In the earlier discussion of the United States and neighborhood crime trend questions, the suggestion was made that respondents tended to view the world outside their own neighborhoods as an undifferentiated place, impressions of which were compared to

Table 7-2. Comparative Neighborhood Danger, by Race and Family Income of Respondent, Eight-City Aggregate, 1972[a]

	Comparative Neighborhood Danger (percent)					Total persons sixteen years of age or older[b]
	Much more dangerous	More dangerous	About average	Less dangerous	Much less dangerous	
White	1	5	36	43	14	100% (1,849,040)
Less than $5,000	2	8	43	37	11	100% (425,170)
$5,000–11,999	1	5	38	43	12	100% (794,800)
$12,000–24,999	0	4	31	47	18	100% (525,640)
$25,000 or more	0	3	21	49	27	100% (103,430)
Black/Other	2	7	56	30	6	100% (927,530)
Less than $5,000	2	8	60	25	5	100% (360,380)
$5,000–11,999	2	6	56	31	5	100% (410,660)
$12,000–24,999	1	4	50	36	9	100% (144,490)
$25,000 or more	1	4	40	40	14	100% (12,000)

[a]For wording of attitude item, see source code 355 in attitude questionnaire, Appendix A.
[b]Excludes respondents who gave no answer to the attitude item or whose family incomes were not ascertained.

their own local experiences. Support for this suggestion comes from the pattern of responses on the three limiting-of-activity questions. Responses to the question about whether people in general had limited their activity were very homogeneous across demographic subgroups of respondents; young and old, those with low and high family incomes, male and female, white and black/other, and so on strongly agreed with each other that people in general had limited their activities because of crime. However, replies to the neighborhood and personal limiting-of-activity questions exhibited a certain amount, and in some cases a substantial amount, of variability across demographic subgroups of respondents. The frame of reference set by the phrase "people in general" seems to have been similar for all respondents, but when the questions referred to "people in this neighborhood" or "you," the frames of reference became more specified and differentiated among the respondents, allowing them to relate the questions more directly to personal experiences rather than to images received from, for example, the mass media.

Figure 7-1 presents an example of both of the patterns discussed above: the decreasing proportion of affirmative replies as respondents are asked, in turn, whether people in general, people in the neighborhood, and they themselves had limited or changed their activities because of crime; and the increasing heterogeneity of responses—in this case for males and females—across the three questions. Note also the difference between the response *trends* for males and females. The proportion of affirmative replies dropped across the first two questions by similar amounts for males and females. But then the pattern began to level off among females, with 52 percent saying that they had personally limited their activities. For males, on the other hand, the proportion of affirmative replies continued its downward trend, in almost perfect linear fashion, until only 37 percent replied that they had personally limited their activities.

We will say more about male-female response differences, particularly in Chapter 9. For the present it is sufficient to note that, although the pattern of perceiving crime as being more serious and more extensive outside of one's immediate environment repeatedly appeared in the data,[4] there were some variations on this pattern among certain subgroups of respondents.

THE THREAT OF OUTSIDERS

Based on the evidence accumulated through a series of surveys it had sponsored, the President's Commission on Law Enforcement and Administration of Justice (1967:165) concluded that the fear of

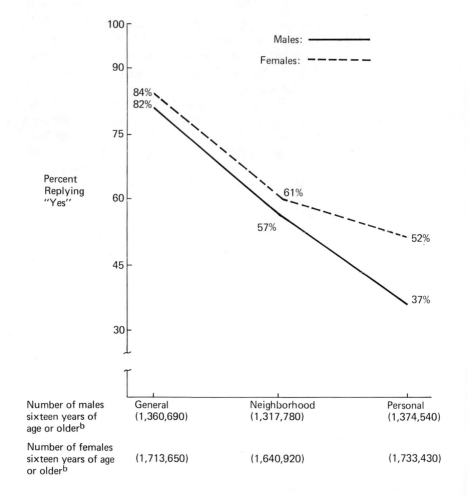

Figure 7-1. Percentages of Respondents Who Said That People in General, People in the Neighborhood, and They Themselves Had Limited or Changed Their Activities Because of Crime, by Sex of Respondent, Eight-City Aggregate, 1972[a]

[a]For wording of attitude items, see source codes 365, 366, and 367 in attitude questionnaire, Appendix A.

[b]Numbers on which percentages were based; excludes respondents who gave no answer for each attitude item.

crime is, "at bottom, a fear of strangers." One component of this fear of strangers was the belief that neighborhood crimes were committed mostly by people from outside the neighborhood. For example, one set of surveys sponsored by the commission was conducted in two Boston and two Chicago police precincts. Among all respondents, 41 percent thought that neighborhood crimes were committed mostly be outsiders, and only 14 percent blamed people living in the neighborhood; 11 percent saw the two groups as equally responsible, and the remaining one-third said they didn't know or gave no answer (Reiss, 1967: Sect. 2, 31). As can be seen from Table 7-3, that distribution of replies is very similar to the one obtained in the eight cities using a similarly worded question.[5]

Table 7-3 displays the beliefs about who commits neighborhood crime broken down by race and family income. At each income level, whites were more likely than black/others to attribute neighborhood crime to outsiders. Among whites, the proportion who blamed outsiders also increased steadily with income, from 41 percent in the lowest income group to 58 percent in the highest. Among black/others, however, there was very little variability across income categories. A convenient summary measure of the extent to which outsiders were blamed for crime in any row of Table 7-3 is the ratio of the proportion who responded "outsiders" to the proportion who responded "people here." From the lowest to highest income categories of whites in Table 7-3, these ratios are 1.9, 2.0, 2.4, and 3.6. The corresponding ratios for black/others are 1.6, 1.7, 1.9, and 2.1. One explanation of these patterns is that respondents were reflecting the commonly held belief that criminal behavior is class linked. Thus residents of high-income areas, in comparison to residents of low-income areas, might tend to believe that a greater proportion of the crimes committed in their areas are attributable to outsiders. The relative lack of variability across black/other income categories is consistent with the finding that income is somewhat less predictive of neighborhood of residence for blacks than for whites (Taeuber, 1968; Erbe, 1975).

There are very few studies that deal with the question of the extent to which crimes in specific areas are committed by residents or nonresidents, and all of the existing studies deal with arrested offenders (Schmid, 1960b; Hoover, 1966:23-25; Normandeau, 1968). Because the property crimes that the eight-city residents saw as increasing in their neighborhoods (see Table 7-1) have low arrest clearance rates, such studies are of limited utility as a check on the accuracy of respondent perceptions of where offenders reside. *But regardless of whether respondents were overestimating or under-*

Table 7-3. Beliefs About Who Commits Crimes in the Neighborhood, by Race and Family Income of Respondent, Eight-City Aggregate, 1972[a]

| | Who Commits Neighborhood Crimes (percent) | | | | Total persons sixteen years of age or older[b] |
	Out-siders	People here	Equally by both	Don't know	
Total	44	21	9	25	100% (2,928,290)
White[c]	47	21	6	25	100% (1,748,900)
Less than $5,000	41	22	6	31	100% (401,460)
$5,000–11,999	45	22	7	25	100% (751,570)
$12,000–24,999	51	21	6	22	100% (497,960)
$25,000 or more	58	16	6	21	100% (97,910)
Black/Other[c]	39	23	15	24	100% (894,690)
Less than $5,000	38	24	15	24	100% (347,630)
$5,000–11,999	39	23	15	24	100% (396,220)
$12,000–24,999	42	22	14	22	100% (139,300)
$25,000 or more	42	20	13	25	100% (11,540)

[a]For wording of attitude item, see source code 347 in attitude questionnaire, Appendix A.
[b]Excludes respondents who gave no answer or who said that there were "no crimes happening in neighborhood."
[c]Excludes respondents whose family incomes were not ascertained.

estimating the relative involvement of outsiders in neighborhood crime, the fact remains that the eight-city residents believed that outsiders were primarily responsible for crimes occurring in their neighborhoods. According to Conklin (1975: 33):

In blaming outsiders for crime, people are able to dissociate themselves from the offenders. This removes the problem from the immediate vicinity, since the criminal is seen as a person who lives elsewhere, journeys to the community, commits a crime, and then returns home. A view of the criminal as a mysterious, unknown predator may increase anxiety about crime, but it also makes continued residence in the community psychologically possible. Denying the indigenous origin of the offender by invoking a we-they dichotomy permits people to condemn offenders more harshly, since they are not then condemning an important part of their own lives, the community in which they live. This permits them to maintain a more positive image of their community.

It appears from the evidence presented in this section that Conklin's observations apply to a wider range of attitudes about crime than just who commits crimes. So far we have seen that the tendency to perceive crime as primarily a nonlocal, nonpersonal problem shows up in beliefs about crime trends, the relative dangerousness of one's neighborhood, and the effects of crime on people within and outside of one's immediate environment, as well as in beliefs about where offenders come from. The next step is to determine if any of the patterns that have been found vary when the actual experiences of respondents with victimization are taken into account.

VICTIMIZATION AND PERCEPTIONS OF THE CRIME PROBLEM

Because the eight-city attitude data were collected in conjunction with a victimization survey, it is possible to analyze attitude responses in terms of the victimizations that respondents reported as having occurred to them in the twelve months preceding the interviews. A reasonable expectation would be that the fact of being victimized should attenuate some of the above noted differences between attitudes about crime in local and nonlocal areas; the experience of being victimized should make crime more of a *personal* reality.

Attitude responses pertaining to the four topics discussed so far—crime trends, comparative neighborhood danger, limiting of activities, and offenders in neighborhood crime—are broken down by the number of personal victimizations that respondents reported to interviewers and are summarized in Table 7-4. Of those who gave usable responses[6] on each of the attitude items in Table 7-4, the overwhelming majority (94 percent) did not report any series or nonseries personal victimizations as occurring during the reference period. About 5 percent reported one victimization, while the remaining 1 percent recalled two or more personal victimizations; these latter respondents also include all who suffered personal victimizations that were classified as series.

Experience with personal victimization does not appear to have had any effect on judgments about the national crime trend; 86 percent of the nonvictims and 87 percent of those victimized once or two or more times said that United States crime had increased. On the other hand, respondents who had suffered one personal victimization (59 percent) or two or more victimizations (66 percent) during the reference period were much more likely than nonvictims (46 percent) to say that neighborhood crime had increased within the past year or two. However, even among those respondents who reported two or more victimizations to interviewers, the proportion who said that United States crime had increased (87 percent) was still substantially greater than the proportion who said that neighborhood crime had increased (66 percent). *Thus, even though direct personal experience with crime did appear to have an effect on perceptions of crime in one's immediate environment, such experiences did not eliminate the tendency to view crime as more of a problem nonlocally then locally.*

The same conclusion can be reached from the pattern of responses to the comparative neighborhood danger question in Table 7-4. The proportion of respondents who said that their own neighborhood was more or much more dangerous than other neighborhoods in the metropolitan area increased from 6 percent among those who suffered no personal victimizations during the reference period to 13 percent for respondents who reported one victimization t) the interviewer, and the figure was only slightly higher (16 percent) among persons who had been victimized two or more times. However, this increasing trend did not change the overall pattern of responses; the 16 percent of those victimized two or more times who rated their neighborhoods as more or much more dangerous still contrasts strongly with the 41 percent in that same group who rated their neighborhoods as less or much less dangerous.[7] *Thus, even when we controlled for personal victimization, respondents were much more likely to view their own neighborhoods as safer, rather than more dangerous, than other neighborhoods in the metropolitan area.*

Responses to the set of three activity-limiting questions are shown next in Table 7-4. On each of the three questions, respondents who were victimized during the reference period were at least *slightly* more likely than nonvictims to say that crime had resulted in a limiting or changing of activities. The differences became greater as the frames of reference of the questions moved closer to the respondent personally. When the question referred to people in general there was almost no difference between nonvictims and respon-

Table 7-4. Responses to Selected Attitude Questionnaire Items, by Number of Personal Victimizations Suffered by Respondent, Eight-City Aggregate, 1972[a]

	Total Number of Personal Victimizations		
	None	*One*	*Two or more*[b]
Crime in United States has increased	86% (2,790,777)[c]	87% (143,833)	87% (35,513)
Crime in respondent's neighborhood has increased	46% (2,524,828)[c]	59% (132,999)	66% (33,694)
Comparative neighborhood danger (percent):			
More or much more dangerous	6	13	16
About average	43	46	43
Less or much less dangerous	51	41	41
Total	100 (2,889,657)	100 (148,062)	100 (36,207)
People in general have limited their activities	83% (2,890,421)[c]	85% (147,870)	86% (36,409)
People in the neighborhood have limited their activities	59% (2,781,979)[c]	66% (141,814)	67% (35,263)
The respondent has limited his or her activities	45% (2,922,354)[c]	54% (149,312)	56% (36,659)
Who commits neighborhood crimes (percent):			
Outsiders	44	42	42
People here	21	31	36
Equally by both	9	10	10
Don't know	26	17	12
Total	100 (2,747,748)	100 (144,605)	100 (36,248)

[a]The attitude questionnaire items used in the table are, in order of appearance, source codes 348, 345, 355, 365, 366, 367, and 347. For wording of attitude items, see attitude questionnaire in Appendix A.

[b]All respondents reporting at least one series personal victimization to the interviewer were classified as having two or more personal victimizations.

[c]Numbers in parentheses indicate the bases (numbers of persons sixteen years of age or older) on which the percentages above them were computed. For all attitude items, respondents who replied "don't know" or who gave no answer are excluded. For source code 345, respondents who said that they "haven't lived here that long" are excluded; for source code 347, respondents who said that there were "no crimes happening in neighborhood" are excluded.

dents who had been victimized two or more times (83 percent versus 86 percent); the difference increased to eight percentage points for the question referring to people in the neighborhood (59 percent versus 67 percent), and to 11 percentage points for the question referring to the respondent personally (45 percent versus 56 percent.) *But again, the fact of being victimized did not change the pronounced tendency for decreasing proportions of respondents to say, in turn, that people in general, people in the neighborhood, and they themselves had limited or changed their activities.* There was a gap of 38 percentage points between the proportions of nonvictims who said that people in general and that they themselves had limited their activities (83 percent versus 45 percent), and the corresponding gap of 30 percentage points (86 percent versus 56 percent) among respondents who suffered two or more personal victimizations during the reference period was not much smaller.

The final portion of Table 7-4 deals with the relationship between experiences with personal victimization and perceptions of who committed crimes in the neighborhood. Regardless of whether or not the respondent had been personally victimized, the tendency to attribute the commission of neighborhood crimes to outsiders showed a negligible amount of variation and was consistently the modal response category. Because the victimizations reflected in Table 7-4 all involved contact between the victim and the offender, it is not surprising that respondents who had suffered such victimizations were less likely than nonvictims to claim that they didn't know who the offenders in neighborhood crimes were. Interestingly, however, this decrease in "don't know" responses was matched by an increase in the proportion of respondents who attributed neighborhood crime to *local residents; only 21 percent of the nonvictims blamed "people here," but the proportion increased to 31 percent for respondents victimized one time during the reference period and to 36 percent for those victimized more than once.* If we can assume that those who had been victimized held a more realistic view of who committed crimes in the neighborhood, then it appears that nonvictims (the overwhelming majority of the eight-city population) underestimated the extent to which crime was a "homegrown" problem.

DISCUSSION

In this chapter, evidence has been presented that tends to support the notion that people generally conceive of crime as something removed from themselves: crime is increasing *elsewhere; other* neighborhoods are more dangerous; the activities of *other* people are more affected by crime; *outsiders* are mostly responsible for local crime. Although response patterns do show variability in relation to certain demographic characteristics of respondents and to actual experiences with victimization, the overall patterns remain strong.

Several brief comments have been made about possible mechanisms that could be producing these response patterns. A simple distrust of the unfamiliar may be at work, or, as described earlier in a quote from Conklin, a psychological defense mechanism may be operating to distort reality and to allow the individual to feel at least a minimal degree of security in his or her own environment, regardless of objective risk. Another mechanism that could account for the results obtained depends upon the perceptual referent to which respondents were comparing their local environments. The observed response patterns could result from perceiving "elsewhere" as an undifferentiated place to which all the evils recorded in the mass media were attributed; then "elsewhere" could be compared with "here," lacking an exact notion of proportionality in terms of the size of the populations at risk. On the other hand, "elsewhere" could be perceptually associated with some single, stereotyped "worst place" outside the local environment. This "worst place" could have some specific referent (e.g., a Denver resident comparing his neighborhood with what he "knows" about New York City) or be nonspecific (e.g., a composite drawn from the numerous crime shows on television). In either case, the local environment would have to be thoroughly ridden with crime in order for it to compare unfavorably with such a perceived "elsewhere." The available data are not sufficient to test the alternatives just mentioned.

This chapter has shown that perceptions of "the crime problem" are not simple reflections of respondent knowledge about actual events, but research that is more focused than the broad attitudinal coverage of the NCS is needed in order to isolate the perceptual influences involved. For example, a great deal of work needs to be done regarding the effects of the media on attitudes about crime. Though some investigations of the treatment of crime, deviance, and social problems in the media have been reported (Cirino, 1972: ch. 18; Cohen and Young, 1973; Hubbard, DeFleur and DeFleur, 1975), mostly we have speculation about the effects of media presentations on perceptions of crime (e.g., Quinney, 1973:155-62).

The sole question in the eight-city surveys dealing with this issue asked the respondents whether they thought crime was less, more, or about as serious as the newspapers and television say. Fewer than 10 percent of the respondents said that crime was less serious than reflected in the media; the remainder were fairly equally divided between saying that crime was more serious or about the same as shown in the media. Because there were virtually no differences between victims and nonvictims in these judgements about the media (Garofalo, 1977:Table 6), and because the research literature generally shows that the media disproportionately present the more "sensational" crimes in both news and dramatizations, the fact that more than 40 percent of the respondents said that crime was actually *more* serious than in the media is not only intriguing but highlights our lack of knowledge about the processes of attitude formation in this area.

Although this entire chapter has been concerned with the idea that crime is often perceived as a nonlocal, nonpersonal problem in many respects, this does not mean that the eight-city residents did not express fear of crime. This issue is the object of our analyses in the next chapter.

NOTES

1. In this book we use the term "attitude" in a very broad, nontechnical sense to refer to all of the attitude instrument items (see Appendix A) that deal with attitudes, beliefs, or opinions about crime. The only items that will not be included within the term are those that apply to specific factual situations—for example, source code 338: "How often do you go out in the evening for entertainment, such as to restaurants, theaters, etc.?"

2. Throughout the attitude instrument, there are a number of items that refer to the respondent's neighborhood. We cannot be certain, however, that "neighborhood" was similarly defined by all respondents because the Bureau of Census instructions to interviewers were: "This term is defined, loosely, as the general area in which a person lives. The boundaries of this area would be whatever each individual feels is his 'neighborhood' " (U.S. Bureau of the Census, 1975: D5-2).

3. The items are source codes 365, 366, and 367 in the attitude questionnaire in Appendix A. Note that there is a subtle wording change in these items. For the first two (people in general and people in this neighborhood), respondents were asked if other people had changed their behavior "because they are afraid of crime." In the third item (have *you* limited or changed your activities), the phrase becomes "because of crime," with the component of fear being dropped. However, the three questions were asked in succession, and their wording was *virtually* identical. It therefore seems likely that the respondents would have developed a single mode of interpretation for answering all three questions. Our analysis will proceed as if the questions were all worded the same.

4. For example, 81 percent of the white respondents said that people in general had limited their behavior; 51 percent said the same about people in the neighborhood and 41 percent said that they personally had limited their behavior. Among black/others the corresponding percentages were 83, 65, and 54.

5. Source code 347: "Would you say they [neighborhood crimes] are committed mostly by the people who live here in this neighborhood or mostly by outsiders?"

6. Cases in which a response was not ascertained, in which the respondent replied "don't know," and in which the respondent was not eligible to answer the particular question (i.e., had not lived in the neighborhood long enough to estimate the crime trend) are excluded from the table.

7. Of course, some of the victimizations may have occurred outside of the victim's neighborhood.

✳ *Chapter 8*

The Fear of Crime

In the eight-city surveys there were two sets of questions that dealt with the issue of fear. The first set asked: "How safe do you feel or would you feel being out alone in your neighborhood (at night, during the day)?" Questions in the other set were a bit more complex: "Are there some parts of this metropolitan area where you have a reason to go or would like to go (during the day, at night), but are afraid to because of fear of crime?"

It would have been helpful to be able to use these two sets of questions in the preceding chapter to examine another aspect of the differences between local and nonlocal perceptions of crime. Unfortunately, the questions diverge too much in wording to allow meaningful comparisons. For one thing, the neighborhood questions directed the respondent to think about being *alone*, but the metropolitan area questions were not explicit on this point. More importantly, the metropolitan area questions contained a qualification about places "where you have a reason to go or would like to go." It seems reasonable to assume that many respondents would be less likely to have had a reason or a desire to go to high-crime places in the metropolitan area than to other places. This qualification in the metropolitan area questions, then, invited respondents to ignore the very places of which they might have been most fearful. For both of these reasons, comparisons were not made between the two sets of questions; for the latter reason, the metropolitan area questions will not be used in this chapter.[1]

With respect to the two neighborhood questions, attention will focus on the one that refers to fear of being alone at night. The great majority (91 percent) of the respondents said that they felt either very safe or reasonably safe about being out alone in their neighborhoods during the *day;* the same was pretty much the case for victims and nonvictims (90 percent versus 91 percent) and for respondents with differing demographic characteristics (Garofalo, 1977:Table 15). However, only 55 percent of all respondents said that they felt very safe or reasonably safe about being out alone at *night*, and there was much more variation in these responses across demographic subgroups than on the daytime question.

Of course, the neighborhood safety questions did not refer specifically to crime. As inspection of the attitude instrument in Appendix A reveals, however, the neighborhood safety question followed a series of crime-related questions, thus establishing crime as the general referent in the interview. It seems reasonable to assume, then, that when respondents said that they felt unsafe, their feelings were based primarily on a fear of being victimized.

FEAR OF CRIME AND RESPONDENT CHARACTERISTICS

Because the attitude item used to measure fear of crime referred to the respondent's own neighborhood, we would expect replies to be related to those respondent characteristics that are also relatively good indicators of area of residence within cities. Table 8-1 presents responses to the question about neighborhood safety at night. The table shows that 40 percent of the whites and 55 percent of the black/others reported feeling either somewhat or very unsafe about being out alone in their neighborhoods at night. When the responses were broken down simultaneously by race and family income, these two variables were independently related to the fear of crime. Whites at each income level expressed slightly less fear of neighborhood crime—that is, reported feeling either somewhat or very unsafe—than black/others of similar incomes, and the fear of crime decreased as income increased within each racial group.

There was some difference in the way that income was related to fear of crime within each racial group. Focusing on the response extremes ("very safe" and "very unsafe") in Table 8-1, we find that there was a bit more variability across income categories for whites than there was for black/others. Although the proportion of white respondents who said they felt very *safe* was more than twice as great in the highest income category than in the lowest income category (32 percent versus 15 percent), the corresponding range

Table 8-1. Feeling of Safety When Out Alone in Neighborhood at Night, by Race and Family Income of Respondent, Eight-City Aggregate, 1972[a]

	Neighborhood Safety at Night (percent)				Total persons sixteen years of age or older[b]
	Very safe	Reasonably safe	Somewhat unsafe	Very unsafe	
White	21	39	20	20	100% (1,870,200)
Less than $5,000	15	32	22	32	100% (432,270)
$5,000–11,999	20	41	21	19	100% (802,410)
$12,000–24,999	26	43	18	13	100% (530,660)
$25,000 or more	32	39	17	12	100% (104,860)
Black/Other	11	34	24	31	100% (934,720)
Less than $5,000	10	29	23	39	100% (363,330)
$5,000–11,999	12	37	24	27	100% (413,370)
$12,000–24,999	15	39	24	22	100% (146,050)
$25,000 or more	18	43	16	23	100% (11,970)

[a]For exact wording of attitude item, see source code 350 in attitude questionnaire, Appendix A.
[b]Excludes respondents who gave no answer to the attitude item or whose family incomes were not ascertained.

among black/others was from 18 percent to 10 percent. At the same time, the proportion of "very *unsafe*" responses decreased from 32 percent to 12 percent across the income categories of whites and from 39 percent to 23 percent across the income categories of black/others. It may be useful to examine these differences in terms of the ratio of "very unsafe" to "very safe" response percentages in each income row in Table 8-1. For whites this ratio was five and one-half times greater among those with family incomes of less then $5,000 than it was for respondents with incomes of $25,000 or more (2.13 versus 0.38). On the other hand, the ratio was only three times greater for low income than for high income black/others (3.90 versus 1.28). This pattern probably results from income being a stronger indicator of area of residence among whites than among black/others; racial segregation tends to restrict the housing market of black/others, regardless of their income (Taeuber, 1968; Erbe, 1975).

But race and income were not the only respondent characteristics associated with variation in fear of crime. Table 8-2 shows the effects of sex and age, two variables that can be assumed to have much less of a connection with area of residence than do race and income. As with race and income, sex and age had independent effects on the fear of crime. Males at each age level expressed much less fear than females, and fear tended to be greater for older respondents of both sexes. And, just as income had less of an effect among black/others than among whites, age was less strongly related to fear of crime among females than among males. In this case the disparities were very pronounced. Computing the ratio of "very unsafe" to "very safe" response percentages (as was done above for income categories in Table 8-1), we find that the ratio for the oldest male age group was more than twelve times as large as the ratio for the youngest male age group (1.47 versus 0.12). Among females, however, the ratio in the oldest age group was less than three times as large as in the female age group with the smallest ratio, twenty-five to thirty-four year olds (7.00 versus 2.55).

The findings here with respect to race, income, and sex are in agreement with the ones reported by Ennis (1967:73) using the data from the national victimization survey conducted in 1966 for the President's Commission on Law Enforcement and Administration of Justice. Ennis even reported an interaction between race and income similar to the one pointed out above; in his data, fear of walking alone in the neighborhood at night was associated with income among whites, but not among blacks. National public opinion surveys conducted by the Gallup organization also concur

Aggregate, 1972[a]

... Sex and Age of Respondent, Eight-City

	Neighborhood Safety at Night (percent)				Total persons sixteen years of age or older [b]
	Very safe	Reasonably safe	Somewhat unsafe	Very unsafe	
Male	28	45	16	11	100% (1,376,510)
16–24	34	50	12	4	100% (333,730)
25–34	33	48	13	6	100% (263,280)
35–49	28	47	16	10	100% (304,980)
50–64	24	43	19	15	100% (293,880)
65 or older	17	36	22	25	100% (180,640)
Female	9	31	26	34	100% (1,732,170)
16–24	9	36	27	28	100% (392,530)
25–34	11	35	26	28	100% (307,920)
35–49	11	32	25	32	100% (377,990)
50–64	9	28	26	38	100% (370,020)
65 or older	7	21	22	49	100% (283,710)

[a] For exact wording of attitude item, see source code 350 in attitude questionnaire, Appendix A.
[b] Excludes respondents who gave no answer to the attitude item.

that, at least on the bivariate level, fear of walking alone in the immediate area at night is related to race, sex, and age in the same manner as reported here for the eight cities (Hindelang, 1974b: 103-105).

VICTIMIZATION AND FEAR

Fear and Risk of Personal Victimization

We have seen that fear of crime varied across several demographic subgroups in the eight cities. The next question is whether this variation can be explained in terms of the differing risks of victimization faced by these subgroups—that is, to what extent is the heightened fear expressed by low income black/others and older females related to their objective risks of being personally victimized?

In this section, the idea of risk will be expressed by the number of personal victimizations suffered by a subgroup standardized by the number of persons in that subgroup (the *rate* of victimization). Note that this does not indicate the proportion of distinct individuals in a subgroup who were victimized (the *likelihood* of victimization) because some individuals incurred more than one victimization during the reference period. There can be some argument as to whether the victimization *rate* or the *likelihood* of victimization is the preferable measure of risk, especially because in Chapter 6 it was shown that the probabilities of second and subsequent victimizations for a person were not simple multiplicative functions of the probability of a single victimization. The assumption here, however, is that, to the extent that people do form a subjective probability of being victimized from the experiences of others, they do so on the basis of some impression of the number of victimizations suffered by "people like themselves." In other words, for example, knowing that two of her friends were each victimized *twice* will probably have more of an effect on an elderly woman than simply knowing that the two friends were victimized.

To facilitate examination of the relationship between fear of crime (as indexed by the proportion of respondents who said they felt either somewhat or very unsafe about being out alone in their neighborhoods at night) and risk of victimization (the total nonseries personal victimization rate), both indicators have been transformed to a standard metric, and the results are plotted by race and income and by sex and age in Figures 8-1 through 8-4. The transformation performed on the data is based on a generalization of a technique described by Hovland, Lumsdaine, and Sheffield (1955). Hovland et al. proposed the technique as a method of measuring improve-

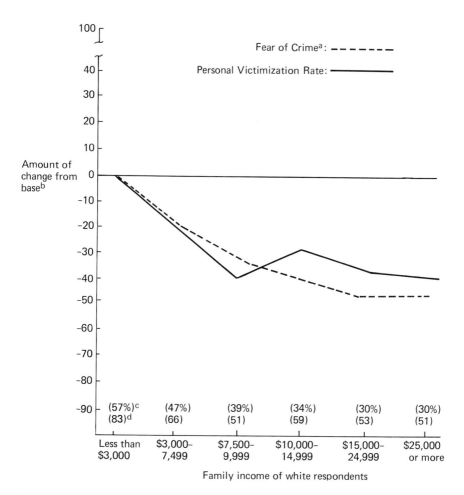

Figure 8-1. Covariation of Fear of Crime and Personal Victimization Rate, by Family Income of White Respondents, Eight-City Aggregate, 1972

[a]Defined as the proportion of white respondents in each income category who replied either "somewhat unsafe" or "very unsafe" to source code 350 in attitude questionnaire; see Appendix A.

[b]See text for explanation.

[c]Percent who responded somewhat unsafe or very unsafe.

[d]Total personal victimization rate per 1,000 persons.

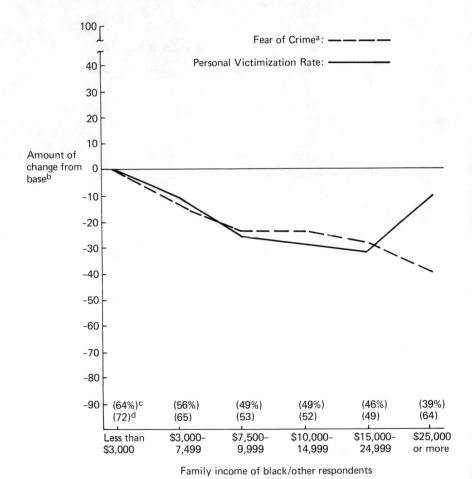

Figure 8-2. Covariation of Fear of Crime and Personal Victimization Rate, by Family Income of Black/Other Respondents, Eight-City Aggregate, 1972

[a]Defined as the proportion of black/other respondents in each income category who replied either "somewhat unsafe" or "very unsafe" to source code 350 in attitude questionnaire; see Appendix A.
[b]See text for explanation.
[c]Percent who responded somewhat unsafe or very unsafe.
[d]Total personal victimization rate per 1,000 persons.

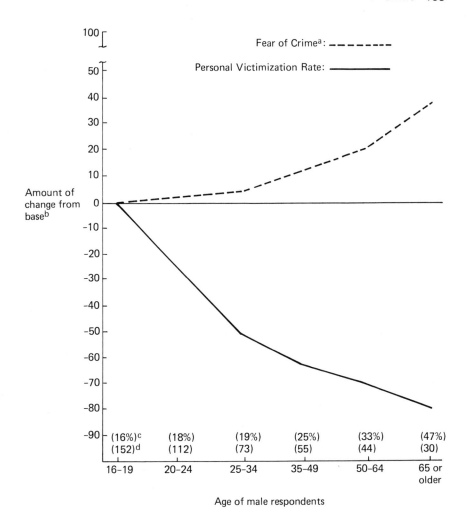

Figure 8-3. Covariation of Fear of Crime and Personal Victimization Rate, by Age of Male Respondents, Eight-City Aggregate, 1972

[a]Defined as the proportion of male respondents in each age category who replied either "somewhat unsafe" or "very unsafe" to source code 350 in attitude questionnaire; see Appendix A.

[b]See text for explanation.

[c]Percent who responded somewhat unsafe or very unsafe.

[d]Total personal victimization rate per 1,000 persons.

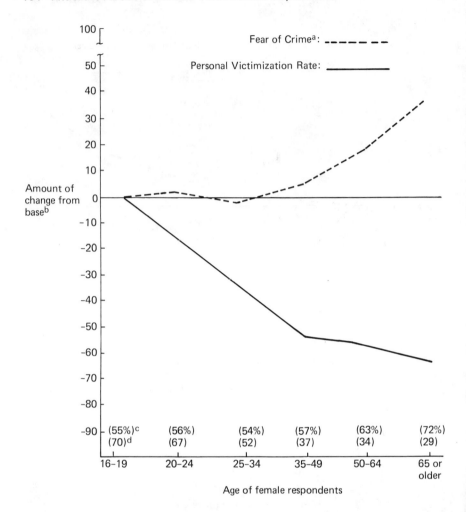

Figure 8-4. Covariation of Fear of Crime and Personal Victimization Rate, by Age of Female Respondents, Eight-City Aggregate, 1972

[a]Defined as the proportion of female respondents in each age category who replied either "somewhat unsafe" or "very unsafe" to source code 350 in attitude questionnaire; see Appendix A.

[b]See text for explanation.

[c]Percent who responded somewhat unsafe or very unsafe.

[d]Total personal victimization rate per 1,000 persons.

ments or deteriorations of subjects' scores while taking into account the amount of improvement or deterioration that was possible given baseline scores. For the present purposes, the victimization rates and proportions of responses indicating fear of crime among the lowest income and age groups (within each race or sex category, respectively) were used as baseline scores; this is the "zero" point on Figures 8-1 through 8-4. Subsequent scores across the income and age categories reflect increases (positive scores) or decreases (negative scores), from the baseline, in victimization rates and fear of crime.[2] It must be emphasized that in this section we are comparing fear of crime and rates of victimization for respective *subgroups* of respondents. It is not until later in this chapter that our attention will return to individual-level data.

Figures 8-1 and 8-2 show that, among both whites and black/ others, fear of crime and victimization rate change scores *both* tended to decrease as income increased. The only exceptions were caused by a slight upturn in the personal victimization rate for whites with family incomes between $10,000 and $14,999 and a sharp jump in the rate for black/others in the highest income category.[3] In contrast, fear of crime and victimization rates moved in *opposite* directions across age groups for both males and females (Figures 8-3 and 8-4). Personal victimization rates decreased quite dramatically from the youngest to oldest male and female age groups, but the fear of crime became greater with age, especially in the two oldest age groups.

The results for income are readily understandable, particularly because this variable is a rough indicator of area of residence; we would expect people who live in low-income areas, areas generally characterized by high crime rates, to have high victimization rates, and we would also expect them to express fear about being out alone in their neighborhoods at night. Although not apparent from Figures 8-1 and 8-2 because of the data transformation technique used, fear of crime and victimization rates did not vary together as neatly across racial categories as they did across income categories. Whites in the eight cities had a total personal victimization rate of 60 per 1,000, which was almost identical to the rate for black/ others, 61 per 1,000. However, black/others did express somewhat more fear of crime, as measured here, than did whites (40 percent versus 55 percent).

The age findings in Figures 8-3 and 8-4 lead to the conclusion that it was not objective risk, at least as the concept is operationalized here, that created the disproportionate fear of crime exhibited by older respondents. Some speculation can be made about what factors produced this effect among older respondents, and there are also some clues in the data that bear on the issue.

First, fear of crime among the elderly may stem less from perceptions of absolute risk than from the belief that, if confronted by an offender, they would not have much success in thwarting a victimization—for example, by fleeing or by physically resisting—because of decreased physical prowess. In addition, they may believe that they would be more likely than younger persons to suffer injury in a victimization event and that, for them, any injury would have seriously debilitating consequences. The eight-city data did reveal that the proportion of victimizations that were completed, as opposed to attempted, tended to be higher for older victims, but older victims of personal crime were no more likely than younger victims to be injured in a personal victimization (Hindelang, 1976:134, 250–51). But, regardless of the actual situation, it seems likely that older persons, whose physical capacities are weakened by age, might *believe* that they will be less able to foil an offender and more likely to suffer an incapacitating injury.

Second, it seems reasonable to assume that as older persons, who are less mobile than younger persons, see their neighborhoods changing, they may translate these perceived changes into a fear of unknown persons in their neighborhoods. At least one portion of the eight-city data supports this possibility. Recall that there were two portions of the NCS attitude questionnaire: one portion for all sixteen year old or older members of households that were in the random half of households selected for the attitude surveys and another portion for persons designated as household respondents within those households. All household respondents in the attitude surveys were asked: "Is there anything you don't like about this neighborhood?" As Table 8–3 shows, the majority of respondents (61 percent) had no complaints concerning their neighborhoods, and satisfaction did not vary drastically by age, even though household respondents in the twenty-five to thirty-four year old age category did express the least satisfaction.

People who said that there was something about their neighborhood that they didn't like were asked to identify the problem; if more than one problem was mentioned, they were asked to designate one as the most important. In the lower portion of Table 8–3 it can be seen that, among those household respondents who expressed dissatisfaction, the distribution of neighborhood problems identified as most important was quite stable across age groups, with one major exception. There was a dramatic increase, from the youngest to the oldest age categories, in the proportion of

Table 8-3. Perceived Neighborhood Problems, by Age of Household Respondent, Eight-City Aggregate, 1972[a]

Anything you don't like about this neighborhood?	Age of Household Respondent					
	16-24	25-34	35-49	50-64	65 or Older	Total
Yes	40%	44%	39%	36%	34%	39%
No	60%	56%	61%	64%	66%	61%
Total number of household respondents[b]	100% (224,750)	100% (318,830)	100% (370,380)	100% (376,820)	100% (296,030)	100% (1,586,810)
Most important neighborhood problems[c]						
Traffic, parking	11%	12%	10%	10%	7%	10%
Environmental problems: trash, noise, etc.	28%	30%	29%	30%	29%	29%
Crime or fear of crime	26%	19%	18%	18%	18%	19%
Public transportation problem	1%	1%	1%	2%	1%	1%
Inadequate schools, shopping facilities, etc.	4%	6%	5%	2%	1%	4%
Neighborhood changing; bad element moving in	8%	11%	18%	23%	25%	17%
Problems with neighbors (or visitors to neighborhood)	15%	14%	12%	10%	12%	13%
Other	7%	8%	6%	5%	5%	6%
Total number of household respondents[d]	100% (87,730)	100% (136,340)	100% (137,500)	100% (132,050)	100% (97,600)	100% (591,220)

[a] For wording of attitude item, see source code 328 in attitude questionnaire, Appendix A.

[b] Excludes respondents who gave no answer.

[c] For wording of attitude items, see source codes 329 and 330 in attitude questionnaire, Appendix A.

[d] Includes only household respondents who said there was something they didn't like about the neighborhood and who designated a problem as most important.

respondents who cited problems of the type, "neighborhood chang-ing; bad element moving in." Only 8 percent of the youngest house-hold respondents who had a complaint about the neighborhood mentioned this as the most important problem, but the percentage increased steadily, reaching 25 percent among household respondents sixty-five years old or older.[4] This finding supports the notion that the generally higher fear of crime found among older respondents may have been more reflective of an uneasiness stemming from the disruption of long-term familiarity with people in their neighbor-hoods, rather than from the actual threat of being victimized.

As was the case for age, fear of crime and risk of victimization were negatively related across sex groups; because the data in Figures 8-3 and 8-4 were standardized within sex groups, this relationship is not apparent in these figures. Males in the eight cities had a per-sonal victimization rate (75 per 1,000) that was more than half again as large as the rate for females (47 per 1,000), but Table 8-2 showed that females expressed more fear of crime than did males. Although 60 percent of the female attitude respondents said that they felt either very or somewhat unsafe about being out alone in their neighborhoods at night, the same was true for only 27 percent of the males.

The fear-risk discrepancy for males and females could be due to sex role differences operating in one or both of two ways. First, socialization into the female sex role in American society has tra-ditionally been geared toward producing passivity and dependency in the role occupant. Griffin (1971) argued that one of the ways in which this is accomplished is by instilling a fear of strangers in young women, especially in terms of a fear of being raped, and she contended that socialization in this manner is intended to make women feel dependent on men for protection. Regardless of the purpose, though, if female sex role socialization is geared toward producing passivity and dependency, it could easily produce fear that is incommensurate with the risk of victimization. Second, sex role socialization may also affect the responses of males. If we assume that part of the traditional American male role model places a negative evaluation on any display of fear, then it is logical to expect that males would *express* less fear of crime than females, regardless not only of their objective risk of personal victimization but also of their actual feelings of fear.[5]

In addition to sex role differentiation, differences between males and females in sheer physical strength may result in women feeling more vulnerable because of their being less able to resist offenders (who are generally males). Furthermore, excluding homicide, there is probably no crime that induces more fear than does rape, a crime that, for all practical purposes, affects only females as victims.[6]

One more issue concerning the age and sex patterns of fear and risk must be noted. A definite possibility exists that a high level of fear of crime *produces* a low risk of victimization. That is, females and older people may have more fear of crime and, therefore, take more precautions against crime than males and younger people. Such precautions may not be entirely effective for people living in high crime areas; thus it is possible to have a positive association between fear and risk across income categories. But when people are considered without regard to income (e.g., by sex and age), the effects of the precautions would become apparent. This possibility is not inconsistent with the hypotheses discussed above about why older people and females in the eight cities expressed more fear of crime. It merely suggests that after fear of crime has been produced, there may be a causal connection between that fear and a reduced risk of being victimized. The relationship between fear of crime and actual experience with personal victimization, with *individuals* as the units of analysis, will be examined momentarily.

To sum up, fear of crime and risk of victimization co-varied (positively) with family income for each racial group, two variables that can be viewed as imperfect indicators of area of residence. However, there was a negative relationship between fear and risk across age and sex subgroups. Some hypotheses about why older people and females expressed a fear of crime disproportionate to their risk of victimization have been discussed, and the possibility of a causal link between fear and decreased risk of victimization has been mentioned briefly.

Fear and Victimization Experiences

In contrast to the preceding discussion, in which risk was defined as the personal victimization rate for a *subgroup* of the population, we will now examine the question of whether any association exists between fear of crime and *individual* experiences with personal victimization during the twelve months preceding the interviews.

There is a problem with the fear of crime indicator when its relationship to experience with personal victimization is being examined. The fear of crime question asked respondents about how safe they felt about being *out alone* in their *neighborhoods* at *night*. Many of the personal victimizations suffered during the reference period, on the other hand, occurred inside buildings, while the victim was accompanied, away from the victim's neighborhood, or during the day. Thus, the hypothetical situation set up by the fear question may not be completely relevant to the victimization experiences of the respondents.[7] Nevertheless, of the items available in the NCS attitude data set, the question about fear of being out alone at night most closely measures what is generally meant by the fear of crime, and it is comparable to questions used in other surveys.

Examination of the top portion of Table 8-4 reveals that there was virtually no relationship between the number of series and nonseries personal victimizations reported to interviewers and how safe the respondents claimed to feel about being out alone in their neighborhoods at night. However, this distribution of responses is influenced by the fact that both variables in the top portion of the table were strongly related, in opposite directions, to sex and to age. The problem of interrelationships between the variables will be analyzed shortly.

In the bottom portion of Table 8-4, the distributions of responses on the fear indicator are presented for respondents who reported suffering one or more of five different types of nonseries personal victimizations.[8] Rape, robbery, and larceny victims exhibited the greatest fear, but again we must be aware of the confounding influences of sex and age; virtually all of the rape victims were female, and older persons were more highly represented among victims of robbery and larceny than among victims of personal crimes not involving theft (Hindelang, 1976:113).[9]

The most that can be said from Table 8-4 is that, overall, the fear of crime was not closely associated with the number of personal victimizations suffered by respondents during the reference period. Victims of various types of crime did differ from each other in fear of crime, but the relationship between fear and experience with victimization was probably confounded by the effects of respondent characteristics such as sex and age. It is necessary to explore these issues further with multivariate techniques. In addition, we cannot dismiss the previously noted possibility that some people with a high level of fear may have taken measures to avoid victimization and thus reported both a great fear of crime and no experiences with victimization.

REGRESSION ANALYSIS OF THE FEAR OF CRIME

Regression analysis was used to help untangle the relationships of the fear of crime with demographic characteristics, personal victimization experiences, and other attitudes. Throughout, responses to

Table 8-4. Feeling of Safety When Out Alone in Neighborhood at Night, by Number and Type of Personal Victimizations Suffered by Respondent, Eight-City Aggregate, 1972[a]

	Neighborhood Safety at Night (percent)				Total persons sixteen years of age or older[b]
	Very safe	Reasonably safe	Somewhat unsafe	Very unsafe	
Number of personal victimizations:					
None	18	38	21	23	100% (2,922,779)
One	17	31	20	32	100% (149,511)
Two	21	32	19	28	100% (18,967)
Three or more[c]	19	32	21	28	100% (17,771)
Victims of at lease one[d]:					
Rape	7	25	18	50	100% (6,441)
Robbery	15	28	20	36	100% (58,312)
Aggravated Assault	26	34	17	23	100% (44,312)
Simple assault	21	38	18	23	100% (49,214)
Larceny from the person	10	23	23	44	100% (30,022)

[a] For wording of attitude item, see source code 350 in attitude questionnaire, Appendix A.
[b] Excludes respondents who gave no answer to the attitude item.
[c] All respondents reporting at least one series personal victimization to the interviewer were classified as having three or more personal victimizations.
[d] Includes only nonseries victimizations.

the question about how safe the respondent felt about being out alone in his or her neighborhood at night were used as the dependent variable.

Measurement Issues

There are some problems in using linear regression as an analytic tool with these data. The dependent variable, fear of crime, does not meet the statistical assumption of interval measurement; responses are in the form of four ordered categories. However, the Pearson's product moment coefficient is a robust statistic, and regression results are not strongly affected when an ordinal variable is treated as if it were measured on an interval scale (Labovitz, 1967). In fact, Boyle (1970:464) has pointed out that "correlation coefficients computed in terms of an arbitrary equal-interval assumption will be *conservative* estimates of the true correlation."

The "experience with victimization" variables have a different measurement problem. Because they represent the number of total personal victimizations (or rapes, robberies, and so on) suffered by a respondent during the reference period, they meet the interval scaling requirements. However, the distributions of these variables are extremely skewed, with an overwhelming majority of respondents (more than 90 percent) having a score of zero. The resulting lack of variation in the experience with victimization variables limits the size that a Pearson's r can attain in any correlation between one of the victimization variables and some other variable that has a less skewed distribution of respnses, such as the fear of crime indicator. When Pearson's r is interpreted in terms of the amount of variation explained (r^2), one would expect the coefficient for the regression of, for example, fear of crime on number of personal victimizations to be small; there simply are not a sufficient number of victims in the sample to account for a major portion of the variability in the fear of crime. Despite these problems, it was decided that regression analysis could help to elucidate some of the relationships existing between fear of crime and other variables.

The first task was to determine the extent to which fear of crime is predictable from the demographic and victimization variables. A description of the variables used and of the way the variables were coded appears in Appendix C. A stepwise multiple regression analysis was conducted;[10] variables were selected for inclusion in the regression equation on the basis of their relationship to the dependent variable, controlling for the effects of variables already in the equation.

Table 8-5 shows the first ten independent variables that entered the regression equation using the stepwise method. The first five

Table 8-5. Multiple Regression Results of Fear of Crime with Ten Independent Variables, Eight-City Aggregate, 1972[a]

Independent variable[b]	Simple r	Regression Results		
		Multiple R at each step	Multiple R^2 at each step	Beta weight in final equation
Sex	.36	.36	.13	.34
Age	.19	.40	.16	.18
Race	.16	.43	.19	.14
Household tenancy status	.11	.45	.20	.09
Family income	-.19	.45	.21	-.06
Total personal victimizations	.02	.46	.21	.04
Education	-.18	.46	.21	-.06
Total robberies	.04	.46	.21	.03
Employment status	.03	.46	.21	.01
Marital status	.05	.46	.21	-.01

[a]The dependent variable, fear of crime, is defined as responses to the question
about feeling of safety when out alone in neighborhood at night. For wording of
the item, see source code 350 in attitude questionnaire, Appendix A.
[b]For definitions and coding of independent variables, see Appendix C.

variables entering the equation all pertained to demographic characteristics: sex, age, race, household tenancy status (whether the
housing unit was owned or being rented), and family income. Only
after these variables had been included did a victimization variable
(total personal victimizations) enter the equation. However, it can
be seen from the columns in Table 8-5, showing the step-by-step
results of the procedure, that the addition of any independent
variables beyond the first two brought about only negligible increases in explanatory power.

The initial implication from Table 8-5 is that any relationship
between experience with victimization and fear of crime is eliminated
once the various demographic variables that enter the solution earlier
are controlled. But this is actually not the case. In Table 8-6 the
initial correlations (simple rs) between fear of crime and various
indicators of victimization experience are presented along with the
partial rs between the same variables, when sex, age, and race were
controlled. The table provides some important information. First,
the partials for total rapes and total personal larcenies show virtually
no change from the simple correlations. Second, compared to their
corresponding simple correlations, the partial correlations of fear of
crime with total personal victimizations, total seriousness score, and
total robberies do not show a decrease in size as might have been
anticipated from Table 8-5; to the contrary, the coefficients for

Table 8-6. Simple and Partial (Controlling for Sex, Age, and Race) Correlations of Fear of Crime with Seven Victimization Experience Variables, Eight-City Aggregate, 1972[a]

	Correlation Coefficients	
Correlation of fear of crime with[b]:	Simple r	Partial r[c]
Total personal victimizations	.024	.072
Total seriousness score	.001	.062
Total rapes	.023	.022
Total robberies	.036	.063
Total aggravated assaults	−.017	.021
Total simple assaults	−.013	.023
Total larcenies from the person	.029	.026

[a]The dependent variable, fear of crime, is defined as responses to the question about feeling of safety when out alone in neighborhood at night. For wording of the item, see source code 350 in attitude questionnaire, Appendix A.

[b]For definitions and coding of independent variables, see Appendix C.

[c]Partial correlations controlling for sex, age, and race.

these variables show a slight increase.[11] Although all of the zero-order and partial coefficients are extremely small, one must note, as was pointed out earlier, the victimization variables are extremely skewed, and the maximum attainable correlation coefficients are correspondingly attenuated.

The reason for the shifts shown in Table 8.6 lies in the inter-relationships among fear, victimization, and various respondent characteristics, particularly sex and age. On the bivariate level, the relationships between fear and total personal victimizations, seriousness score, and robberies are depressed by the counteracting relationships between these variables and sex and age.

The measurement problems that exist for both the fear of crime and experience with victimization variables have already been discussed. In particular, the extreme skewness of the response distributions on the experience with victimization variables acts to limit the potential size of coefficients measuring the relationship between experience with victimization and the fear of crime. For example, in Table 8-6 we saw that the simple r between perceptions of neighborhood safety at night and total number of personal victimizations suffered during the reference period was very small (0.024). The partial r did increase to 0.072 when sex, age, and race of respondent were controlled—a relationship that is very small in correlational terms.

In Table 8-7, the same relationships are illustrated with tabular methods. In this table, race, sex, age, and victimization status are simultaneously examined in relation to perceived neighborhood safety at night. Consistent with the regression analysis, as can be seen from the bottom of Table 8-7, there was, overall, only a small difference between the proportions of nonvictims and victims who said that they felt either somewhat unsafe or very unsafe when out alone in their neighborhoods at night (44 percent versus 51 percent). But when race, sex, and age are controlled, the nonvictim-victim differences in the eight resulting subgroups were accentuated. Only among young white males and young white females did small differences maintain. The reason for these accentuations, as suggested in the regression results above, lies in the interrelationships among fear, victimization, and various respondent characteristics, particularly sex and age.

It is important to note in Table 8-7 the very substantial variation across groups in the percentages feeling somewhat unsafe or very unsafe when out alone in their neighborhoods at night. Among white males under thirty-five years of age the figure was 13 percent for nonvictims and 21 percent for victims; at the other extreme, the respective percentages for black/other females thirty-five or older were 72 percent for nonvictims and 82 percent for victims.

Thus, it appears that simple and partial Pearson's *rs* do reflect the behavior of the relationships in the data, but the nature of the distributions being examined tends to produce coefficients that are misleadingly small.

It might also be argued that the victimization variable, simply reflecting whether or not a personal victimization occurred, is not a good indicator of experience with victimization when our purpose is to examine fear-producing effects. The variable lumps together personal victimizations that were only attempted with those that were completed, events that resulted in serious injury with those that involved minor jostling, and so on. In Figures 8-5 and 8-6, we can look at the fear of crime expressed by victims with victimizations differentiated by the amount of physical harm suffered by the victim. Sex and age are controlled in the figures; only male victims are included, and Figure 8.5 deals with victims less than thirty-five years old, while Figure 8-6 deals with victims thirty-five years old or older.[12] The victimizations are first trichotomized according to whether the victim was neither attacked nor threatened, threatened but not attacked, or actually attacked. Then, within the group of victimizations that involved a physical attack, the subset in which the victim suffered some injury and the even smaller subset in which the victim required medical attention are displayed.

Table 8-7. Feeling of Safety When Out Alone in Neighborhood at Night, by Race, Sex, Age, and Victimization Status of Respondent, Eight-City Aggregate, 1972[a]

	Neighborhood Safety at Night (percent)		Total persons sixteen years of age or older [b]
	Very safe or reasonably safe	Somewhat unsafe or very unsafe	
White male			
Less than 35			
Nonvictim[c]	87	13	100% (341,157)
Victim	79	21	100% (46,269)
35 or older			
Nonvictim	73	27	100% (524,755)
Victim	51	49	100% (25,131)
Black/other male			
Less than 35			
Nonvictim	77	23	100% (189,992)
Victim	65	35	100% (19,622)
35 or older			
Nonvictim	54	46	100% (217,548)
Victim	31	69	100% (12,121)
White female			
Less than 35			
Nonvictim	52	48	100% (386,561)
Victim	45	55	100% (29,205)
35 or older			
Nonvictim	41	59	100% (695,405)
Victim	24	76	100% (22,838)
Black/other female			
Less than 35			
Nonvictim	38	62	100% (267,812)
Victim	25	75	100% (16,897)

Table 8-7 continued

| | Neighborhood Safety at Night (percent) | | Total persons sixteen years of age or older [b] |
	Very safe or reasonably safe	Somewhat unsafe or very unsafe	
35 or older			
Nonvictim	28	72	100% (299,380)
Victim	18	82	100% (14,166)
Total			
Nonvictim	56	44	100% (2,922,610)
Victim	49	51	100% (186,249)

[a]For wording of attitude item, see source code 350 in attitude questionnaire, Appendix A.

[b]Excludes respondents who gave no answer to the attitude item.

[c]The nonvictim-victim dichotomy was formed on the basis of whether or not the respondent had suffered at least one series or nonseries personal victimization during the reference period.

Among those victimizations that involved males less than thirty-five years old (Figure 8-5), the victims did not show much variation in fear of crime according to the amount of physical coercion in the event. Victims who required medical attention gave a response of "very unsafe" more often than other victims, but only by a slim margin. However, they also said that they felt very safe slightly more often than did the other victims in Figure 8-5. Turning our attention to Figure 8-6, we see that fear of crime was greater among older male victims (thirty-five or older) than among younger male victims when the amount of physical coercion in the victimization was held constant; that is, more fear of crime is reflected in the cells of Figure 8-6 than in the corresponding cells of Figure 8-5. Within Figure 8-6 itself, there was some variation in fear of crime; older males who were threatened but not attacked exhibited the least fear, while those who were attacked (including those who were injured and required medical attention) exhibited the most fear. But the differences in the fear of crime were not large compared to the ones previously found across age and sex groups.

From the data in Figures 8-5 and 8-6 we can conclude that failure to differentiate among victimizations with different characteristics did mask some of the relationship between fear of crime and ex-

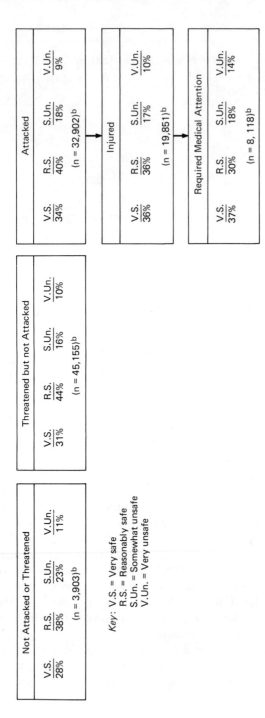

Figure 8-5. Feeling of Safety When Out Alone in Neighborhood at Night, by Personal Victimization Outcomes, Among Male Respondents Less Than Thirty-Five Years Old, Eight-City Aggregate, 1972[a]

[a]For wording of attitude item, see source code 350 in attitude questionnaire, Appendix A.
[b]Number on which percentages are based; represents the number of males less than thirty-five years old in the victimization outcome category, excluding those who gave no answer to the attitude item.

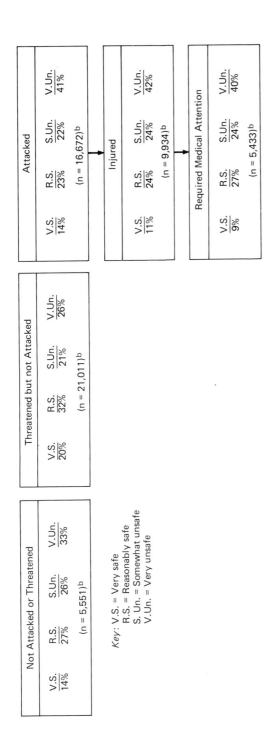

Figure 8-6. Feeling of Safety When Out Alone in Neighborhood at Night, by Personal Victimization Outcomes, Among Male Respondents Thirty-Five Years of Age or Older, Eight-City Aggregate, 1972[a]

[a]For wording of attitude item, see source code 350 in attitude questionnaire, Appendix A.
[b]Number on which percentages are based; represents the number of males, thirty-five years of age or older, in the victimization outcome category, excluding those who gave no answer to the attitude item.

perience with victimization. But these effects were not great in comparison to the previously discussed effects of variables such as age and sex or race and income on the fear of crime.

Fear, Limitations on Behavior, and Victimization

Several times in this chapter, mention has been made of the possibility that the fear of crime may lead some people to restrict their activities in ways that would decrease their risk of being victimized. This possibility appears especially appealing when we try to explain the inverse relationship that existed between fear of crime and rate of victimization across age and sex *groups* (see Figures 8-1 and 8-2);[13] if the high levels of fear among older people and females can be interpreted as *causing* their low victimization rates, then the relationship between fear and risk can be explained.

First impressions may seem to indicate that the variables necessary to test whether such a link between fear and risk exists are present in the NCS data: we have been using a reasonable fear of crime indicator throughout this chapter; respondents were asked whether they had limited or changed their own behavior because of crime; and both likelihood and rate indicators of the risk of personal victimization are available. However, initial optimism is dampened when we realize that these variables are not sensitive to the time ordering of effects in a model postulating that the fear of crime leads to limitations on behavior which, in turn, leads to a decreased risk of victimization. That is, respondents were interviewed about victimizations occurring during the twelve-month period prior to the interview, about whether they limited their behavior because of fear of crime at any time during "the past few years," and about their fear of crime at the time of the interview. Thus, as fear of crime is measured, it is clearly subsequent to any victimizations or limiting of behavior that may have occurred at times prior to the interview; this is, of course, not the time ordering suggested by the hypothesis that fear leads to limiting, which in turn lowers the risk of victimization. An adequate test of this and competing models in which the time ordering of these variables is crucial requires that we have information about attitudes, behavioral limitations, and victimization experiences from a panel study over a fairly long period of time.[14] Although we do not have the requisite data to disentangle the time-dependent nature of these effects, we will give substantial attention in Chapter 9 to limitations on behavior and in Chapter 11 to a discussion of theoretical mechanisms involving these variables.

To summarize, using perceived danger of being out alone in one's neighborhood at night as an indicator, we have analyzed fear of crime in terms of respondent characteristics, risk of victimization, and actual experiences with victimization. Fear of crime was found to be positively related to the risk of victimization across family income categories for each racial group, inversely related to the risk of personal victimization faced by different age and sex groups, and only marginally related to the experiences of respondents with personal victimization during the twelve months preceding the interviews. However, the variation in fear of crime across age and sex groups was found to be substantial; older respondents and females expressed much more fear of crime than their younger and male counterparts. Because the variations across sex and age groups could not be attributed to variations in objective risks, several alternative explanations were discussed—for example, the effects of sex role socialization, and the greater fear of injury and fear of strangers among older persons.

Multivariate analyses of the fear of crime indicator confirmed the explanatory importance of sex and age, and the marginal effects of experience with personal victimization. However, the NCS data could not be used to test the possibility that fear of crime leads to limiting of behavior, which in turn reduces the chances of victimization. In the next chapter, the question of how attitudes about crime are related to respondents' limitations on behavior will be discussed in detail.

NOTES

1. Responses to the questions concerning fear of places in the metropolitan area are reported in Garofalo (1977: Tables 12 and 13).

2. The actual formulas used were (Hovland et al., 1955: 79):

$$\text{Score} = \frac{P_2 - P_1}{100 - P_1} \text{ , (whenever there was an increase) and}$$

$$\text{Score} = \frac{P_2 - P_1}{P_2} \text{ , (whenever there was a decrease), where}$$

P_1 = the baseline score, and

P_2 = the observed score for any subgroup.

The formula was constructed to be used with percentages; thus the "100" in the first formula reflects the maximum possible score. There would be some problem trying to use the first formula with victimization rates because a maximum possible score is not really definable. Fortunately (for computational reasons), the groups used for baseline purposes in Figures 8-1 through 8-4 (lowest income, youngest) had higher victimization rates than the other income and age groups, so it was only necessary to use the second formula with victimization rates.

3. Note that the highest income category contained fewer than 1 percent of the black/others in the population.

4. The increase was somewhat greater among white (8 percent to 28 percent) than among black/other (4 percent to 16 percent) household respondents.

5. More will be said about this possibility in the next chapter.

6. A very small number of male rapes were reported in the survey.

7. Unfortunately, the NCS data do not allow us to determine where a victimization occurred in terms of neighborhood–not neighborhood.

8. Exclusion of the small number of series crimes did not affect the results.

9. Interestingly, data not presented here indicate that, among persons victimized, the fear of crime is not strongly related to whether the victimization was committed by a stranger or by someone known to the victim.

10. In this chapter, "stepwise" refers to the technique used in the Statistical Package for the Social Sciences. See Nie et al. (1975: ch. 20).

11. It should also be noted that the change in signs for aggravated and simple assaults is consistent with this shift.

12. Although the data are not presented here, the results are similar for females. Only the data for males are presented because there were more male than female victims.

13. It should be reemphasized that Figures 8-1 and 8-2 dealt with *groups* of respondents. As was shown in Table 8-7, for example, there was a slight direct relationship between fear of crime and actual experiences with victimization when individuals were the units of analysis.

14. The national component of the National Crime Survey uses a panel design, but there are no attitude data currently being collected in the national surveys.

 *Chapter 9*

The Effects of Crime and the Fear of Crime on Behavior

In the two preceding chapters we have discussed images of "the crime problem" held by respondents in the eight cities and some of the determinants of the fear of crime expressed by those same respondents. Although it was pointed out in Chapter 8 that the NCS data can not be used to test the notion that people who fear crime limit their behavior and, therefore, decrease their chances of victimization, the issue of whether concern about crime affects behavior can be examined with the NCS data. In a different context, early in Chapter 7, we dealt briefly with one NCS attitude item that deals with effects on behavior: "In general, have you limited or changed your activities in the past few years because of crime?" Responses to that item will be analyzed in more detail in this chapter. Also, we will examine the extent to which respondents felt that crime and the fear of crime had influenced some specific behavior, such as where one shops for food.

PERSONAL LIMITING OF ACTIVITIES—
A BROAD PERSPECTIVE

Simply asking people whether they had limited or changed their activities can only elicit a very general indication of the effect of crime and fear of crime on behavior. There are, obviously, a rather large number of activities that could be limited or changed in a variety of ways. In a sample of respondents from four police districts (two in Boston and two in Chicago) for example, Reiss (1967: Sec. 2, 102-12) found that people used techniques ranging from riding in taxis or cars rather than walking at night, to not talking to strangers, and even to carrying weapons to protect themselves from crime. The broad question about whether respondents had limited their activities, then, can give us only a very general picture of behavioral responses to crime in the eight cities.

As was mentioned in Chapter 7, slightly less than half (46 percent) of the eight-city respondents said that they had limited or changed their activities because of crime. In Chapter 7, that figure was contrasted to the greater proportions of respondents who thought that people in general (83 percent) and people in their neighborhoods (59 percent) had limited their activities. It was also noted, however, that substantial variation in replies to the personal limiting-of-activity question existed across subgroups of respondents; specifically, in Chapter 7, the response differences between males and females were shown. Furthermore, responses concerning the personal limiting of activities are related to the fear of crime. Tabular data not presented here show that only 22 percent of the eight-city respondents who felt very safe about being out alone in their neighborhoods at night said that they had limited their activities because of crime; the figure was 33 percent for those who felt reasonably safe, 57 percent for those who felt somewhat unsafe, and 72 percent for those who felt very unsafe at night in their neighborhoods.

Given the close association between these two items, it is not surprising that the relationships between personal limiting of activity and various respondent characteristics are similar to the relationships, shown in Chapter 8, between the fear of crime and the same respondent characteristics. Table 9-1, for example, shows that both race and family income were related to whether or not respondents said that they had limited or changed their activities because of crime. Among whites, 41 percent said they had limited their activities, but among black/others the figure was 55 percent. There was also a tendency, within both racial groups, for the proportion of respondents who said they had limited their activities to decrease at higher family income levels. Finally, in Table 9-1, the response differences between whites and black/others occurred for each family income category; that is, regardless of family income, black/others were more likely than whites to say that they had limited or changed their activities because of crime.[1]

Limiting of activity was also related to sex and age in the same way that the fear of crime was, as can be seen in Table 9-2. Males were much less likely to say that they had limited or changed their activities than were females (37 percent versus 52 percent), and, in both sex groups, the same held true for younger respondents relative

Table 9-1. Personal Limiting of Activities Because of Crime, by Race and Family Income of Respondent, Eight-City Aggregate,1972[a]

	Personal Limiting of Activities (percent)		Total persons sixteen years of age or older[b]
	Yes	No	
White	41	59	100% (1,868,770)
Less than $5,000	46	54	100% (433,010)
$5,000-11,999	41	59	100% (801,510)
$12,000-24,999	37	63	100% (529,660)
$25,000 or more	39	61	100% (104,590)
Black/Other	55	45	100% (935,310)
Less than $5,000	59	41	100% (364,440)
$5,000-11,999	53	47	100% (412,810)
$12,000-24,999	50	50	100% (146,090)
$25,000 or mroe	43	57	100% (11,970)

[a]For wording of attitude item, see source code 367 in attitude questionnaire, Appendix A.
[b]Excludes respondents who gave no answer to attitude item.

to older respondents. Among males, one quarter of the youngest (sixteen to twenty-four year old) respondents reported limiting of behavior, and the proportion increased steadily with age, reaching 47 percent for males who were sixty-five years old or older. The same pattern was present but less pronounced, among females; the percentage of affirmative replies to the question increased from 42 percent to 57 percent across the age groups.

Finding that the personal limiting-of-activity item and the fear of crime item were so closely related and that both items showed a similar pattern of relationships to various demographic variables is not really surprising. We can even conceptualize the items as two indicators of the fear of crime. Thus, the question about how safe respondents feel about being alone in their neighborhoods at night is an *affective* indicator of fear, while the personal limiting of activity

Table 9-2.   Personal Limiting of Activities Because of Crime, by Sex and Age of Respondent, Eight-City Aggregate, 1972[a]

	Personal Limiting of Activities (percent)		Total persons sixteen years of age or older[b]
	Yes	*No*	
Males	37	63	100% (1,374,540)
16-24	25	75	100% (332,870)
25-34	33	67	100% (263,020)
35-49	41	59	100% (303,890)
50-64	44	56	100% (293,610)
65 or older	47	53	100% (181,150)
Females	52	48	100% (1,733,430)
16-24	42	58	100% (171,200)
25-34	49	51	100% (528,560)
35-49	54	46	100% (377,360)
50-64	57	43	100% (370,330)
65 or older	57	43	100% (285,980)

[a]For wording of attitude item, see source code 367 in attitude questionnaire, Appendix A.
[b]Excludes respondents who gave no answer to attitude item.

item can be construed, at least partially, as a *behavioral* indicator of fear. All of the suggestions that were offered in Chapter 8 to explain variability in the affective indicator of fear—for example, the effects of area of residence, feelings of vulnerability associated with aging, and differences due to sex role socialization—are also applicable as potential explanations of variability in the behavioral indicator. We will not repeat all of the hypotheses that were discussed in Chapter 8; instead, our attention will focus on the reasons for differences between males and females in limiting of behavior because of crime.

There are several justifications for concentrating our attention on the variable of sex rather than, for example, race, income, or age. First, response differences between males and females cannot be attributed to the special circumstances faced by an identifiable group that is in a *numerical* minority, such as racial minorities or the very poor. Second, response differences related to sex cannot be readily attributed to the possibility that males and females differ in their likelihoods of living in certain high- or low-crime areas of the city. That argument can be made for differences associated with race or income (as was done previously) because of residential segregation patterns, but residential segregation based on sex is much less likely. Finally, in addition to showing response differences on many attitude items, males and females also differ considerably in rates and likelihoods of personal victimization.

Recall from Chapter 7 (Figure 7–1) that when males and females were compared on the three limiting-of-activity items (general, neighborhood, personal), their responses diverged only on the item referring to personal limiting of activity. At that point we noted that the general pattern across the three items dealing with limiting of activity was for a decreasing proportion of affirmative responses as the frame of reference moved closer to the respondent (i.e., from people in general, to people in the neighborhood, to the respondent). But Figure 7–1 showed a difference between males and females in the pattern. Among males, 57 percent thought that people in their neighborhoods had limited or changed their activities because of crime, but only 37 percent said that they themselves had done so. Females had a comparable proportion of affirmative replies to the neighborhood question (61 percent) but more than half (52 percent) said that they had personally limited their activities.[2] In Chapter 7, discussion focused on the reasons for the decreasing proportion of affirmative replies across the three questions. The sex-specific nature of the pattern, however, demands that we explore the question of why females were more likely than males to say that they had personally limited or changed their activities because of crime. Several suggestions can be made.

First, it is possible that males were less likely than females to believe that they would be victimized. Second, regardless of what they believed were their probabilities of being victimized, males may have had less fear of the victimization itself than females. Third, males may have been less *able* to limit or change their activities because they were more likely than females to be employed outside of the home. Finally, because of traditional conceptions of sex roles, males may have been less likely to *admit* that the fear of crime had in fact motivated them to change their behavior. The available information does not allow us to select the best hypothesis (or combination of hypotheses) from the four listed. However, some of the survey data are relevant, at least to the first three of these hypotheses.

The first hypothesis may not seem compatible with a finding that has been noted frequently in this book; namely, that males had higher personal victimization rates than females. Furthermore, respondents who had suffered one or more personal victimizations during the reference period were more likely than nonvictims (55 percent versus 45 percent) to say that they had limited or changed their activities—and, of course, males were disproportionately represented among persons who had suffered personal victimizations. Just as with the fear of crime indicator used in Chapter 8, response differences between males and females do not appear to be accounted for by differences in objective risk of, or experience with, personal victimization.

But the first hypothesis was that males *believed* they had a low risk of being victimized, and measures of objective risk and actual experiences really do not tap that belief. However, one of the attitude items in the survey may be useful in this regard. Respondents were asked whether their own "chances of being attacked or robbed" had gone up, gone down, or remained the same in the past few years.[3] Females were slightly more likely than males to have said that their chances of being attacked or robbed had gone up (69 percent versus 62 percent), indicating that males may have felt more immune from victimization than was justified by their objective risk, but the size of the difference between males and females was quite small.[4] In addition, when we cross-tabulate the two items (personal limiting of activity and perceived changes in chances of being attacked or robbed) in Table 9–3, we see that the relationship between the two items was similar for males and females. Among males, 46 percent of those who thought that their chances of being attacked or robbed had gone up said that they had limited their activities, but the figure was only 24 percent for males who thought that their chances of being attacked or robbed had stayed the same or gone down.[5] For females, the comparable figures were 60 percent and 38 percent. Although males were slightly less likely than females to believe that their chances of being attacked or robbed had gone up, the effect of perceived increases or decreases in vulnerability to victimization on decisions to limit one's activities appears to have been as strong among males as among females.[6] Thus, the first hypothesis is not supported by the data.

Table 9-3. Personal Limiting of Activities Because of Crime, by Perceived
Changes in Chances of Being Attacked or Robbed and Sex of Respondent,
Eight-City Aggregage, 1972[a]

Chances of Being Attacked or Robbed	Personal Limiting of Activities (percent)		Total persons sixteen years of age or older[b]
	Yes	No	
Males			
Gone up	46	54	100% (830,970)
Same or gone down	24	76	100% (507,940)
Females			
Gone up	60	40	100% (1,146,680)
Same or gone down	38	62	100% (521,340)

[a]For wording of attitude items, see source codes 367 and 363, respectively, in
attitude questionnaire, Appendix A.
[b]Excludes respondents who gave no answer to either attitude item or who replied
"no opinion" to the item about chances of being attacked or robbed.

The second hypothesis was that males had less *fear* of being
victimized, even if they viewed their *chances* of being victimized as
high. Some support for this hypothesis is provided by Table 9-4
in which the perception of changes in chances of being attacked
or robbed is cross-tabulated with the fear of crime indicator from
Chapter 8 (feelings of safety when out alone in one's neighborhood
at night) for males and females separately. The differences between
the amount of fear expressed by males and females was virtually
independent of respondent estimations of changes in chances of
being attacked or robbed. Among those who thought that their
chances of being victimized had gone up, two-thirds (68 percent)
of the males, but only about one-third (35 percent) of the females,
felt either very safe or reasonably safe about being out alone in
their neighborhoods at night. When we examine those who perceived
either no change or a decrease in chances of victimization, the gap
between the proportions of males and females who felt very or
reasonably safe remains about the same (82 percent versus 51 percent). Clearly, the difference between the fear of crime expressed
by males and females was not a function of differences in percep-

Table 9-4. Feeling of Safety When Out Alone in Neighborhood at Night, by Changes in Chances of Being Attacked or Robbed and Sex of Respondent, Eight-City Aggregate, 1972[a]

Chances of Being Attacked or Robbed	Neighborhood Safety at Night (percent)				Total persons sixteen years of age or older[b]
	Very safe	Reasonably safe	Somewhat unsafe	Very unsafe	
Males					
Gone up	23	45	19	13	100% (831,750)
Same or gone down	36	46	11	7	100% (507,760)
Females					
Gone up	7	28	27	37	100% (1,146,410)
Same or gone down	14	37	22	27	100% (519,970)

[a]For wording of attitude items, see source codes 350 and 363, respectively, in attitude questionnaire, Appendix A.
[b]Excludes respondents who gave no answer to either attitude item or who replied "no opinion" to the item about chances of being attacked or robbed.

tions of changing probabilities of being attacked or robbed; males were less fearful than females regardless of their estimations of such probabilities. There is some support in the data, then, for the second hypothesis.

The third hypothesis—that occupational requirements did not allow people to limit or change their activities because of crime and that this affected males more than females—can be evaluated partially by examining the limiting-of-activity responses for males and females after respondents have been categorized according to what they normally did during the week. If the hypothesis is correct, there should be little or no response differences on the limiting-of-activity question between males and females within the same employment status category. Table 9-5 shows, however, that the response differences remained even when employment status was controlled; within each category, a greater proportion of females than males said that they had limited or changed their activities because of crime. The difference was small (seven percentage points) within the "keeping house" category, but fewer than 1 percent of the males were in that category, so the estimate based on that relatively small number of cases is the least reliable in Table 9-5. In any case, the response distribution in Table 9-5 clearly militates against the third hypothesis; the greater propensity of females, relative to males, to say that they had limited or changed their activities because of crime cannot be attributed to sex-related differences in employment status.

The fourth hypothesis was that, because of traditional conceptions of sex roles, males might be less likely than females to *admit* limiting their activities as a response to crime, regardless of their actual behavior. Unfortunately, this hypothesis is not testable with the NCS data. In fact, if it is true that traditional conceptions of sex roles strongly influenced what respondents were willing to admit—distinguished from what they believed or did—there is no reason to assume that the effect would be restricted to responses concerning personally limiting one's activities because of crime. Answers to other attitude items in the NCS (e.g., feeling of safety in one's own neighborhood at night) could have been influenced in the same way. A generalized "sex role response set" as an explanation for male-female response differences on all attitude questionnaire items that related to the behaviors and fears of the respondent personally cannot be tested with the NCS data.

So far we have seen that a rather large proportion of the eight-city respondents replied affirmatively to the very broad question of whether they had personally limited or changed their activities in

Table 9-5. Personal Limiting of Activities Because of Crime, by Sex and Employment Status of Respondent, Eight-City Aggregate, 1972[a]

	Personal Limiting of Activities (percent)		Total persons sixteen years of age or older[b]
	Yes	No	
Employment status[c] of males			
Has employment	37	63	100% (982,260)
Unemployed	32	68	100% (44,430)
Keeping house	46	54	100% (9,300)
Going to school	23	77	100% (68,870)
Retired or unable to work	48	52	100% (193,180)
Other	33	67	100% (67,840)
Employment status[c] of females			
Has employment	51	49	100% (763,700)
Unemployed	54	46	100% (63,220)
Keeping house	53	47	100% (632,480)
Going to school	44	56	100% (66,290)
Retired or unable to work	60	40	100% (128,590)
Other	51	49	100% (79,130)

[a]For wording of attitude item, see source code 367 in attitude questionnaire, Appendix A.

[b]Excludes respondents who gave no answer to either the attitude item or the employment status item.

[c]Refers to status during the week preceding the interview. See source code 048 in victimization questionnaire, Appendix A.

the past few years because of crime. It was shown that various subgroups of respondents differed in their replies to this item, and a somewhat extensive treatment was given to the possible reasons for the response differences shown by males and females. But the respondents were also asked about some very specific behaviors in the course of the interviews. We will now turn to the question of what effects (if any) crime and the fear of crime had on these specific behaviors.

GOING OUT FOR ENTERTAINMENT

All respondents to the attitude portion of the eight-city surveys were asked: "How often do you go out in the evening for entertainment, such as to restaurants, theaters, etc?" Of more interest here is the follow-up question: "Do you go to these places more or less now than you did a year or two ago?"

Only about one of five (18 percent) of the respondents said that they go out more now than a year or two ago. There were virtually no response differences between males and females or between whites and black/others, while the differences between victims and nonvictims were only slight (Garofalo, 1977: Table 35). However, some interesting variations appeared across age and family income groups, as can be seen in Table 9-6. Although 37 percent of the sixteen to twenty-four year old respondents said that they go out more, the proportion dropped substantially to 19 percent for the next age group (twenty-five to thirty-four); the proportion continued to decline slowly, reaching 5 percent for respondents sixty-five years old or older. Surprisingly, this declining pattern was not matched by a corresponding variation in the proportions of respondents who said they go out *less;* instead, the proportion of respondents who said their frequency of going out for entertainment was *about the same* as a year or two ago increased from 31 percent in the youngest to 58 percent in the oldest age groups.

Variation across income categories was not as pronounced as across age categories, but a pattern did emerge. As shown in Table 9-6, only 13 percent of the respondents from families earning less than $5,000 annually said that they go out more, and the figure rose to 23 percent for respondents in the two highest family income categories. Unlike the pattern shown above for age, however, there was not a tendency for the proportion of "same" responses to vary in the opposite direction of "more" responses. In fact, the pattern across income groups was for the proportion of respondents who said "same" to parallel the increase in the proportion who said "more." On the other hand, while the proportion of respondents who said they go out less showed little variation across age groups, the corresponding proportions decreased from 41 percent to 23 percent from the lowest to highest family income groups.

There are, of course, a number of explanations that can be offered

Table 9-6. Changes in Frequency of Going Out in the Evening for Entertainment, by Age of Respondent and by Family Income of Respondent, Eight-City Aggregate, 1972[a]

	Go Out for Entertainment (percent)			Total persons sixteen years of age or older[b]
	More	Same	Less	
Age				
16–24	37	31	33	100% (726,720)
25–34	19	41	40	100% (570,150)
35–49	14	53	33	100% (681,490)
50–64	10	58	32	100% (664,850)
65 or older	5	58	37	100% (466,870)
Family income[c]				
Less than $5,000	13	45	41	100% (794,270)
$5,000–11,999	18	47	35	100% (1,214,900)
$12,000–24,999	23	48	29	100% (676,760)
$25,000 or more	23	54	23	100% (116,890)

[a]For wording of attitude item, see source code 339 in attitude questionnaire, Appendix A.
[b]Excludes respondents who gave no answer to attitude item.
[c]Excludes respondents whose family incomes were not ascertained.

for the patterns displayed in Table 9-6. With respect to age, for example, it was shown in Chapter 8 that older persons exhibited more fear of crime, so it could be that this higher level of fear led to the relative rarity of older people going out in the evening for entertainment more now than a year or two ago. But such an explanation does not account for the fact that there was hardly any variation across age groups in proportions of respondents who said they go out *less*. One would think that, if the fear of crime was a strong influence on such behavior, its effects would be apparent in a *decrease* in the behavior. It seems more likely that the response patterns in Table 9-6 can be attributed to differences in lifestyles rather than to the fear of crime. For example, the younger respondents who said they go out more now than a year or two ago may have become independent of their families and taken their first full-time jobs during the time period referred to in the question. On the other hand, the lifestyles of older respondents were probably more stable, thus resulting in much higher proportions saying that their frequency of going out has stayed the same (rather than decreased).

The response patterns associated with family income are also somewhat amenable to an explanation that is independent of the fear of crime, namely the very direct effect of differential economic resources. The greatest response differences across income groups in Table 9–6 were for people who said that they go out less, with 41 percent of those in the lowest income group giving that response. Remembering that the interviews were conducted in the early 1970s, at a time when the economy was experiencing a high rate of inflation, it is quite understandable that people with lower family incomes would be forced to cut back on nonessentials such as going out in the evening for entertainment. People with higher incomes would be more able to absorb the effects of inflation so that they could maintain, or even increase, their frequency of going out for entertainment.

Fortunately, the relative influence of the fear of crime and other factors on the frequency of going out for entertainment can be examined further with the NCS data. Respondents who told interviewers that they go out either more or less frequently than a year or two ago were asked, "Why?" If more than one reason was mentioned, the interviewer asked: "Which reason would you say is the most important?" Although the data are not shown here in tabular form, people with higher family incomes ($12,000 or more) were most likely to name money as the most important reason why they go out more. On the other hand, among respondents who said they go out less, it was only in the lowest income group (less than $5,000) that money was the most frequently cited reason.

Table 9–7 displays the reasons named as most important by respondents who said they go out for entertainment less than a year or two ago; the responses are shown by age. Crime or the fear of crime was mentioned as most important by 12 percent of the respondents who said they go out less. As expected from the fear of crime findings in Chapter 8, the frequency with which this reason was cited increased with age,[7] and it was the modal response category for respondents between the ages of fifty and sixty-four. It must be noted that the percentages in Table 9–7 overstate the total effect of crime and the fear of crime on the entertainment-seeking behavior

Table 9-7.   Most Important Reason for Going Out Less in the Evening for Entertainment, by Age of Respondent, Eight-City Aggregate, 1972[a]

Most Important Reason (percent)	Age of Respondent					
	16–24	25–34	35–49	50–64	65 or older	Total
Money situation	20	20	18	12	5	16
Less opportunity (places to go, people to go with)	9	6	6	5	3	6
Convenience	1	1	1	1	1	1
Own health	1	1	5	13	23	8
Transportation	2	1	1	1	2	1
Age	2	2	5	15	27	9
Family reasons (marriage, children, parents)	24	32	18	8	4	18
Activities, job, school	16	12	11	8	2	10
Crime or fear of crime	5	7	14	19	18	12
Want to (personal preference)	13	11	13	13	7	12
Other	3	2	2	2	2	2
No answer	5	6	5	6	6	5
Total number of respondents[b]	100 (236,960)	100 (226,240)	100 (225,360)	100 (213,450)	100 (174,100)	100 (1,076,110)

[a]For wording of attitude item, see source codes 340 and 341 in attitude questionnaire, Appendix A.
[b]Includes only respondents who said they go out less often than a year or two ago and who designated a reason for doing so.

of the eight-city residents. Remember that Table 9–7 includes only persons who said they go out less, and they comprised only one-third of the cities' population sixteen years old or older. The other two-thirds said that they go out just as often as, or even more than, a year or two ago. Respondents who indicated that they go out less and that crime or the fear of crime was the most important reason for their change constituted only 4 percent of the eight-city population sixteen years old or older.

The effects of lifestyle variations across age groups show up in several portions of Table 9–7 From the youngest to the oldest age groups, the proportions of respondents who named health or age as the most important reason for going out less increased dramatically—from 1 percent to 23 percent and from 2 percent to 27 percent, respectively. Correspondingly, family reasons were cited by one-quarter to one-third of the respondents less than thirty-five years old, and persons in that age group are the most likely to have been living with their parents, newly married, or having young children. At higher age levels, the frequency with which family reasons were mentioned declined rapidly, reaching 4 percent among those in the oldest age group. There is even an indication that among younger respondents a decrease in the frequency of going out for entertainment did not necessarily mean staying at home more, but that among older respondents it did. This can be inferred from the decline (16 percent to 2 percent), as age increased, in the proportion of respondents who cited other activities (e.g., school, job) as the most important reason for going out for entertainment less. Finally, younger respondents were much more likely to attribute the decrease in their frequency of going out to their money situation. Because this reason was given relatively often even by respondents in their peak earning years, with only respondents sixty-five or older failing to cite the reason in a substantial proportion of cases, one is tempted to speculate that "going out in the evening for entertainment" generally involved a more expensive outing for younger persons than for older persons (or, of course, that noneconomic reasons were more compelling among older respondents).

More will be said about the effects of lifestyles in the concluding chapter of the book. For now, one more indication of the minimal effect that crime and the fear of crime had on going out in the evening for entertainment can be mentioned. Respondents who said they go out for entertainment less were categorized according to whether or not they mentioned crime or fear of crime as their most important reason and how many series or nonseries personal victimizations they suffered during the reference period.

Although people who were victimized at least once during the reference period cited crime or fear of crime more often than non-victims, the differences were only slight (18 percent versus 11 percent).[8]

This section has shown that crime and the fear of crime did not have major effects on the willingness of people to go out in the evening for entertainment. Although, as expected, a greater effect was found among certain respondent subgroups (e.g., the elderly, victims), most of the variations in willingness to go out appear to be related to lifestyle differences. We will now turn to another specific behavior about which respondents were asked.

LEAVING AND SELECTING NEIGHBORHOODS

Although going out for entertainment was the only specific behavior about which all the attitude respondents were asked, a series of behavioral questions was answered by the household respondent in each household in the attitude subsamples. The household respondent was an adult—generally the head of household or the head's spouse—who was knowledgeable about the affairs of the household as a unit (see Appendix B). The behavioral questions fell into the two general areas of choosing neighborhood of residence and shopping. Neighborhood choice will be examined in this section.

The first attitude questionnaire item directed at the household respondent was used to determine how long the household had lived at its current address. For households that had been at the address for five years or less, the household respondent was asked: (1) why the current neighborhood was selected, and (2) why the household left its previous neighborhood.[9] More than half (53 percent) of the estimated one and a half million households in the eight cities had been located at their current addresses for five years or less.

Of those households that had resided at the current address for no more than five years, the modal response given as the most important reason for leaving their old neighborhood was that the present location was more convenient (closer to job, family, friends, shopping, school, etc.); almost one-quarter of the household respondents gave that reason. Fear of crime in the old neighborhood was one of the least frequently cited reasons for leaving (3 percent).

Table 9-8 shows the distribution of most important reasons for leaving the old neighborhood, broken down by race and family income. It is obvious from the table that both race and income were

Table 9-8. Most Important Reason for Leaving Old Neighborhood, by Race and Family Income of Household Respondents, Eight-City Aggregate, 1972[a]

Most Important Reason for Leaving (percent)	Family Income of White Household Respondents				Family Income of Black/Other Household Respondents			
	Less than $5,000	$5,000–11,999	$12,000 or more	Total	Less than $5,000	$5,000–11,999	$12,000 Or more	Total
Location: closer to job, family, friends, school, shopping, etc. here	31	26	30	28	14	14	15	14
Needed larger/smaller house/apartment	10	15	17	14	17	19	18	18
Wanted better housing, own home	10	18	20	16	19	25	30	23
Wanted cheaper housing	8	5	2	5	9	4	2	6
Evicted; building demolished, condemned, etc.	8	5	3	6	12	8	5	10
Marital status changed	10	12	11	11	9	11	11	10
Old neighborhood run down; bad element moving in	4	4	4	4	5	4	5	5
Crime in old neighborhood; afraid	3	2	2	2	5	4	3	4
Other	13	10	9	11	7	7	8	7
No answer	3	2	2	3	3	3	2	3
Total number of household respondents[b]	100 (148,916)	100 (223,971)	100 (125,518)	100 (498,405)	100 (129,538)	100 (111,168)	100 (31,081)	100 (271,787)

[a]For wording of attitude item, see source codes 326 and 327 in attitude questionnaire, Appendix A. Item was only asked in households that had been at current address for five years or less.

[b]Excludes household respondents who gave no answer to the attitude item or whose family income was not ascertained.

associated with the factors that influenced people to leave their old neighborhoods. Whites, for example, were twice as likely as black/others (28 percent versus 14 percent) to name the location of their new residence as the most important reason for leaving their old neighborhood, while black/others were somewhat more likely than whites to be motivated to leave by a desire for better housing (23 percent versus 16 percent). Within both racial groups, the proportion of household respondents who said that the desire for better housing was their most important reason for leaving increased with income—from 10 percent to 20 percent among whites, and from 19 percent to 30 percent among black/others. Correspondingly, the proportions of household respondents who cited the fact that they had been evicted from their previous residences, or that the building had been demolished or condemned, decreased as income went up for each racial group.

The factor of crime or the fear of crime in their old neighborhoods, however, showed up as only a minor influence for each racial group and all income categories; at its high point in Table 9–8, crime was only mentioned as the most important reason by 5 percent of the black/other household respondents with family incomes of less than $5,000. Even if we consider the response "old neighborhood run down; bad element moving in" as a crime-related reason for leaving one's neighborhood, no more than 10 percent of the households in any of the race-family income categories of Table 9–8 could be interpreted as having left their old neighborhood primarily because of a fear of crime. For the majority of households in both racial groups, the decision to move from the old neighborhood stemmed, most importantly, from a desire to obtain a dwelling of a different type (smaller, larger, better, cheaper, etc.) or with a convenient geographic location. Just as was shown with going out in the evening for entertainment in the preceding section, crime or the fear of crime did not appear to play a predominant role in decisions to leave a neighborhood.

If crime was not a major influence on *leaving* a neighborhood, it was even less of a factor in the decision, by the same households, about what neighborhoods to move *into*. Table 9–9 displays, for those households that had not lived at the surveyed address more than five years, the most important reason cited by the household respondent for selecting the current neighborhood of residence; as in Table 9–8, the responses in Table 9–9 are shown by race and family income.

The perception that the current neighborhood was safe from crime apparently played a negligible role in the decision to select

Table 9-9. Most Important Reason for Selecting Current Neighborhood of Residence, by Race and Family Income of Household Respondents, Eight-City Aggregate, 1972[a]

Most Important Reason for Selecting Neighborhood (percent)	Family Income of White Household Respondents				Family Income of Black/Other Household Respondents			
	Less than $5,000	$5,000– 11,999	$12,000 or more	Total	Less than $5,000	$5,000– 11,999	$12,000 or more	Total
Like neighborhood (type of neighbors, environment, streets, parks, etc.)	15	19	23	19	19	26	34	24
Good schools	2	2	5	2	1	1	2	1
Safe from crime	2	1	1	1	2	2	3	2
Only place housing could be found	14	9	4	9	28	19	11	23
Price was right	15	14	8	13	13	11	8	12
Location: close to jobs, family, friends, school, shopping, etc.	39	39	38	39	20	21	19	21
Liked the house/apartment or property (size, quality, yard space, etc.)	6	9	13	9	9	12	16	11
Other	5	4	4	5	5	4	4	4
No answer	3	3	4	3	2	3	3	3
Total number of household respondents[b]	100 (148,916)	100 (223,971)	100 (125,518)	100 (498,405)	100 (129,538)	100 (111,168)	100 (31,081)	100 (271,787)

[a]For wording of attitude item, see source codes 321 and 322 in attitude questionnaire, Appendix A. Item only asked in households that had been at current address for five years or less.
[b]Excludes household respondents who gave no answer to the attitude item or whose family income was not ascertained.

the neighborhood. The proportion of household respondents who cited "safe from crime" as their most important reason varied between 1 percent and 3 percent across the race-family income groups. On the other hand, there was substantial variation across the race and income groups in the proportion of household respondents who cited some of the other reasons. Whites, for example, were more likely than black/others to name "location" as their most important reason (39 percent versus 21 percent), while black/others were more likely than whites to say that their current neighborhood was the "only place housing could be found" (23 percent versus 9 percent). As income increased in each racial group, there was an increasing tendency to mention the aesthetic qualities of the neighborhood ("like neighborhood") as the most important reason for selecting it; however, this trend was somewhat stronger among black/others (from 19 percent to 34 percent) than among whites (from 15 to 23 percent). Mirroring this pattern for what might be called a positive reason for selection was a pattern for a negative reason: in each racial group, household respondents with the lowest family incomes were most likely to say that their neighborhood at the time of the interview was the only place in which they could find housing.

Taken together, responses to the questions examined in this section support the notion that economic and social barriers and advantages were the primary factors involved in selecting a residence. The decision to leave a particular neighborhood appeared to be contingent on such things as job or marital status changes or on the desire to obtain a more suitable housing unit; selection of a new neighborhood was based on factors such as convenience of location and the availability and cost of housing. Crime or the fear of crime did not appear to be salient motivating factors in either aspect of mobility.

SHOPPING

All household respondents in the attitude subsamples were asked about where they shopped for food and for clothing and general merchandise, and they were also asked to indicate their reasons for selecting particular areas for shopping. We will discuss the responses to these items only briefly because the findings do not shed much light on the effects of crime or the fear of crime on behavior.

Household respondents who gave a negative reply to the question, "Do you do your major food shopping in this neighborhood?" were requested to name their reasons for this decision and, if more than one reason was mentioned, to designate which reason was most important. The results are not presented here in tabular form, but not more than 2 or 3 percent of the household respondents who were asked the question—regardless of race or family income—mentioned crime or the fear of crime as their most important reason for not doing their major food shopping in their own neighborhoods. More than four-fifths of the respondents voiced very pragmatic reasons: there were no stores in their neighborhoods; neighborhood food stores were inadequate relative to those in other neighborhoods; prices were too high in their neighborhood food stores.

The questions dealing with nonfood shopping were a bit more ambiguous. Household respondents were asked: "When you shop for things other than food, such as clothing and general merchandise, do you usually go to *suburban or neighborhood shopping centers* or do you shop '*downtown*'?" (emphasis added). Clearly, interpretation of the responses to this question, and to the follow-up questions associated with it, are hampered by the ambiguous nature of the choices presented to the respondents. Just as with the food shopping responses, then, we will present no tables and simply discuss the results briefly.

After respondents had indicated whether they did their nonfood shopping in "suburban or neighborhood shopping centers" or "downtown," each group was asked to give the reasons for their preference and to designate one reason as most important. Among white household respondents who said they preferred "suburban or neighborhood shopping centers," the most important reasons cited tended to fall in the categories of "more convenient" (60 percent) and "better parking; less traffic" (13 percent). "Afraid of crime" was mentioned by only 4 percent of these white household respondents. Black/other household respondents in the same group also tended to designate convenience (48 percent) and parking/traffic (10 percent) as most important reasons, but they also mentioned "better prices, credit" (16 percent) and "better selection" (15 percent) more often than whites, while mentioning "afraid of crime" (1 percent) less often. Within both racial groups, variations associated with family income were slight.

As might have been expected, household respondents who said that they usually did their nonfood shopping "downtown" virtually never mentioned "afraid of crime" as a reason—let alone a most important reason—for that preference. White and black/other household respondents in this group were very similar in their choices of a reason as most important: more than 40 percent cited convenience, while almost 30 percent referred to the better selection of stores and merchandise "downtown." Again, there was hardly any variability in these responses associated with family income.

SUMMARY AND DISCUSSION

In this chapter we have utilized data from the eight-city attitude subsample of the NCS to examine the effects of crime and the fear of crime on behavior. The analysis started with a very broad issue: whether respondents had limited or changed their activities (in any, unspecified way) in the past few years because of crime. We found that slightly less than half of the eight-city respondents said that they had made such alterations in their behavior, but variations were apparent, especially in relation to sex and age.

Attention then shifted to some specific behaviors dealt with in the NCS attitude questionnaire, and indications that crime and the fear of crime had affected the activities of respondents began to slip away. Only a small proportion of the respondents who said that they had decreased their frequency of going out in the evening for entertainment during the last year or two gave crime or the fear of crime as the reason for doing so; moving from or selecting a new neighborhood of residence did not appear to depend much on crime-related factors, and in choosing where to shop for both food and other items, respondents emphasized factors such as convenience, price, and variety, while hardly ever mentioning the fear of crime.

Do the results pertaining to specific behaviors mean that people's behaviors are *not* influenced, to any significant extent, by crime or the fear of crime? We think that the evidence from other sources (Biderman et al., 1967: 128–29; Ennis, 1967: 77–78; Reppetto, 1974: 150) and from daily experience must lead us to reject such a conclusion. Instead, the most reasonable inference we can make from the eight-city data, as well as other sources, is that, for most people, the behavioral effects of crime or the fear of crime appear more as *subtle adjustments* in behavior than as major shifts in what can be called "behavioral policies." That is, rather than making substantial changes in *what* they do, people tend to change the *ways* in which they do things. For example, an individual might continue to go out in the evening for entertainment about as often as a year or two ago, but the same individual might modify his or her behavior by taking a taxi rather than walking, by going out with others rather than alone, or by avoiding places that have "bad reputations."[11] Likewise, the same individual, when at home, may begin to take extra precautions such as installing dead-bolt locks or leaving lights on.

On another level, people can make choices that insulate them from crime even though crime avoidance is not a conscious motivation in reaching the decision. When a family selects a house in a neighborhood characterized by green lawns, quiet streets, good schools, and the absence of bars and adult bookstores, the decision may be experienced as aesthetic, but the aesthetic qualities are highly correlated with the absence of crime. Even more indirectly, people who shop at suburban shopping centers having huge parking lots and a wide variety of stores may not be choosing these comparatively low-crime locations because of a salient fear of crime.[12] Instead we can say that, to some extent at least, businesses may have moved to such shopping centers to escape the congested, high-crime areas of the city, and it is the presence of the businesses rather than the absence of crime that attracts shoppers to the centers. From this perspective, the shoppers are insulating themselves from crime not by deciding to avoid high-crime areas but by responding to business owners who opted to avoid high-crime areas. It would not be surprising to find that businesses take the initiative in such cases because many businesses, particularly retail establishments, have much higher risks of being robbed or burglarized than do individuals or private households.[13]

There are, of course, some individuals for whom the fear of crime is a primary factor in determining what to do; the evidence indicates that such a situation is most likely to occur among the elderly. For most people, however, social or economic roles or positions (e.g., age, sex, race, income) appear to be the primary forces influencing behavior. Concern about crime is evidently a subsidiary factor that can affect subtle modifications in the content of behavior that is chosen for other reasons. In Chapter 11 we will attempt to fit both social or economic roles or positions and attitudes about crime within a tentative theory of criminal victimization.

NOTES

1. However, the difference was quite small (four percentage points) between whites and black/others with family incomes of $25,000 or more.

2. The discrepancy between males and females held even when age, race, and whether or not the respondent had suffered a personal victimization were taken into account.

3. See source code 363 in attitude questionnaire, Appendix A.

4. Unfortunately, the attitude item refers to *changes* in chances of being

attacked or robbed, and the same results may not have been observed if the question referred to chances of being attacked or robbed at a given time.

5. In this analysis, the response categories of "haven't changed" and "gone down" are combined because only 5 percent of the respondents chose the latter category.

6. An indication of the similarity of effects is the measures of association for the two "partial" tables in Table 9-3. For males and females, the strength of association between personal limiting of activities and perceived changes in chances of being attacked or robbed was similar: Yule's $Q = 0.47$ and 0.43, respectively.

7. Although not shown here, females named fear of crime slightly more often than males (14 percent versus 10 percent). The pattern across age groups was present for both males and females.

8. Further analysis using the total Sellin-Wolfgang seriousness scores of respondents did not change this finding significantly.

9. See source codes 320, 321 and 322, and 326 and 327 in the attitude questionnaire, Appendix A.

10. It must be noted, however, that among older respondents who said that they go out less, crime or the fear of crime does play a role; it was mentioned as the most important reason by almost 20 percent of those fifty years old or older who said that they go out less (see Table 9-9).

11. This is illustrated by the fact that the Pearson's product moment correlation between the fear of crime indicator (feeling of safety when out alone in neighborhood at night) and the personal limiting of activities item is higher than the correlation between fear of crime and changes in the frequency of going out in the evening for entertainment (0.39 versus 0.16). Responses to the personal limiting of activity question—as noted in the first part of this chapter—can reflect some of the relatively minor behavioral adaptations that we are discussing here.

12. By "low-crime" here we mean in terms of rape, robbery, assault, and larceny with contact. Suburban shopping centers may have fairly high levels of noncontact property crimes such as larceny and vehicle theft.

13. In the eight cities, the personal robbery rate was 19 per 1,000 residents twelve years old or older, while the commercial robbery rate was 90 per 1,000 businesses; the household burglary rate was 137 per 1,000 households, while the commercial burglary rate was 480 per 1,000 businesses.

✳ *Chapter 10*

A Methodological Postscript

Before proceeding to our last chapter, which suggests a theoretical framework within which to view criminal victimization, it is important to pause briefly in order to take a look back at the empirical work that has been presented. We are particularly interested in discussing some of the limitations of the data and the methods that we have used.

VALIDITY AND RELIABILITY OF VICTIMIZATION SURVEYS

The technique of victimization surveying is only about a decade old. Although careful methodological work designed to improve the technique has been undertaken by LEAA and the Bureau of the Census, it is erroneous and naive to believe that victimization survey results tell us what the "true" crime rate is. Just as traditional police statistics on offenses known have shortcomings that limit their utility, so too do victimization surveys. In fact, victimization surveys have been criticized both for undercounting (Maltz, 1975) and overcounting (Levine, 1976) victimizations. Although the developmental work bearing on these and other important methodological questions has been reviewed in detail elsewhere (Hindelang, 1976: chs. 2 and 3), it may be useful here to give some consideration to questions of the reliability and validity of reports of victimization experiences provided by respondents.

To the extent that the criterion variables that we have used are not reliable or valid, the utility of subsequent analyses—for example, analytic solutions for injury and loss—are decreased. Obviously, no analytic method could differentiate meaningful subgroups if the criterion variables were unreliable or invalid. Assessing the validity of the criterion is clearly a difficult task. There are two general potential sources of bias: (1) persons who had actually been victimized during the reference period may have reported to the interviewer that they had not been victimized; and (2) persons who had not actually been victimized during the reference period may have reported that they had been victimized. Each of these potentially biasing influences has several components. For persons who did in fact suffer a victimization but who reported that they did not, the report may not be valid due to: (1) the respondent deliberately not telling the truth (for a variety of reasons, including such factors as perceived stigmatizing effects, disregard for the survey itself, etc.); (2) memory effects (some respondents may have forgotten that they had been victimized during the reference period, or alternatively, some respondents may have erroneously believed that a victimization occurring during the reference period actually took place before the reference period); or (3) the respondent may not have perceived a relevant victimization as having fallen within the scope of the survey (e.g., some forms of domestic assault). The bias associated with persons who had *not* been victims during the reference period, yet who reported to the interviewer that they had, also has several potential components: (1) the respondent may have not told the truth deliberately (perhaps by trying to "please" the interviewer with positive responses or because of disregard for the survey itself); (2) memory effects (e.g., some respondents may have erroneously reported a victimization that actually occurred prior to the reference period as having occurred during the reference period); or (3) the victim may have erroneously believed that she or he was victimized when she or he was not (e.g., a respondent may have reported a misplaced wallet as a pocket picking).

The major question of concern in the study of correlates of victimization revolves around the extent to which biases are associated with respondent characteristics. If these biases were found not to exist, or were found to be randomly distributed across respondent characteristics, then there would be less cause for concern. Unfortunately, the available research that bears on these questions is limited.

Prior Research on the Validity
of the Criterion

The potentially biasing effect of memory on victimization estimates has substantial implications for the research reported in the
previous chapters. For example, if respondent characteristics were
related to memory effects, then the associations between respondent
characteristics and the probability of victimization as measured by
the respondents' reports—a key concern for victimization risk analyses—would be equivocal. It would not be known whether a personal
characteristic was actually related to victimization or whether the
obtained relation was an artifact of memory. The research of Biderman et al. (1967), Ennis (1967), the U.S. Bureau of the Census
(1970a, 1970b), and LEAA (1972) clearly indicates that there are
considerable memory effects in retrospective surveys of victims of
crimes; however, these studies only serve to underscore the potential
for the bias that is of primary concern here—that is, the association
between respondent characteristics and memory biases. In order for
these memory biases to have an effect on a classification of victims,
it must generally be the case that the characteristics of respondents
associated with the criterion are also associated with memory biases.

The relationship between memory biases and respondent characteristics in victimization surveys was investigated in an earlier work
(Gottfredson and Hindelang, 1977). Of special interest here is that
the memory biases studied were found to be virtually unrelated
to characteristics of respondents such as age, race, sex, family income, employment status, and the educational attainment of the
the respondent. Thus, although there are clearly substantial memory
effects in victimization surveys that would certainly caution against
the notion that such surveys somehow measure the "true" level of
criminal activity, the currently available evidence indicates that
these effects do not appear to be strongly correlated with characteristics of victims.

Reverse Record Check Results

The reverse record check studies also bear on the validity of the
victimization classifications developed here. The study of most
direct relevance to the issue of bias associated with respondent
characteristics is the *San Jose Methods Test of Known Crime Victims* (LEAA, 1972). In that study, persons known to be crime
victims on the basis of police offense reports were interviewed to
see if they would report the crime to survey interviewers. It was

found that of those known victims of assault, robbery, rape, burglary, and larceny who were interviewed (64 percent of those selected), 26 percent did not report the incident to the interviewers; for the crime of assault, the crime proportionately least often reported to interviewers, about half of the known victims failed to mention the victimization to the interviewer. Indications are, then, that the validity of the victimization estimates is far from perfect, especially for assaultive crimes. More important, however, is the question of whether there is systematic bias due to a relationship between respondent characteristics and the failure of known victims to report to survey interviewers that they were victimized. Unfortunately, there are no reverse record checks in which this question has been satisfactorily addressed.

Therefore, the reverse record check research does not adequately answer the question of differential bias (associated with respondent characteristics) in the criteria used in earlier chapters. Additionally, because these reverse record check studies have relied upon validation samples drawn from police offense reports, there are no data bearing on victims who do not report the offense to the police and the extent to which the survey method is capable of eliciting such incidents of victimization.

Studies of response biases resulting from reports to interviewers of incidents that are not crimes and of biases related to the failure to report incidents because respondents do not conceive of them as crimes have not yet been undertaken. To some extent the design of the survey instrument, in which there is a great variety of detailed information collected about each reported incident, may serve to minimize fabrication, and the instrument is constructed in such a way as to weed out many noncrime incidents that may be reported. On the other hand, because the screen questions are asked in nontechnical terms (e.g., "Did anyone beat you up, attack you or hit you with something, such as a rock or bottle?"), the instrument may elicit incidents not previously considered crimes by the respondent.

Prior Research on the Reliability
of Respondent Reports

As part of its effort to maintain quality control of the victimization survey data collected, the Bureau of the Census conducts reinterviews with a sample of the respondents interviewed as part of the NCS program. This reinterview procedure is used as a check on the quality of the completed interviews submitted to the bureau by its interviewers and as a means of informing users about the impact of response errors on the accuracy of the data. Census interviewers are aware that their work is checked on a sampling basis, and it is believed by supervisory personnel that this continuous reinterviewing contributes to accuracy in three ways. First, interviewers are more conscientious in collecting and recording data in the original interviews. Second, discrepancies that are isolated can be used to retrain particular interviewers and to give an indication of items in the interview schedule that may have to be explained more fully in the training of all interviewers. Third, when an inconsistency is found, it can be resolved and the record can be corrected.

In the Bureau of the Census reinterview procedures in the city surveys, a subsample of approximately 4 percent of the households originally visited were revisited by a census interviewer. In these households, respondents were told that the bureau was checking to be sure that the data recorded by the original interviewer were correct. The procedures followed in the original survey were followed in the reinterview. For example, individual interviews were conducted with all household members fourteen years of age or older and with proxy interviewees for twelve and thirteen year old household members; interviews were only conducted for those who were interviewed in the original survey. In the reinterview, a shorter interview schedule, containing a subset of the original items, was used.

For our purposes, we are most interested in the test-retest consistency between the original response and the reinterview response. In its reinterview reports (e.g., Schreiner, 1974; Graham, 1974a, 1974b, 1974c, 1974d) one such measure of consistency used by the Bureau of the Census was the ratio of the number of discrepancies to the maximum number of possible discrepancies between interview and reinterview. This ratio was computed for victimizations that were reported in the original and in the reinterview. For purposes of computing the ratio, incident questions were grouped into fourteen areas; the maximum number of discrepancies for a given victimization was fourteen. This grouping procedure was followed so that only one discrepancy was counted when it led to another discrepancy in succeeding items that probed the same area. In the national sample for the July 1973 to the June 1974 period, the matched incidents (original and reinterview) showed discrepancies for only about 2 percent of the items in which discrepancies could have appeared (Graham, 1974d: Table 4).

In the reinterview study conducted in the eight cities, more than 5,000 persons in 2,500 households were reinterviewed. Although ratios comparable to those reported above for the national sample have not been published for the reinterviews conducted in the eight cities, there are other results reported that give an indication of the interview-reinterview consistency. One such measure results from a cross-tabulation of the responses to detailed incident questions asked of respondents who reported incidents at both times. As a measure of inconsistency, the Bureau of the Census uses the L-fold Index of Inconsistent Responses (U.S. Bureau of the Census, 1969). The index varies from 0.00, indicating no inconsistency between the original and the reinterview responses, to 1.00, indicating no consistency between original and reinterview responses. As a rule of thumb, the bureau considers values of less than 0.20 as small, indicating "that the response variability is not a major problem"; values of 0.20 to 0.50 as moderate, "indicating that there is some problem with inconsistent reporting"; and values of more than 0.50 as large, "indicating that improvements are required in the method used to collect these data or that the category concepts themselves are ambiguous" (Graham, 1974b: 3).

In the eight-city reinterview study, most of the indexes of inconsistent reporting were less than 0.20. The most inconsistent item was one designed to determine whether or not the incident was a series victimization (see Check Item A, Appendix A). The index of inconsistent response for this item was 0.29. Most of the remaining indexes of inconsistency were low. For example, the question: "Was something stolen or taken without permission . . .," produced an index of 0.02, indicating a great deal of consistency (Graham, 1974b: Table A). The question regarding a need for medical attention produced an index of 0.19, suggesting that responses to it were more inconsistent than the responses to the theft question (Graham, 1974b: Table A). On the other hand, the question regarding whether the respondent received any treatment at a hospital had an index of 0.00 (Graham: Table B). However, it should be noted that, because injury is a relatively rare phenomenon, the number of cases on which the medical attention and hospital treatment indexes were based was small (unweighted N = 15), while the theft question was based on a much larger number of cases (unweighted N = 669). In the reinterview report, the author concluded: "The overall results indicated that most of the answers to the questions on the reinterview survey were fairly consistent with responses obtained on the initial interview" (Graham: 1974b: 5). On the basis of evidence currently available from interview-reinterview studies, it appears that the instruments, procedures, and interviewers used produced reasonably reliable results. Furthermore, because the persons who conducted the reinterviews were more experienced and used deeper probing techniques, the reinterview consistency provides some confidence in the validity of the original interview results reported by less experienced interviewers.

THE ADEQUACY OF THE ANALYTIC METHODS USED

When we began our analytic work, we considered a variety of alternative techniques for exploring the data. Our first efforts relied primarily on traditional tabular procedures (Hindelang, 1976), but we have explored multiple regression, discriminant function, path, log-linear, and predictive attribute analyses as methods for analyzing the victimization results. Each of these methods has serious shortcomings for the kinds of work presented in this book.

In our preliminary work, multiple regression and discriminant function analyses were attempted, particularly in conjunction with the victim-nonvictim types of analyses. As anticipated, the extreme skewness of the dependent variables (or attributes) resulted in unsatisfactory and generally unenlightening solutions. The skewness of an attribute like injury versus no injury—but even the more general attribute, victim versus nonvictim—was so extreme that even variables shown in other analyses to be powerfully related to the criterion (in terms of very substantial rate differences) had small Pearson's rs, multiple Rs, and beta weights. Thus, in a stepwise regression procedure, the variability of the zero-order correlations of the predictors with the criterion was so small that it was difficult for the program to select the best predictors in a reliable fashion. Furthermore, our tabular work had indicated that the data were replete with interactions that would have been very cumbersome to handle and difficult to interpret with multiple regression. For similar reasons, as well as because of time-ordering problems (see Chapter 8), path analytic solutions proved difficult to evaluate. Despite the fact that we report some multiple regresssion results in Chapter 8 (where some of these problems are evident), we concluded that this approach generally would not be sufficient for our purposes in this book.

Log-linear analysis was explored in detail as a technique that might be used in lieu of predictive attribute analysis. Log-linear analysis imposes a practical limitation on the number of variables that can be examined simultaneously before the complexity of the models becomes overwhelming and the number of (unweighted) cases within cells is depleted. Furthermore, log-linear analysis is better suited for testing hypotheses about the interrelationships among a limited number of variables than for screening a large number of potentially predictive variables. In addition, we found after using log-linear and traditional tabular approaches independently that they led to virtually identical conclusions.

Predictive attribute and traditional tabular analyses were the techniques selected for presenting the data; obviously, these approaches are not without serious shortcomings. Predictive attribute analysis with a large number of predictors virtually requires that the predictors be dichotomized.[1] Because most of the predictors of interest are polychotomous nominal variables, this means that dummy coding or some recoding into "natural" dichotomies was necessary. Dummy coding often results in unusual attributes being isolated in a solution. For example, in the PAA solution for injury (Chapter 3, Table 3-9), the attribute "loss ≠ $10–49" emerged in the solution. The emergence of attributes of this type is often difficult to explain. However, one of the primary aims of using PAA in this connection is for its heuristic value. Because PAA uses a strictly empirical search technique, reasons for the emergence of particular attributes are not always obvious.[2] In some analyses, we might be tempted to write off some of the less interpretable solutions to unreliability; this possibility is reduced here by our demonstration that when the resultant solutions were forced on a split half of the sample, generally consistent results were obtained. Some might suggest that the attributes should have been created primarily or exclusively on theoretical grounds. For example, why not simply dichotomize loss into "high" and "low?" Although this procedure helps to eliminate an air of "brute empiricism" and to reduce the interpretability problem, at the same time this orientation tends to convert an exploratory analysis into a confirmatory one. We agree that at some point such a shift should take place, but it is probably more fruitful for it to take place after the phenomenon of interest has been adequately studied and movement toward theory construction has advanced sufficiently. At the outset, we believed that such theoretical advancement had not yet taken place in the study of victimization.

The use of PAA might also be faulted on the grounds that the solutions that it generates are too unwieldy. It is undoubtedly true that the PAA solutions present a challenge to the English language; they are certainly difficult to discuss. It is also the case, however, that traditional multiple regression solutions are too simplistic, in the sense that they mask a good deal of what is going on in the data. By assuming a noninteractive linear model, the empirical complexities that are often present in data are ignored by traditional multiple regression.[3] PAA is more sensitive to these complexities and hence often yields complex solutions. It would be convenient if at each level in the solution, the same variable emerged as the best predictor in each branch (as traditional multiple regression assumes). Unfortunately, the data are not generally cooperative in this respect, and hence the solutions are often difficult to interpret. One of the consequences of this lack of neatness is that, beyond the first break, it is not generally easy to quantify the importance of variables in explaining variability in the dependent variable. Despite these shortcomings, PAA seemed to us to be the most appropriate technique for those kinds of analyses in which it was used.

One other aspect of our analytic stance is relevant to the predictive attribute analyses but is also relevant to most of the other analyses presented throughout this book. It is our use of terms such as "association," "correlate," and "relationship." In conjunction with our PAAs, Somers' d was used as the measure of association to gauge the strength of the relationships between the available predictors and the respective criterion variables. Somers' d in the 2×2 case is equal to the percentage difference on the dependent variable between the two categories of the predictor variable; thus, whether the Somers' d or the percentage difference is discussed, each is equally indicative of the strength of the relationship.

In other analyses, we discuss patterns of percentages (e.g., across age) and sometimes refer to these patterns as showing a "relationship" or "association" between the two variables under discussion. In this context, the fact of variations in percentages reflects a relationship between the two variables. At the same time it is true, however, that substantial variations in percentages across categories of an "independent" variable may reflect only a weak correlation depending on the marginal distribution of the predictor variable—for example, a substantial percentage difference on a dependent variable between the oldest and youngest respondents may translate into a small correlation coefficient if the number of cases in either of the extreme age groups is small. However, because of the nature of the data on which we focus, we believe that it is more useful to consider conditional probabilities, which ignore marginal distributions on the "independent" variables, than to focus exclusively on measures of association that are strongly affected by marginals and hence may mask important detail. Obviously, this is of particular importance when we are considering differences between victims and nonvictims. Throughout, we gave particular attention to the bases on which percentages were calculated, in order to avoid giving too much weight to percentages that applied to trivial numbers of cases.

Finally, although not precisely an analytic method, we have sometimes—particularly in Chapters 7 and 8—used the race and income characteristics of *individuals* as a rough indicator of the race and income characteristics of the *areas* in which those individuals reside. As noted, there was no areal information available from the NCS city surveys, but data from the NCS national surveys can be broken down by the characteristics of the neighborhoods in which interviewed households were located. The 1975 national data show that using individual race and income characteristics as a rough indicator of neighborhood characteristics works reasonably well. For example, more than one-half of the households headed by blacks were located in neighborhoods in which at least half of the residents were black. The 1975 national data also show that about 60 percent of the households with annual incomes of less than $3,000 were located in neighborhoods having a median income of $8,000 or less while the same was true for only about 15 percent of the households with incomes of $15,000 or more.

SERIES VICTIMIZATIONS

The questions of whether and how best to use series victimizations in our analyses have been of some concern to us. Consideration of these questions has been given elsewhere (Hindelang, 1976: Appendix F), but for us the questions are not resolved. In the previous chapters we used a mixed strategy. In general, when our analyses were primarily concerned with the association of various characteristics of the victimizations with some criterion, series victimizations were excluded. This seems reasonable in that one of the prime criteria for events being categorized by the interviewer as belonging to a series was that the victim was not able to recall the circumstances of the events in the series sufficiently well to report on the victimizations individually. Thus, by definition, in series victimizations there was more ambiguity regarding what actually happened during the event than in nonseries victimizations. Hence, only nonseries victimizations, which are inherently relatively more reliable, were used when what happened during the event was particularly crucial— for example, in analyzing the kinds of victimizations most likely to result in injury or loss (e.g., Chapters 3 and 4). However, when the focus was on whether or not the person was victimized at all (e.g., Chapters 6, 7, 8, and 9), series victims were included, because these respondents were apparently victims of something; *precisely what* seems less crucial in these analyses. In Chapter 5, series victims were excluded because one of the aims of the chapter was to analyze separately persons suffering loss and persons suffering injury victimizations. In any event, in the eight-city data, the proportion of persons who were not victims of a nonseries crime, but who were victims of a series crime (and who would be counted as nonvictims when series victimizations are excluded) was very small.[4] This implies that for simply classifying respondents as victims or nonvictims the inclusion or exclusion of the series respondents had little practical effect on the solutions. However, when the interest is in estimating the absolute level of victimization or in comparing levels of victimization with the *Uniform Crime Reports*—neither of which have been addressed in this book—whether or not series victimizations are included is a crucial decision.[5]

LIMITATIONS IN THE
SURVEY INSTRUMENTS

The National Crime Survey data collection effort has provided researchers with a wealth of systematic data that have heretofore been unavailable. These data permit analyses the depth and breadth of which were well beyond the realm of feasibility as little as two decades ago. Despite their richness, the instruments currently in use have some shortcomings that limit the interpretation of the data.

One important aspect of our victimization analysis in which lack of data was very problematic was in the loss and injury areas, in which we could only speculate about the order in which events occurred: Did the offender attack the victim without "provocation" or did the victim *first* resist the property demands of the offender, who then resorted to an attack on the victim? Did some victims avoid injury simply by giving up their property rather than resisting? Without more information on precisely how these events unfolded it is not possible to resolve these questions. Clearly, the answers to these questions, especially the means that victims can use to avoid injury, are of such importance that more detail about how the events transpired must be collected in future surveys.

Another aspect of the survey that requires some attention is the attitude portion. As noted in the attitude chapters, there are some unfortunate shifts in wording and emphasis from question to question that reduce the utility of the attitude data. Furthermore, the items dealing with attempts of respondents to protect or insulate themselves from victimization are much too limited. The fact that the attitude supplement has not been used in the national panel surveys prevents us from examining the effects of attitudes and behavioral changes on future victimizations; a definitive resolution of some of the time-ordering problems can only be achieved through panel studies. These are just some shortcomings of the attitude portion of the surveys as it now exists. One factor explaining a variety of the shortcomings is that the attitude instrument was not subjected to the extensive pretesting that preceded the use of the other interview instruments.

One final area in which we believe additional data need to be collected revolves around the victim's activities just prior to victimization: What was the victim doing when he or she was victimized? Was the victim in what he or she believed was a high crime or high risk area? How close was the location of the victimization to the residence of the victim? These questions will help to assess risk factors associated with variations in victimization rates across demographic subgroups of the population.

Similarly, it would be helpful theoretically if the victimization survey could collect information from victims and nonvictims about how time is spent. With such data, it would be possible to study the correspondence between how and where time is spent and the likelihood of various types of victimization. Our final chapter suggests a theoretical framework within which victimization experiences can be viewed; part of this theoretical analysis postulates an association between lifestyles and daily activities on the one hand and the likelihood of victimization on the other.

NOTES

1. Variations on the technique using polychotomous predictors have been used; see, for example, Cohen (1975).

2. Parenthetically it should be noted that this problem is not peculiar to PAA. Whenever dummy coding is used—for example, in multiple regression analysis (Kerlinger and Pedhazur, 1973)—this problem exists.

3. Dummy and effect coding, as well as interaction vectors, can be used to isolate more complex patterns in the data, but these adaptations of traditional multiple regression lead to similarly (or more) complex results.

4. See Chapter 6.

5. See Hindelang (1976: Appendix F) for some empirical illustrations.

Part IV

A Theoretical Model

In the first three parts of this book and in earlier efforts, we have given extensive empirical attention to the nature and correlates of personal victimization. These analyses have encompassed characteristics of victims and offenders, the prior relationships between victims and offenders, the elements and consequences of personal victimizations, attitudes of respondents, and the reactions of victims who are caught up in the victimization experience.

In Chapter 11 we attempt to synthesize these findings and put forth some propositions to account for variations in risks and consequences of personal victimization. We propose a grounded theoretical model—what we refer to as the lifestyle/exposure model—that we believe is compatible with the victimization survey findings and general criminological literature on the common law personal crimes of rape, robbery, assault, and larceny.

This lifestyle/exposure model of personal victimization is in its early stages of development. We anticipate that as more is learned about criminal victimization, the model will have to be modified. At our current level of understanding of personal victimization, however, the model seems quite useful, both as a summarizing and as a deductive device.

Chapter 11

Toward a Theory of Personal Criminal Victimization[1]

INTRODUCTION

To this point, our work with the victimization survey data—and the work of most of those who have used the data—has been almost wholly empirical and methodological. On the basis of what is now known about victimization experiences, it is time to attempt to move beyond the data in order to postulate a theoretical model to help to account for these phenomena. Owing largely to the recency of victimization data and the complexity of victimization experiences, the theoretical model proposed in this chapter is a tentative, first step in constructing a theory of personal victimization. Although the theoretical model proposed here is, by and large, grounded in data about victims of crime, for many of the *explanatory mechanisms* that are postulated no data are currently available. Nonetheless, what is proposed in this model appears to be compatible with what is known about victims of personal crime from victimization surveys and other data.

Our theoretical model of the likelihood that an individual will suffer a personal victimization depends heavily on the concept of *lifestyle.* Briefly, lifestyle refers to routine daily activities, both vocational activities (work, school, keeping house, etc.) and leisure activities. What is offered is a theoretical model that postulates the antecedents of lifestyle and the mechanisms that link lifestyle with victimization. The findings that have been presented both in the earlier chapters and in other criminological research are then discussed within the context of the model.

The basic model is shown in Figure 11-1. We postulate that role expectations and social structure impose constraints to which persons must adapt if they are to function smoothly in society.[2] Role expectations and structural constraints for any individual depend upon that individual's constellation of demographic characteristics. The use of dashed lines in connection with demographic characteristics in Figure 11-1 is meant to indicate that these characteristics do not cause role expectations and social structural constraints.

Role expectations as used here refers to cultural norms that are associated with achieved and ascribed statuses of individuals and that define preferred and anticipated behaviors. The role expectations with which we are concerned are those that pertain to central statuses of individuals—central in the sense of having a diffuse influence on the person occupying the status.[3] For example, role expectations vary dramatically with the age of the person; what is expected and/or deemed appropriate behavior for a child is generally not what is expected of an adult. Similarly, traditional American childrearing practices involve implicit and explicit definitions of role expectations—the differential propriety of dress, manner, expression of emotion, choice of play objects, etc.—depending on the sex of the child. Also, with respect to marital status, there are different role expectations for married versus unmarried persons; the former are generally expected to spend more time at home and in general to lead a more settled existence.

The other source of constraints identified in Figure 11-1 is the social structure. The *structural constraints* originating from this source can be defined as limitations on behavioral options that result from the particular arrangements existing within various institutional orders, such as the economic, familial, educational, and legal orders. For example, economic factors impose stringent limitations on the range of choices that individuals have with respect to such fundamentals as area of residence, nature of leisure activities, mode of transportation, and access to educational opportunities; to some extent racial barriers, particularly with regard to area of residence, are economically based. In addition, in the United States, the decline of the extended family structure has had an impact on the behavioral choices of family members. For example, parents must assume at-home responsibilities—including child supervision, cooking, and cleaning—that in former times were shared with grandparents and other relatives in the household.

No attempt is made to assign priorities to these institutional orders; they are certainly interdependent, and most people, at various times in their lives, are simultaneously constrained by several of them. By

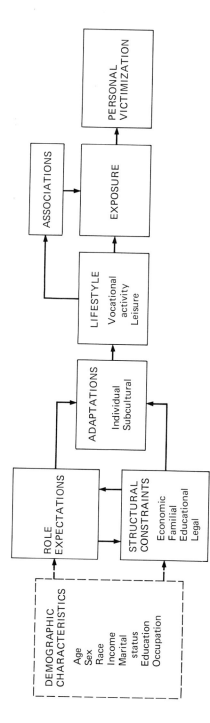

Figure 11-1. A Lifestyle/Exposure Model of Personal Victimization

way of illustration, adolescents under a certain age are constrained by both legal and educational institutions. That is, the structure of the educational system (e.g., school calendar and class times) as well as legal requirements (e.g., compulsory attendance laws and child labor laws) limit the behavioral options of adolescents.

Note that in Figure 11-1, role expectations and structural constraints are reciprocally related. In recent years, for example, sex role expectations have been modified so that there has been some convergence in the role expectations for males and females. This change, in turn, has been translated into structural changes, particularly in the family and, to a lesser extent, in the economic realm. One might argue that role expectations and structural constraints are indistinguishable, that social structure is simply a composite of social roles. However, we believe the two are analytically distinct; for example, the expectations associated with the role of parent may be quite different in a social structure characterized by detached nuclear families than in one characterized by an extended family structure of communal childrearing.

As pointed out earlier and as illustrated in Figure 11-1, members of society adapt to role expectations and structural constraints. Such *adaptations* occur on both the individual and group levels. Each person learns skills and attitudes that allow him or her to operate with some individuality within the constraints imposed by role expectations and social structure. Among the skills and attitudes that an individual acquires in adapting to role expectations and structural constraints, of particular interest in connection with personal victimization are attitudes and beliefs about crime, including fear of crime. Once learned, these attitudes and beliefs are often incorporated into the routine activities of the individual, frequently as limitations on behavior.

Role expectations and structural constraints have similar effects for people with the same demographic characteristics. Thus, *shared* adaptations also emerge and can even be incorporated as norms among subgroups of society. Such group adaptations are postulated in Cohen's (1955) description of the "delinquent subculture" and Wolfgang and Ferracuti's (1967) "subculture of violence" theory.

Individuals adapt to structural constraints and role expectations in ways that result in regularities in behavioral patterns. What is important for our purposes is that these include such routine activities as working outside of the home, going to school, or keeping house, as well as typical leisure time pursuits. These daily routines constitute *lifestyle* as we use the term here.

Our usage of lifestyle is similar to Havighurst's (1961:333): "a characteristic way of distributing one's time, one's interest, and one's talent among the common social roles of adult life—those of worker, parent, spouse, homemaker, citizen, friend, club or association member, and user of leisure time." Our definition differs from Havighurst's in that ours is not limited to adults; furthermore, our emphasis is heavily on *routine* activities.

In our model, lifestyle differences result from differences in role expectations, structural constraints, and individual and subcultural adaptations. Variations in lifestyles are related differentially to probabilities of being in particular places at particular times and coming into contact with persons who have particular characteristics; because criminal victimization is not randomly distributed across time and space and because offenders in personal crimes are not representative of the general population—but rather there are high-risk times, places, and people—this implies that lifestyle differences are associated with differences in *exposure* to situations that have a high victimization risk.

In the course of vocational and leisure pursuits, individuals spend a disproportionate amount of their time with others who have similar lifestyles. One reason why vocation—whether it be keeping house, going to school, or being employed—is so central to lifestyle is that it structures a large portion of daily activities. To the extent that these vocational activities are carried out as formal roles within institutional structures, the nature of an individual's interactions with others has a greater degree of predictability. That is, formal roles generally define socially acceptable daily routines that structure the lifestyles of those involved.

As shown in Figure 11-1, the major linkage between lifestyle and exposure to high victimization risk situations is direct. There is, however, another indirect link, which operates through associations. *Associations* refer to more or less sustained personal relationships among individuals that evolve as a result of similar lifestyles and hence similar interests shared by these individuals. Because offenders disproportionately have particular characteristics, association with people having these characteristics serves to increase exposure to personal victimization.

Personal victimization, the final element in the model, follows probabilistically from exposure to high victimization risk situations. Below, we will give additional attention, primarily in the form of a series of propositions, to the model and how it helps to explain variations in the likelihood of personal victimization. Before doing so, however, it is necessary to discuss more fully the key component in our model, lifestyle.

LIFESTYLE

Such diverse phenomena as life expectancy, morbidity, automobile accidents, suicide, and criminal victimization are all closely associated with demographic characteristics. For example, the life expectancy for women is about eight years longer than that for men and the life expectancy for whites is about seven years longer than for blacks (U.S. Bureau of the Census, 1974:58). Blacks have higher infant and maternal death rates than do whites (U.S. Bureau of the Census, 1974b:60). Younger drivers are more likely than middle-aged drivers to be involved in automobile accidents. Persons who have never married or who are separated, widowed, or divorced have suicide rates that are substantially higher than those for married persons (Gibbs, 1966). Males have higher suicide rates than females, particularly in older age groups (U.S. Bureau of the Census, 1974b:63). As we have shown throughout this book, demographic characteristics are also related to differential probabilities of personal victimization.

In terms of our model, these relationships between demographic variables and these diverse consequences, particularly personal victimization, can be attributed to differences in lifestyle. This is because various constellations of demographic characteristics are associated with role expectations and structural constraints that, mediated through individual and subcultural adaptations, channel lifestyles. For example, the lifestyles of young drivers can help account for their relatively high accident rates. They have less driving experience and relatively immature judgment; they are more likely to socialize in groups and to be influenced by group pressures to drive recklessly, drag race, and so on. Younger persons are typically more mobile and active than older persons and hence have a greater *exposure* to risks of automobile accidents. Similar inferences about differential lifestyles can be suggested to account for the relationship of demographic variables to the other consequences noted above: men are more likely than women to be exposed to the health hazards related to occupation; because of the relative economic constraints impinging on blacks and whites, blacks are more likely to live under conditions conducive to ill-health and are less able economically to take advantage of preventive medical care; unattached persons (single, divorced, widowed, or separated) may tend to spend more time alone and to have fewer dependents who rely upon them for nurturance and support.

It should not be surprising that lifestyle is closely tied to the most fundamental aspects of human existence: how long we live, how well we live, and how we die. The antecedents of lifestyle not only affect life chances in the long run, but also affect short-term life experiences. As conceptualized in our model, variations in lifestyles are attributable to the ways in which persons with various constellations of demographic characteristics adapt to role expectations and structural constraints. Our attention will now turn briefly to some examples of how lifestyle can be traced back to demographic characteristics in our model.

Age

Perhaps the clearest example of a demographic variable that dramatically affects lifestyle is age. Role expectations vary as a function of age. In addition, a variety of structural constraints—kinship, economic, educational, and legal—differentially impinge upon individuals according to age. In infancy and early childhood, the child's existence is highly structured according to parental expectations; that is, such things as when the child is fed, the stimuli within the child's environment, where the child is permitted to play, and with whom the child comes into contact are all largely under parental control. However, as the child approaches school age and begins to associate increasingly with others outside of the immediate family, parental control is less influential in restricting the extrafamilial exposure of the child—where the child is, with whom she or he comes into contact, and generally how the child's time is spent outside of the home.

During the years in which the child is completing her or his education, the child's lifestyle begins to shift dramatically. The waking hours spent outside of the home are largely structured by the activities involved in traveling to school, participating in curricular and extracurricular activities, and returning from school. As the child moves into adolescence, there is increasing autonomy; a greater proportion of time is spent in association with peers, and, by late adolescence, the activities of the child are by and large no longer within the institutional control of family or school. During early adulthood, lifestyles become increasingly determined by adaptations to the constraints of educational and occupational (economic) structures. For those pursuing neither occupational nor educational careers, there is considerably less institutional structure. The occupation of the person—that is, the role that the individual assumes within the economic structure—will have a substantial impact on that person's lifestyle throughout adulthood. This impact manifests itself with respect to where, when, and with whom time is spent. Of course, throughout the occupational career, age itself will also have an impact on lifestyle, especially in terms of time spent outside of the home, restrictions imposed by childrearing, and leisure time activities. As retirement years are reached, individuals begin to experience another dramatic shift in daily activities: mobility decreases, the number of interpersonal contacts decreases, and the experiential world of the individual becomes constricted generally. One of the important *adaptations* that occurs as age increases is a shift in attitudes, including an increased fear of crime. This increased fear contributes to limitations of activities, mobility, and contacts with strangers. By virtue of adaptations to role expectations and structural constraints that vary as a function of age, age itself an important indicator of lifestyle.

Parenthetically, it is important to note that throughout the life cycle, individuals are more likely to associate with and to come into contact with those occupying similar age-linked roles than with those occupying different roles: students with students, workers with workers, homemakers with homemakers, and retired persons with retired persons.

Sex

Despite the growing movement toward sexual equality in all institutional spheres and away from sex role differentiation, there remain structural constraints and differences in sex role expectations. Adaptations to these make sex an important indicator of lifestyle. Traditionally, the sex role socialization of females has been different from that of males. Because of sex role differentiation, sex is related to daily activities such as where time is spent, the number of interpersonal contacts, and the likelihood of encountering strangers. For example, females spend a greater proportion of their time inside the home because as adolescents they are more closely supervised than males, and as adults they are more likely than males to assume housekeeping responsibilities. Although sex is a major indicator of lifestyle, it is a weaker indicator for the youngest and oldest members of society. That is, in preadolescent and postretirement age groups, the lifestyles of males and females are less differentiated than in the intervening years, during which sex-linked differences in structural constraints and role expectations are more pronounced. For example, after retirement, both men and women are likely to be less mobile, to spend more time at home, and to have fewer contacts with persons outside of their primary groups; at this point in the life cycle (and in preadolescence as well), the role expectations and structural constraints associated with age tend to take precedence over those associated with sex.

Marital Status

Another variable that is closely tied to lifestyles through the processes shown in our model is marital status. Among adults, the lifestyles of those who are married can be expected to differ in several important respects from those who are not married. The common living arrangements associated with marriage (or cohabitation) introduce a form of structure that is less prominent in the lives of "unattached" persons. For example, married persons would be expected to spend proportionately more time within the home than would single persons; this is especially true of those who have children. Marital and familial ties result in an increased number of at-home responsibilities. In addition, leisure time spent out of the home is likely to be in the company of partners or with other persons of similar marital and familial statuses. Also, because the marital bond brings together two extended family networks, the likelihood of spending time with family members increases. On the other hand, single persons are likely to spend their time outside of the home more often unaccompanied or in the company of other single persons. The transition from an "unattached" to an "attached" status (e.g., single to married) generally implies a dramatic shift in lifestyle; this transition involves a shift in role expectations and structural constraints to which individuals must adapt. Thus, marital status is another indicator of where, when, and with whom individuals routinely spend their time.

Family Income and Race

Family income is closely associated with life chances and life experiences because it is reflective of one's position in the economic structure, which is one of the most important constraints on behavioral options. As family income increases, so too does the flexibility to adjust one's lifestyle to one's wishes. This flexibility includes the ability to select the area in which to live, the mode of transportation that will be used in daily activities, the proportion of time spent in private surroundings versus public places, and the very nature of leisure time activities. It is important to note that the choices provided to those with sufficient family income often result in an income-linked segregation in housing, transportation, privacy, and many leisure time activities. Thus, patterns of *association* are also income-linked: those living in suburbs are likely to be of at least moderate income; those relying primarily on public modes of intracity transportation are likely to be less affluent; members of country clubs are likely to be relatively wealthy. Thus, those of similar family incomes tend to cluster in particular residential, recreational, and other social settings.

Like family income, race is closely tied with life chances and life experiences. Some of the importance of race as an indicator of lifestyle derives from its association with family income. However, whites and blacks of the same socioeconomic stratum live in quite different worlds. For example, noneconomic structural constraints associated with race result in segregated housing patterns, and thus blacks tend to live in more economically heterogeneous areas than do whites (Taeuber, 1968; Erbe, 1975). Such housing patterns have particularly strong implications for patterns of associations among blacks versus whites; among the latter, patterns of association will be more income-segregated than among the former. These differences are apparent throughout the life cycle, especially in the educational and recreational realms. For example, attending private schools and belonging to private clubs are much more common among whites than among blacks.

Our attention will now turn to an examination of some of the major victimization findings and to a discussion of ways in which patterns of victimization can be related to variations in lifestyles. Our discussion will draw on the analyses presented both in earlier chapters and in Hindelang (1976). In order to assist the reader, references to the tables in which particular findings are presented will be given as those findings are discussed. In addition, to the extent that the data are available, our discussion below will draw upon relevant findings of prior research.

VICTIMIZATION AND LIFESTYLE—A SET OF PROPOSITIONS

For a personal victimization to occur, several conditions must be met. First, the prime actors—the offender and the victim—must have occasion to intersect in time and space. Second, some source of dispute or claim must arise between the actors in which the victim is perceived by the offender as an appropriate object of the victimization. Third, the offender must be willing and able to threaten or use force (or stealth) in order to achieve the desired end. Fourth, the circumstances must be such that the offender views it as advantageous to use or threaten force (or stealth) to achieve the desired end. The probability of these conditions being met is related to the life circumstances of members of society.

Lifestyle is the central component in our theoretical model. In our view, the centrality of lifestyle derives primarily from its close association with *exposure* to victimization risk situations. Victimization is not a phenomenon that is uniformly distributed; it occurs disproportionately in particular times and places; it occurs disproportionately by offenders with particular demographic characteristics; it occurs disproportionately under certain circumstances (e.g., according to whether or not the person is alone); it occurs disproportionately according to the prior relationship between the potential victim and the potential offender; and so forth. Because different lifestyles imply different probabilities that individuals will be in particular places, at particular times, under particular circumstances, interacting with particular kinds of persons, lifestyle affects the probability of victimization. In the following discussion, we will suggest ways in which particular lifestyles have implications for exposure to personal victimization in light of the empirical properties of these victimizations. Although the format we will use involves the statement of a single proposition followed by a discussion of its theoretical and empirical tenability, it should be stressed at the outset that these propositions are interdependent. Therefore, for each proposition, the phrase "other things being equal" is implied.

Proposition 1: *The probability of suffering a personal victimization is directly related to the amount of time that a person spends in public places (e.g., on the street, in parks, etc.), and particularly in public places at night.*

Systematic analysis of the occurrence of criminal events has demonstrated repeatedly that the likelihood of a crime occurring is not uniformly distributed by time or place. In his study of robbery in Philadelphia, Normandeau (1968:221) found that 38 percent of the robberies studied occurred in the six-hour period from 8 P.M. to 2 A.M. Similarly, findings from both the President's Commission on Crime in the District of Columbia (1966:58) and McClintock and Gibson's (1961:131-2) London study are congruent with Normandeau's finding that robbery occurs disproportionately in the late evening and early morning hours.

In studies of police offense reports, rape has also been found to occur disproportionately in the late night and early morning hours. Chappell and Singer (1973:60) found that in New York City 37 percent of the rapes reported to the police occurred between the hours of 8 P.M. and 2 A.M.; Amir's (1971:84) study of Philadelphia rapes showed that nearly one-half of the rapes recorded in the police files occurred during the same time period. Likewise, the President's Commission on Crime in the District of Columbia (1966:48) found that nearly three-fifths of the rapes reported to the police in that city occurred between the hours of 6 P.M. and 3 A.M.—a finding congruent with MacDonald's (1971:30) study showing that 53 percent of the reported rapes in Denver occurred in the six-hour period between 10 P.M. and 4 A.M. The available studies using official data on assaults suggest that the majority of these crimes fall within the 6 P.M.–12 A.M. time period (President's Commission on Crime in the District of Columbia, 1966:70; Pokorny, 1965: Fig. 1; Pittman and Handy, 1964:45). Without exception, these studies of robbery, assault, and rape using police data demonstrate that late night and early morning carry the greatest risk of personal victimization. In the eight cities studied here, it was found that 40 percent of the total personal incidents occurred during the six-hour period from 6 P.M. to midnight (Hindelang, 1976:204).

What can the available data tell us about the places in which personal victimizations occur? Studies of robbery have uniformly shown that by far the greatest proportion of robbery incidents take place on the street. For example, Normandeau (1968:244), McClintock and Gibson (1961:130), Reiss (1967:22), Mulvihill, Tumin and Curtis (1969:221), and the President's Commission on Crime in the District of Columbia (1966:66) each found that about one-half of the robbery incidents recorded in police files took place on the street. For assault, similar findings have been reported (Pittman and Handy, 1964: Table 3.3; Reiss, 1967:34; Mulvihill et al., 1969:221), though the dominance of public places as the location of the crime is less than for robbery; in one study (President's Commission on Crime in the District of Columbia, 1966:79) assaults were found to have occurred more often in a residence than on the street (47 versus 37 percent). The results of studies of rapes known to the police indicate that this offense—unlike the crimes of robbery and aggravated assault—is most likely to occur within the residence of the victim or the offender (Amir, 1971:145; MacDonald, 1971:33; Reiss, 1967: 105; Mulvihill et al., 1969:221; Chappell and Singer, 1973:62). However, this finding is tempered by data that show that the most frequent place in which the victim and the offender came into initial contact is the street (Amir, 1971:139; MacDonald, 1971:32).[4]

Victimization survey results are consistent with studies of robbery and assault using official police data. About seven out of ten robberies and one out of two assaults occurred on the street and in other public places (Hindelang, 1976:206). In fact, victimization results indicate that this finding even holds for rape. In 1974, almost half of the rapes reported in the national sample were reported to have occurred on the street or in other open public places, compared to about one-third reported to have occurred inside of a home or other

building (Hindelang, Dunn, Sutton, and Aumick, 1976:356).[5] Overall, these data on personal victimizations suggest that the street and
other public places are the places in which personal victimizations,
especially robberies, are most likely to occur. There is evidence, then,
to support the notion that personal victimizations occur disproportionately at night and in public places.

Proposition 2: *The probability of being in public places, particularly at night, varies as a function of lifestyle.*
In our earlier discussion of lifestyles, we suggested that, as a result
of adaptations to role expectations and structural constraints, particular demographic characteristics are predictive of lifestyle differences. We suggested that younger persons (e.g., adolescents and
young adults) are more likely than older persons to spend time outside of the home. Similarly, we posited that males and single persons
are apt to spend a higher proportion of their time away from home
than their similarly situated counterparts. Also, those whose daily
routines are highly structured by involvement in conventional
vocations (e.g., working or attending school)—although they spend a
relatively high proportion of their time outside of the home—are
more likely than those not involved in conventional vocations (e.g.,
unemployed or school dropout) to spend time in relatively structured, sheltered environments.[6] Finally, we argued that the higher
one's family income, the greater the likelihood that time will be
spent in semiprivate or private environs.
Some data supporting our contentions are available from studies
of how people spend their time. DeGrazia (1961:121–124) found
that away from home leisure activity tends to drop off sharply after
the fifteen to nineteen year old group and then decline slowly, almost
to zero among persons sixty or older; these age-specific differences
were less pronounced for females than for males. Similarly, Chapin
(1974:113) found that young persons and the elderly had more "free
time" than persons in the middle age groups, but the elderly disproportionately spent their free time resting and watching television.
Examining several variables simultaneously, Chapin (1974:144) discovered that "working full time, being a female, and having young
children in the household each put constraints on the amount of
discretionary time available".
How do these demographic characteristics, which we argue are
predictive of lifestyle differences, relate to rates of personal victimization? As noted in Chapters 1 and 5, each of these lifestyle indicators is associated with rates of personal victimization. In the eight
cities, rates of personal victimization are strongly related to *age*

(Table 1-1): those under twenty years of age had a rate of victimization that was three times the rate for those sixty-five years of age or older; to *sex* (Hindelang, 1976: Table 5-5): males had a rate that was 50 percent greater than the rate for females; to *marital status* (Hindelang, 1976: Table 5-7): those who were never married, divorced, or separated had total personal victimization rates that were more than twice as large as the rates for those who were married or widowed; to *vocation* (Figure 5-1): for example, young (sixteen to nineteen years old) males who were not in school had a risk of personal victimization that was 50 percent greater than the risk for young males who were in school, and young (sixteen to nineteen years old) females who were unemployed had a risk of personal victimization that was 50 percent greater than that of young females who were not unemployed; to *family income* (Hindelang, 1976: Table 5-7): there was a trend for rates of personal victimization to decrease as family income increased.

It should be pointed out here that although demographic indicators of lifestyle have been discussed as though they are independent of each other, clearly this is not the case. For example, in the earlier discussion of sex as predictive of lifestyle, it was suggested that sex would appear to be a poorer predictor of lifestyle for older persons than for young adults; that is, as dependent children leave the home and as retirement age approaches, the daily activities of males and females become more similar. The impact on personal victimization rates of this decreasing sex-based differentiation in lifestyles as a function of age was evident in the victimization survey results. In the youngest age groups surveyed (twelve to fifteen and sixteen to nineteen years old), males had a victimization rate that was nearly twice that of females; as age increased, the male-female rate differences decreased until in the sixty-five or older age category the rates of total personal victimization for males and females were virtually identical (Hindelang, 1976: Figure 5-2).[7]

Demands of lifestyle influence where an individual spends time. Those who work have a large portion of their daily activities structured in and around the workplace; those who raise children have a large portion of their time structured in and around the home; those in school have their time structured by school activities. Lifestyle includes not only these structured activities but also how leisure time is typically spent.

Both leisure time and work time activities are shaped by adaptations to structural constraints and role expectations. Earlier it was pointed out that attitudes are an important component of these adaptations. Of particular relevance to our present concern are attitudes about crime. Chapter 8 as well as prior research (Hindelang, 1974b; Ennis, 1967) indicate that fear of crime and victimization are closely linked to respondent characteristics such as age and sex. For example, one of the most frequently asked "fear of crime" questions is: "Is there any area right around here—that is, within a mile—where you would be afraid to walk alone at night?"[8] Responses to this and similar questions consistently indicate that age and sex are both related to fear of crime. Older persons and females are more fearful than younger persons and males, respectively. These differences are especially pronounced when the referent is "on the streets."[9] Such fears would be expected to be translated by the respondent into avoidance of the feared situation whenever possible. The key words in the question quoted in the text above are "area" (i.e., public place), "alone," and "at night." Because these are the very conditions under which victimization is most probable, it follows that those who are fearful of these conditions and who therefore presumably try to avoid them will have a decreased *exposure* to personal victimizations.[10] Behavioral avoidance may be a powerful means of reducing one's likelihood of victimization. As pointed out in Chapter 9, however, such reductions may come about not by complete avoidance of exposure, but by subtle changes in such things as the times and the conditions (e.g., accompanied rather than alone) under which exposure occurs. As discussed in Chapter 8, in conjunction with age and sex, those with the highest levels of fear (older persons and females) have the lowest rates of personal victimization. These findings are quite consistent with the proposition that lifestyle (particularly leisure components), and hence, exposure to situations in which the risk of victimization is high, are shaped by personal attitudes and beliefs.

On the basis of a simultaneous consideration of Propositions 1 and 2, we are postulating that lifestyles are related to the probability of being in places (street, parks, and other public places) at times (especially nighttime) when victimizations are known to occur disproportionately. As will become clear below, lifestyle is related to victimization not only because it correlates with place-time exposure, but for other important reasons as well.

Proposition 3:   *Social contacts and interactions occur disproportionately among individuals who share similar lifestyles.*

Because they are predictive of lifestyle, demographic characteristics—such as family income, race, age, education, and marital status—are indicative of stratification processes that pattern social interactions. Not only are neighborhoods often segregated by race and income, but there are also housing developments and apartment complexes that are often segregated by age and marital status. Working, being in school, keeping house, as well as being unemployed and being a school dropout (routine activities that are a major component of lifestyle), all differ from each other along demographic dimensions.

People who are employed are different demographically from people who are unemployed. The latter are more likely to be younger, have less education, and be black (Executive Office of the President, 1973:113-14). Among the employed, people are more likely to interact with persons of similar socioeconomic statuses—blue collar workers with blue collar workers and white collar workers with white collar workers (Laumann, 1966). Within each of these groups (e.g., blue collar workers), patterns of interactions are likely to be further segregated by race, age, and sex. The interactions to which we refer here include both the formal structured aspects of the job as well as the informal unstructured aspects such as coffee breaks, lunch breaks, and relatively brief social interactions that occur in the process of going between work and home (e.g., stopping at a bar for a drink).

Just as those who are employed differ demographically from those who are not, so too do those in school differ from those of the same age who are not in school. Among those in school, segregation similar to that among workers is also evident. Those in school are obviously segregated by age. In addition, they tend to be segregated by income and race. Even within schools that are heterogeneous, the informal interactions are typically segregated by race, family income, sex, and age. Most of what we have said about those who are employed and those in school can be generalized to the other activities and statuses mentioned earlier.

The demographically segregated social interactions that occur within the structured school and work environs are also in evidence in the less structured social interactions that typically occur during leisure hours. As a result of role expectations and structural constraints, social interactions during leisure hours tend toward demographic homogeneity. Not only are the social interactions themselves segregated along demographic dimensions, but the places and situations in which these interactions occur are markedly different. For example, young single males and older married females might both go out of the home for entertainment during leisure hours, but the places they go are likely to be quite different from each other in the patrons they attract.

One of the consequences of the tendency toward demographically homogeneous social interactions is that criminal offenders have a greater probability of interacting with people who are demographically similar to themselves.

Proposition 4: *An individual's chances of personal victimization are dependent upon the extent to which the individual shares demographic characteristics with offenders.*

Data from the Federal Bureau of Investigation's *Uniform Crime Reports* show that individuals arrested for the personal crimes of interest here—rape, robbery, assault, and larceny—are much more likely (in relation to their representation in the general population) to be male, young, and black than female, old, and white. Data on arrests reported in the UCR for 1975 show that virtually all of those arrested for rape, about 90 percent of those arrested for robbery and aggravated assault, and nearly 70 percent of those arrested for larceny were males (Kelley, 1976:183).[11] About one-half of those arrested for index violent crimes and 60 percent of those arrested for larceny, were between the ages of fourteen and twenty-four (Kelley, 1976: 189), but only one-third of the general population fell into this age group (U.S. Bureau of the Census, 1974:31). The UCR data on race indicate that 31 percent of those arrested for larceny, 40 percent for aggravated assault, 45 percent for rape, and 59 percent for robbery were black (Kelley, 1976:192). For each of these crimes, the representation of blacks among arrestees is substantially above their 11 percent representation in the general population (U.S. Bureau of the Census, 1974b:33).

Data on the residence of the arrestee (e.g., urban versus rural) are not available from the UCR. However, arrest rates—the number of arrests divided by the general population—are available in the UCR for various city size groups. These data indicate that rates of arrest are related to extent of urbanization in much the same way as offense rates are related to extent of urbanization. In 1975, the arrest rate for rape in cities with populations of more than 250,000 was more than twice that in rural areas (21.2 per 100,000 versus 9.9 per 100,000). Similarly, for aggravated assault (163.0 versus 92.7), larceny (589.6 versus 204.6), and particularly robbery (163.1 versus 21.3), the rates of arrest per 100,000 persons in the general population were relatively high in large cities and tended to decrease as the extent of urbanization decreased. These data suggest that urban residence is also a characteristic of offenders, because offenders in personal crimes tend to commit crimes within a short distance of their residence (Turner, 1969; Hoover, 1966:23-27; Normandeau, 1968:249-77).

Although the findings reported above are generally accepted as demonstrating higher rates of offending by males, younger persons, and urban residents in the personal crimes of interest in this book, the findings on race are often questioned on the basis of alleged racial discrimination in the administration of justice (e.g., Quinney, 1970:129-30; Chambliss, 1969:856). In a recent paper (Hindelang, 1978), victimization survey data have been used as a source of information about the race of offenders as reported by victims. These data from the LEAA-Census 1974 national survey indicate that, according to victims' reports, seven out of ten of the offenders in personal larceny victimizations, six out of ten in robbery, four out of ten in rape, and three out of ten in assault are reported by victims to be black. The data, which are not subject to the criticism of reflecting biases in the administration of justice, are in close agreement with the UCR arrest data in showing that in the crimes of rape, robbery, assault, and personal larceny, blacks are substantially overrepresented as offenders in relation to their representation in the general population.

Unfortunately, the UCR arrest data only provide information on the offender's age, race, and sex. Other offender characteristics, however, such as marital status, educational attainment, and income, are available from a variety of other sources. In the National Survey of Jail Inmates conducted by the Bureau of the Census in 1972, it was found that fewer than one-quarter of those being held in jails, as compared to more than 60 percent of those in the general population of males fourteen years of age or older, were married (LEAA, 1977: Table C). This same survey indicated that the median number of years of education for the jail population was two years less than that of the general population of males fourteen years of age or older (ten versus twelve years; LEAA, 1977:Table 4). The income data available from this survey show that 44 percent of the jail inmates had annual incomes in the year prior to arrest and confinement of less than $2,000; this contrasts with 16 percent for males fourteen years of age or older in the general population. Further, only 6 percent of the inmates, but 35 percent of the general population of males fourteen years of age or older, had annual incomes of $10,000 or more (LEAA, 1977:20).[12]

Data available for specific offenses, such as robbery (Normandeau, 1968:ch. 6) and rape (Amir, 1971:ch. 5), are consistent with the profile of offenders conveyed by the jail survey data. In relation to the general population, offenders are less likely to be married and more likely to come from lower status occupations (and inferentially to have lower educational attainment), than the general population.

An earlier work (Hindelang, 1976) examined the joint distributions of victim and offender characteristics for race, sex, and age. These data for total personal incidents indicate that the vast majority of personal victimizations suffered by black/others were committed by black/others; similarly, victimizations suffered by males were committed by males, and those suffered by younger persons were committed by younger persons. Also, offenders with these characteristics were more likely to victimize those with the same characteristics than to victimize those with other characteristics.

To summarize, offenders involved in the types of crimes of interest here are disproportionately male, young, urban residents,[13] black, of lower socioeconomic status, unemployed (and not in school), and unmarried. In our brief review of victim characteristics above, and in earlier chapters, it was seen that victims disproportionately share these characteristics. It is of particular importance to note that when these characteristics are considered simultaneously, they are especially predictive of both rates of offending and rates of victimization. For example, from Figure 5-1 it can be seen that the likelihood of personal victimization for sixteen to nineteen year old males who are not in school was 143 per 1,000—nearly three times the overall likelihood of personal victimization in the eight cities. Data of this kind, which are standardized according to population characteristics, are not generally available in the literature for more than two *offender* characteristics at a time. Normandeau (1968:175) reports such data standardized by age and sex. The overall offending rate for robbery in Philadelphia was 17.7 per 10,000 general population; however, for fifteen to nineteen year olds the rates for males and females, respectively, were 55.6 and 3.1. Further, when race was taken into account, the rates ranged from 218.4 for fifteen to nineteen year old black males to zero for white females of the same age. Although there are some exceptions, the combinations of demographic characteristics that are predictive of offending for the personal crimes studied here are also predictive of victimization for these crimes.

Proposition 5: *The proportion of time that an individual spends among nonfamily members varies as a function of lifestyle.*[14]

Certain lifestyles insulate the individual from contacts with nonfamily members. For example, as children mature from infancy through adolescence, they spend a decreasing proportion of their time with family members. In early adulthood, individuals begin to marry and raise families and, consequently, spend an increasing proportion of time with their family of procreation. Because childrearing responsibilities fall disproportionately on women, the result is that, among those who are married, females spend a greater proportion of their time with family members than do males. Also, as noted in our introductory discussion of lifestyle, as the retirement years approach, contacts outside of the home, and beyond a narrowing circle of close friends and family members, generally decrease. Thus, at the age extremes and among those who are married—particularly those with children—the proportion of time spent with nonfamily members is less than that for persons with other characteristics.

Proposition 6: *The probability of personal victimization, particularly personal theft, increases as a function of the proportion of time that an individual spends among nonfamily members.*

Our discussion regarding the general homogeneity of the victim-offender dyad does not necessarily imply, of course, that victims and offenders are likely to know each other. In fact, the victimization data from the eight cities indicate that four out of five personal victimizations reported to survey interviewers involved strangers as offenders (Hindelang, 1976:Table 7-1).[15] Offenders who were strangers predominated, particularly in theft-related offenses; in robberies, about 90 percent, and in personal larceny, about 95 percent of the victimizations reported to interviewers involved strangers. For assaultive victimizations not involving theft, the proportion of all offenders who were strangers was smaller; about seven out of ten of the rape and assault victimizations were by strangers (Hindelang, 1976:Table 7-1).

Studies using official statistics have repeatedly found that more than four out of five robbery victimizations involve strangers (Mulvihill et al., 1969; Normandeau, 1968; and McClintock and Gibson, 1961). Thus, for robbery, official statistics and victimization survey results are in agreement on this point. The official and victimization data on assault, and to a lesser extent rape, are not in as close agreement. For aggravated assault, Mulvihill et al. (1969) and the President's Commission on Crime in the District of Columbia (1966) report that only one out of five incidents involved offenders who were strangers to the victim. Thus, official data on aggravated assault show a percentage of stranger crimes that is less than one-third the percentage found in victimization survey data. The official data on rape are also at odds—but much less so than the assault data—with victimization survey results. Although the eight-city data show that about 70 percent of rape victimizations were committed by strangers, the percentages of strangers involved in rape victimizations as measured by official statistics reported in the literature range from 42 to 60 percent (Amir, 1971:42 percent; Mulvihill et al., 1969:53 percent; Chappell and Singer, 1973:58 percent; MacDonald, 1971:60 percent).

Reverse record checks can be used to estimate the extent to which differences between official and victimization data in the proportion of "stranger" offenders are method-linked. In such studies, victims are drawn from police files, and (ideally) interviewed in a double-blind design, about victimization during the reference period. These studies—which were limited to "known victims" (i.e., those selected from police files)—indicate that when the offender was a nonstranger, victims were slightly less likely to report aggravated assaults (50 percent versus 56 percent) to survey interviewers than when the offender was a stranger (LEAA, 1972: Appendix Table 5). According to reverse record checks, victimization surveys apparently undercount aggravated assault victimizations by nonstrangers only slightly (in comparison to official data). When an adjustment is made for this differential, victimization survey data still show that strangers predominate substantially as offenders in aggravated assault. Reverse record check results for rape indicate that when police files showed the offender as a stranger, 84 percent of the victimizations were reported to survey interviewers, compared to 54 percent of the nonstranger victimizations. If the victimization survey data are adjusted for this differential, the survey data for the eight cities would indicate that about 64 percent of the rapes were committed by strangers; this compares to an average of 53 percent for the four studies using official rape data cited above.

A point that is more critical to Proposition 6 is that our focus of interest is on nonfamily members rather than on strangers. We have reviewed the cited literature on *strangers* using official data because much of this literature does not report the results for *family members*. Those studies that do permit an examination of the proportion of offenders who are family members indicate that in rape the non-stranger offender is very rarely a family member. Amir (1971:234) reports for rape incidents that although 58 percent of all offenders were nonstrangers, only 2.5 percent of them were relatives of the victim. Similarly, Chappell and Singer (1973:64) found for rape incidents that 42 percent involved nonstrangers, but only 2.8 percent involved family members.[16] Mulvihill et al. (1969:217) found 47 percent nonstrangers and 6.9 percent family members in rape incidents.[17] For aggravated assault, the President's Commission on Crime in the District of Columbia (1966:78) reports that 60 percent of the victims and offenders were previously acquainted, but only 20 percent were relatives. These figures are similar to those for aggravated assault by Mulvihill et al. (1969:287); although only 21 percent of the aggravated assault victims were strangers, only 14 percent were relatives.

The victimization survey results are in close agreement with these official data in showing that a very small proportion of nonstranger offenders are members of the victim's family. In lone offender assaultive victimizations in the eight cities, only 7 percent were committed by family members (Hindelang, 1976: Table 7-2). Data from the national victimization survey indicate that in rape, 4 percent, and in assault, 7 percent of the victimizations involved offenders who were members of the victim's family. For robbery, victimization by family members accounted for fewer than 1 percent of the victimizations (Hindelang, Dunn, Sutton, and Aumick, 1976: Table 3-27).

Rates of personal victimization by age, race, and marital status are consistent with Propositions 5 and 6, jointly considered. In the eight cities, victimization rates increased through adolescence and decreased monotonically thereafter. Among the marital status categories, even when age was controlled, married persons consistently had rates of personal victimization that were about one-half of the rates for those who were not married. Also, regardless of employment status, available data indicate that females spend a larger portion of their time in "personal and family care" than do males (Executive Office of the President, 1973:214).

Proposition 7: *Variations in lifestyle are associated with variations in the ability of individuals to isolate themselves from persons with offender characteristics.*

In our introductory discussion of lifestyles, we indicated that family income, as it reflects economic structural constraints facing an individual, is an important determinant of lifestyle for a variety of reasons. Among the important consequences of family income are where one lives, how one lives, and with whom one comes into contact. Poor people have little choice about these matters; if the situation is undesirable in any respect, those in poverty have little choice but to cope. Greater family income provides flexibility to move one's place of residence from a less desirable to a more desirable location; to use private (e.g., personal automobiles) or more expensive (e.g., taxicabs, commuter trains, and airplanes) modes of transportation rather than inexpensive public modes of transportation; to change jobs; to have access to private environs for recreation; and to live in apartments and homes with elaborate security measures (e.g., security guards, video surveillance, and burglar alarms). Each of these concomitants of higher income has the effect of isolating the individual from exposure to persons with offender characteristics. Our review of offender characteristics under Proposition 4 indicates that the crimes of common theft and assault are simply much less often *com-*

mitted by those who can make these choices—that is, to live in exclusive suburbs, to ride commuter trains, and to go to the mountains for a weekend. Those with offender characteristics are much more likely to spend their time in core urban areas, to walk or to ride public transportation, and to be restricted to public places for recreation.

The flexibility that family income provides to make these choices in not independent of race. Because of de facto segregated housing patterns, higher income blacks do not have the same flexibility as higher income whites; that is, racial barriers are structural constraints that further limit the behavioral options of blacks. Sections of urban areas in which blacks are concentrated are more heterogeneous in family income than are areas in which whites are concentrated (Taeuber, 1968; Erbe, 1975). Further, the private clubs and environs that are open to higher income whites may be inhospitable or simply closed to blacks. As a result, blacks with incomes equal to those of whites are, in fact, less insulated from those with offender characteristics. All of this suggests that even when family income is controlled, blacks will have a higher rate of personal victimization than whites.

When rates of personal victimization in the eight cities are examined by race and family income, both racial groups showed generally decreasing rates as income increased. This pattern was slightly stronger for whites than for black/others (Hindelang, 1976; Table 5-6). When victimizations were weighted according to seriousness as measured by the Sellin-Wolfgang (1964) scale, the pattern was even more clear. The seriousness-weighted rate for whites in the less than $3,000 category was 70 percent greater than that for whites in the $15,000-24,999 category. For black/others, the rate for those in the lowest income category was 60 percent greater than that for black/others in the $15,000-24,999 category.[18] Furthermore, within each income category, the seriousness-weighted rate of personal victimization was greater, generally about 15 percent, for black/others than for whites (Hindelang, 1976: Table 6-5).

Variations in lifestyle are associated with variations in the ability to isolate oneself from persons with offender characteristics not only because family income affects lifestyle but also because the nature of the vocational activity in which an individual is involved—an important component of lifestyle—itself affects the freedom to isolate oneself from persons with offender characteristics. This vocationally linked potential for isolation is largely independent of income. Those who are students or employed outside of the home, although they are relatively insulated from personal victimization by the formal structure of their vocations once they are "on the job," nonetheless are exposed coming from, and going to, school or work. Those whose vocational activities do not demand that they be in particular places outside of the home at particular times have the ability to isolate themselves to a degree that those involved in vocations that have definite time and place demands do not. Those who are keeping house, retired, or unemployed can, within limits, control whether and when they will leave the relative security of their homes and expose themselves to those with offender characteristics. If she chooses, a housewife fearful of purse snatchers can shop during the day when many potential offenders are not on the streets. Similarly, retired couples need not go out after dark, because they are free to do what they wish to do or must do in public during safer daytime hours. Of course, the *freedom* to choose to isolate oneself from those with offender characteristics does not mean that that choice will be exercised; those who are unemployed have the same freedom to remain in the home and thus to isolate themselves from those with offender characteristics as do retired people and those keeping house. However, the unemployed are disproportionately young, male, poor, and urban, and ethnographic studies indicate that a great deal of their free time is spent on the street in interaction with others who have similar characteristics (Whyte, 1943; Liebow, 1967; Horton, 1972).

Proposition 8: *Variations in lifestyle are associated with variations in the convenience, the desirability, and vincibility of the person as a target for personal victimizations.*

In the preceding seven propositions we have dealt with the implications of lifestyle for potential victims in terms of their exposure to high risk situations. Proposition 8 is concerned with the offender's perception of potential victims. Throughout our discussion of lifestyle, we have repeatedly emphasized the importance of *exposure* to persons with offender characteristics—particularly to persons who are nonfamily members—in public places during nighttime hours. One reason that this is important, we believe, is that the convenience of the victim as a target is a prime concern to the offender. From the offender's perspective, it is *convenient* to wait for a potential victim to come to a place (at a time) that is suitable to the offender for victimization. Public places, such as the streets and parks, offer the offender opportunities to victimize persons who have virtually no effective defensible space. Further, a patient offender can select from among potential victims a person who is most appropriate for the contemplated offense. Because these areas are public, if the victimization can be committed during times when these public places are less heavily traveled, the chances of observation or of intervention by another on the victim's behalf can be minimized. Although some robbery offenders engage, in effect, in door-to-door robberies (Reppetto, 1974), it is clear that from the offender's perspective, selection of targets in this way is extremely inconvenient. In such residential robberies, the offender approaches the victim within the victim's defensible space, in which the number of persons in the residence at the time of the robbery is unknown, in which the characteristics of the victim(s) (e.g., sex, age, and physical stature) may not be known, and in which the victim's access to weapons is increased.

The available literature suggests that offenders tend to commit their crimes within short distances of their residences (Hoover, 1966; Turner, 1969; Reiss, 1967; Normandeau, 1968; Amir, 1971). Amir (1971: Table 31) reports, for example, that seven out of ten of the rapes he studied for which the requisite location data were available were committed within the "vicinity" (five blocks) of the offender's residence. Normandeau (1968) reports that the median distance from the residence of Philadelphia robbers to the location of the robbery was 0.95 miles for juvenile offenders and 1.14 miles for adult offenders. From such data, it follows that those who live in or are frequent visitors to areas in which those with offender characteristics reside—that is, individuals who are convenient potential targets—have an increased risk of personal victimization. This helps to explain the finding that those who are among the least affluent (e.g., poor blacks) have the highest rate of personal theft victimization (Hindelang, 1976: Table 5-6).

The convenience of the target may also be a factor in assaults. Among those who are known to each other, the daily frustrations of living and the frictions that often arise among persons who are known to each other may combine with the result that a period of friction can trigger an aggressive outburst. The aggressor may have been "primed" for the outburst as frustration built up over time. A precipitating event—one that in the absence of the pent up frustration may have passed without incident—results in a convenient target (someone close to the aggressor) being the recipient of the aggression. In a similar way, a victim with no prior relationship with the offender can become a target of convenience in public places.

From the offender's perspective, not all individuals are equally *desirable* targets. In theft-motivated offenses, the apparent affluence of the potential victim may be an important consideration weighed by the offender. Another way that a potential victim's lifestyle influences the offender's perception of that person as a desirable target is whether the offender believes that the person is likely to report the crime to the police. For example, the lifestyles of some persons may occasionally place them in situations that involve violations of legal or other norms (e.g., visiting a prostitute, purchasing drugs, or seeking out a homosexual partner). In such situations, offenders may believe that the person would not report being robbed or assaulted out of fear of revealing the initial illegal involvement. Similarly, school-aged children may be desirable targets for assaults and thefts committed by other adolescents due to peer pressures not to inform the police.

The third component of Proposition 8 is *vincibility*. A person's vincibility to personal victimization increases to the extent that the potential victim is seen by the offender as less able to resist the offender successfully. Persons who are unaccompanied or under the influence of drugs or alcohol are relatively vincible to personal victimization. Although no "at risk" data are available regarding the probability of victimization for those who are alone versus those who are in the company of others when a potential offender is encountered, victimization survey results indicate that, in the eight cities, when personal incidents did occur, about nine out of ten victims were alone; only one out of fifty victims was accompanied by two or more persons (Hindelang, 1976:207). It seems reasonable to suppose that offenders will select lone victims in preference to accompanied victims because the former are liable to be less able and willing to resist; furthermore, the fewer the victims, the less likely it is that the offender will be subsequently identified. In our earlier discussion of lifestyles, we suggested that certain individuals—particularly young, single males—are more likely to be alone in public places. Also, the attitude data presented in Chapter 8 indicate that young males are nearly four times more likely than young females to say that they feel very safe about being out alone in their neighborhoods at night (Table 8-2). Of course, as the number of offenders increases, it becomes more feasible to confront multiple victims. It is interesting to note that although only one out of ten personal incidents in the eight cities involved multiple *victims*, nearly half of the personal incidents involved multiple *offenders*.

In addition to the vincibility indicator of number of victims, the sobriety of the potential victim is another indicator of vincibility. If a potential victim appears to be unable to resist and/or to provide the police with a description of the offender, then that person's apparent vincibility increases the likelihood of personal victimization. It is likely that variables predictive of lifestyle—particularly sex and socioeconomic status indicators—are related to the probability of being in a public place while intoxicated.

A NOTE ON VICTIM PRECIPITATION

One aspect of personal victimization that has had a prominent place in American criminological literature on aggressive crimes is that of victim precipitation. According to Wolfgang (1958:252):

> The term *victim-precipitated* is applied to those criminal homicides in which the victim is a direct, positive precipitator in the crime. The role of the victim is characterized by his having been the first in the homicide drama to use physical force directed against his subsequent slayer. The *victim-precipitated* cases are those in which the victim was the first to show and use a deadly weapon, to strike a blow in an altercation—in short, the first to commence the interplay or resort to physical violence.

A similar notion is embodied in Toch's typology of violent activity, which "is intended as a catalogue of ways of relating to people which carry a high probability of degenerating into contact of an aggressive nature" (Toch, 1969:135).

Compatible with these conceptions of victim precipitation is the notion that individuals and subcultural groups may subscribe to a set of values that result in an increased willingness to exhibit defiant or aggressive reactions to a wide range of stimuli. Wolfgang (1958:188) has pointed out that "the significance of a jostle, a slightly derogatory remark, or the appearance of a weapon in the hand of an adversary are stimuli differentially perceived and interpreted . . . ." These differential perceptions and interpretations can be expected to vary as a function of race, sex, age, and socioeconomic status. Wolfgang and Ferracuti's (1967) subculture of violence thesis postulates that such propensities are disproportionately found among young, black, lower-class males. In connection with assaultive crimes, such propensities on the part of the victim may serve to precipitate an event that might otherwise have not occurred or to escalate the level of violence in an event that otherwise would have been less violent.

Although the victimization survey results contain no information on victimizations that may have been victim-precipitated, the data presented in Chapter 3 do indicate that the rate of injury to victims is substantially greater for those victims who used a physical force self-protective measure than for those victims who did not (Figure 3-1). The victimization results in the eight cities show that males were more likely than females and younger persons more likely than older persons to use physical force self-protective measures; however, no race effects were found (Hindelang, 1976:260). Regardless of the tenability of the subculture of violence thesis, it seems reasonable to postulate that the propensity to precipitate or escalate violent victimization is not uniformly distributed among members of society.

Although a notion such as propensity to precipitate or escalate is implicitly subsumed in our model as a possible individual and/or subcultural adaptation to role expectation and structural constraints, we have not discussed this particular adaptation in our general presentation of the model. Because such a propensity is only one of a variety of possible specific adaptations, we believed that to have displayed it in the model in Figure 11.1 would have given to it undue prominence, perhaps to the exclusion of other important adaptations that are less widely discussed in the literature. In addition, propensity to precipitate or escalate—although it has been discussed and investigated by Normandeau (1968:286–92) in connection with robbery—does not, we believe, have applicability to the vast majority of theft-motivated offenses. It should be stressed that although some adaptations, such as propensity to precipitate, result in an increased likelihood of victimization, our model is equally concerned with common adaptations that decrease the likelihood of victimization. For example, adaptations to the role expectations of parenthood and the constraints of family structure lead to a lifestyle that involves spending more time with family members in the home and therefore decreases the exposure to high risk victimization situations.

INTERDEPENDENCE OF PROPOSITIONS

In this presentation of the lifestyle/exposure model of personal victimization, we have refrained from using the phrase "other things being equal." It should be clear, however, from the propositions themselves, that we have been generally discussing zero-order effects. This in no way implies, of course, that the propositions are independent in their effects on the likelihood of personal victimization. For example, the most desirable targets for theft-motivated crimes, as discussed in Proposition 8 (e.g., the affluent) may simultaneously be the individuals who are least likely to spend time in public places (Proposition 2). Predictions about victimization risks can be derived from a given proposition only when the other propositions are taken into account. Obviously, it would be easier to test this theoretical model if the propositions were independent of each other. This is especially true in light of the fact that many of the data required to operationalize the propositions adequately are not readily available. Unfortunately, the phenomenon of personal victimization, as is the case with most social phenomena, is sufficiently complex to preclude univariate explanations or multivariate explanations in which the critical dimensions are assumed to be orthogonal.

SOME EXPECTATIONS FROM
THE MODEL

In the course of discussing the individual propositions, we pointed to readily available research findings that are compatible with our life-style/exposure model. In addition, there are important expectations that can be derived from this model for which data are not as readily available. We believe that it would be helpful in explicating the model further to give brief attention to illustrations of some of these expectations.[19]

Our model suggests that as sex role expectations become increasingly less differentiated and sex-linked structural barriers become less rigid, with a corresponding convergence of the adaptations and life-styles of males and females, rates of victimization for males and females will tend to converge. This is true primarily for two reasons. First, females generally will increase their exposure to nonfamily members, and hence their victimization rate should increase relative to the male rate. Second, if the *offending* rate among females increases, as some have suggested it will (Adler, 1975:251-52), then the lifestyle/exposure model predicts that females will have higher rates of victimization than would otherwise be expected. This is so because an offender characteristic (sex) would be shifting toward a characteristic of these individuals (female); according to Proposition 4, the more similar an individual's characteristics to those of offenders, the greater the chance of victimization.

To the extent that cohabitation outside of marriage continues to increase, we would expect that marital status will become less predictive of victimization. That is, persons who are not married (e.g., "single") but who are cohabiting will have adopted to some extent lifestyles that are normally associated with marriage. This would be especially true to the extent that cohabiting and married couples are equally likely to incur childrearing responsibilities.

The lifestyle/exposure model also suggests that to the extent that trends toward age segregation in housing patterns increase, rates of personal victimization among age groups will diverge; conversely, to the extent that housing arrangements become age-heterogeneous, rates of victimization among age groups will tend toward convergence. We are not suggesting, of course, that in an age-heterogeneous setting, variations in rates of personal victimization across age groups would not exist; there are too many other factors that affect differential likelihoods of victimization by age.

A society that is fully integrated—in terms of housing patterns, lifestyles, and patterns of personal interactions with regard to such dimensions as race, socioeconomic status, age, sex, etc.—would likely be relatively homogeneous with respect to many important social consequences, including criminal victimization. Conversely, to the extent that patterns of interaction occur more within race-age-sex clusters, rates of victimization for demographic subgroups can, on the basis of our model, be expected to diverge, provided that there are demographic correlates of offending behavior.

SUGGESTIONS FOR ADDITIONAL RESEARCH

There are a number of areas in which further research could have a bearing on our model in terms of refining, confirming, or falsifying portions of it. Some of these were mentioned in our discussion of the limitations of the NCS questionnaire in Chapter 10, but they will be repeated here in an attempt to draw together a group of suggestions for future research.

1. We defined lifestyle in terms of routine vocational and leisure activities. These activities are predictive of when, where, and with whom persons spend their time. Obviously, direct measures of these factors would be invaluable. There has already been a good deal of research in the realm of time budgeting that examines the spatial and temporal distribution of the subject's activities (cf. Chapin, 1974). The specific time, place, and activity categories used in prior time-budgeting research could be modified and used in a study that would yield information about lifestyle that is particularly relevant to the exposure to victimivation risk. If such direct measures of exposure were found to be unrelated to personal victimization, or if demographic characteristics were still found to be substantially related to personal victimization after such refined measures of exposure were controlled, then the model would be untenable as currently postulated.

2. In conjunction with the first suggestion, more information is needed about lifestyle variations within gross categories of major activity. For example, in this chapter we referred generally to persons employed outside the home, in contrast to homemakers, unemployed persons, retired persons, and so forth. But there are certainly variations within these categories—for example, related to *type* of occupation—that have major ramifications for lifestyle. For example, do those whose occupations involve work in public places have higher rates of personal victimization than those who work in private places?

3. To complement more specific information about the lifestyles of potential victims, more complete information about the locales of

victimizations are needed. In this work, we have been dealing with general locales such as "public places," but more specificity in our knowledge of high-risk locales would allow a more precise mapping of lifestyle variations to variations in exposure. If more detailed information about the locales of victimization were available, our model could be tested more precisely. It would have to be found that people with lifestyles that place them disproportionately in these specific types of public places where personal victimizations are likely to occur have higher victimization rates than do others.

4. In relation to victimization events, there is also a need for data about factors that immediately preceded the victimization (e.g., were the victim and offender drinking together in a bar?) and for more detailed information about the victim-offender relationship (e.g., was the offender a co-worker, a fellow student, a rival gang member?). Data of these sorts would be helpful for understanding the links between lifestyle and victimization, especially through the mechanism that was labeled "associations" in Figure 11-1.

5. Among the adaptations to role expectations and structural constraints that were identified were particular attitudes and response sets, such as the fear of crime and the propensity to precipitate or escalate violence. Further research is needed to determine how these adaptations are incorporated into individual lifestyles and how they, thereby, effect the likelihood and nature of personal victimization.

6. The theoretical model that has been postulated is grounded in cross-sectional research. Many of the important linkages in the model, however, can only be tested adequately with longitudinal data. As role expectations change according to the increasing age of the individual, do changing adaptations in fact result in lifestyle shifts that affect exposure and hence the probability of victimizations? Similar questions could be posed with respect to changes in marital status and income. As noted in Chapter 8, longitudinal data are also required to disentangle the time-dependent relationships among fear of crime, personal limiting of behaviors, and likelihood of victimization.

7. One test of our model would be in the realm of comparative research. That is, are the postulated mechanisms applicable under varying sets of role expectations and structural constraints that could be identified in cross-cultural research?

CONCLUDING REMARKS

The theoretical model that has been proposed grows primarily out of our research during the past four years on victimization survey results. Although the data and the theoretical model presented in this book deal with personal victimization, in prior research we have closely examined the correlates of household victimization—burglary, household larceny, and vehicle theft. We believe that with modifications the lifestyle/exposure model has some applicability to household victimization, primarily because lifestyles that disproportionately result in individuals being in public places also tend disproportionately to leave the households of those persons unoccupied and hence more vulnerable to household victimization. For example, age of head of household is inversely related to rates of household victimization; the lifestyles of younger persons which bring them into public places simultaneously tend disproportionately to expose their homes to household victimization. We are, however, pessimistic about the applicability of this model to victimization by corporate crime, white collar crime, and consumer fraud.

This lifestyle/exposure model of personal victimization has evolved as a result of a grounded theoretical approach. Although there are major advantages to a grounded approach to theory construction, there are some substantial shortcomings as well. Among the advantages are an intimate familiarity with the empirical patterns in the data, an empirical stance toward the concepts and indicators that are developed, and an appreciation for some of the measurement limitations inherent in the data. On the other hand, the greatest dangers are that grounded theory may be limited to ex post facto interpretation of the data and may not achieve a sufficiently high level of abstraction and generality. On balance, the advantages of a grounded theoretical approach seem to outweigh the disadvantages and such an approach has the greatest potential for advancing knowledge and explanations of social phenomena such as criminal victimization.

The lifestyle/exposure model is but a preliminary step toward an adequate explanation of personal victimization. Our own research will focus on testing, reformulating, and refining this theoretical model. To the extent that the model stimulates additional empirical and theoretical work on the part of others, it will have served an important function.

NOTES

1. Throughout this chapter, our intent is to construct a theoretical model of the personal victimizations discussed in this book—rape, assault, robbery, and personal larceny. Although the model has some implications for household, business, and other forms of victimization, our discussion is not specifically designed to address these types of victimizations.

2. We are not arguing that behavior is completely determined by role expec-

tations and social structure. The constraints imposed by these factors delimit a range of behaviors from which even conforming members of society can choose. In addition, the individual can, with varying degrees of risk and success, resist or rebel against the constraints. Our argument is that the constraints do act to produce typical ways of behaving.

3. This differentiation is similar to the one used by Becker (1963:31-35) in his designation of "master statuses."

4. MacDonald includes only stranger-to-stranger rapes in reporting this finding. Chappell and Singer (1973) found that in New York, the most frequent place of initial contact between the victim and the offender was a residence.

5. Part of the discrepancy between the official and victimization results is attributable to the greater proportion of rapes in police data committed by non-strangers. When the victim and the offender are known to each other, victimization survey data show that the rape is most likely to occur inside of a home or other building (Hindelang, Dunn, Sutton, and Aumick, 1976:356).

6. There are, of course, some vocations—such as police officer and taxi driver—in which time on the job is not generally spent within a structured, sheltered setting.

7. We suggested earlier that for preadolescents, lifestyles would not be as differentiated by sex as among young and middle-aged adults. Although the victimization survey did not collect data for children under twelve years of age, our theory predicts that the male-female rates for these children would be more similar than those for young and middle-aged adults.

8. See generally, Chapter 2, Hindelang, Gottfredson, Dunn and Parisi (1977).

9. In addition to the question quoted in the text, the question, "Compared to a year ago, do you personally feel more afraid and uneasy on the streets today, less uneasy, or not much different than you felt a year ago?" has also been asked. For males 59 percent and for females 73 percent felt more uneasy. Within each sex group, the percentage tended to increase with age (Hindelang, Dunn, Aumick and Sutton, 1975:173).

10. We will discuss the victimizations of "lone" persons below.

11. The UCR larceny category includes larcenies from stores and homes, which are not counted as personal larcenies by the definition used in this book. Similarly, the UCR robbery category includes robberies of commercial establishments, which do not fall within the definition of personal robbery used herein.

12. Some of these data are also presented in Hindelang, Gottfredson, Dunn, and Parisi (1977: Tables 6-6, 6-9, 6-11).

13. In this book we have reported victimization data for urban areas only. Victimization results from the NCS national survey indicate that rates of personal victimization are positively associated with the extent of urbanization. See Hindelang, Gottfredson, Dunn, and Parisi (1977:368).

14. In our usage here, "family" refers to the extended family.

15. "Stranger" here includes persons whom the victim had never seen before, were known by sight only, or about whom the victim did not know whether or not they were strangers. When multiple offenders were involved in the victimization, if the victim did not know any of them, they were classified as strangers.

16. Chappell and Singer report that for 19 percent of their cases the victim-offender relationship was unknown.

17. It is possible that "rapes" by family members that come to the attention of the police are sometimes categorized as other crimes such as incest or child abuse. In addition, "rapes" by spouses probably do not generally appear in police files as rapes, because in most jurisdictions such events do not meet the legal criteria of rape.

18. In the $25,000 or more income category among black/others, the rate was higher than that for all other income categories except those under $7,500. However, fewer than 1 percent of the black/others in the eight cities had incomes of $25,000 or more; nearly three out of five black/others had incomes below $7,500.

19. Unless otherwise noted, in these illustrations we will be assuming that patterns of offender characteristics remain constant.

 *Appendix A*

National Crime Survey, Central Cities Sample Questionnaires

O.M.B. No. 41-S72036; Approval Expires June 30, 1974

FORM **NCS-3**
(4-25-72)

U.S. DEPARTMENT OF COMMERCE
SOCIAL AND ECONOMIC STATISTICS ADMINISTRATION
BUREAU OF THE CENSUS

NATIONAL CRIME SURVEY

CENTRAL CITIES SAMPLE

BASIC SCREEN QUESTIONNAIRE

Control number

PSU	Serial	Panel	Household	Segment

1. Interviewer identification

(010) Code | Name

2. Record of interview

(011) Line number of household respondent | Date completed

3. Reason for noninterview (cc 29d)

TYPE A

Reason

(012)
1 ☐ No one home
2 ☐ Temporarily absent – *Return date*_____
3 ☐ Refused
4 ☐ Other Occ. – *Specify* _____

Race of head

(013)
1 ☐ White
2 ☐ Negro
3 ☐ Other

TYPE B

(014)
1 ☐ Vacant – Regular
2 ☐ Vacant – Storage of HH furniture
3 ☐ Temporarily occupied by persons with URE
4 ☐ Unfit or to be demolished
5 ☐ Under construction, not ready
6 ☐ Converted to temporary business or storage
7 ☐ Occupied entirely by Armed Forces members
8 ☐ Unoccupied tent site or trailer site
9 ☐ Permit granted, construction not started
10 ☐ Other – *Specify* ➚

TYPE C

(015)
1 ☐ Unused line of listing sheet
2 ☐ Demolished
3 ☐ House or trailer moved
4 ☐ Outside segment
5 ☐ Converted to permanent business or storage
6 ☐ Merged
7 ☐ Condemned
8 ☐ Built after April 1, 1970
9 ☐ Other – *Specify* ➚

TYPE Z

Interview not obtained for—

Line number

(016) _____
(017) _____
(018) _____
(019) _____

4. Household status

(020)
1 ☐ Same household as last enumeration
2 ☐ Replacement household since last enumeration
3 ☐ Previous noninterview or not in sample before

5. Special place type code (cc 6c)

(021) _____

6. Tenure (cc 8)

(022)
1 ☐ Owned or being bought
2 ☐ Rented for cash
3 ☐ No cash rent

7. Type of living quarters (cc 15)

Housing Unit

(023)
1 ☐ House, apartment, flat
2 ☐ HU in nontransient hotel, motel, etc.
3 ☐ HU — Permanent in transient hotel, motel, etc.
4 ☐ HU in rooming house
5 ☐ Mobile home or trailer
6 ☐ HU not specified above — *Describe* ➚

OTHER UNIT

7 ☐ Quarters not HU in rooming or boarding house
8 ☐ Unit not permanent in transient hotel, motel, etc.
9 ☐ Vacant tent site or trailer site
10 ☐ Not specified above— *Describe* ➚

8. Number of housing units in structure (cc 26)

(024)
1 ☐ 1
2 ☐ 2
3 ☐ 3
4 ☐ 4
5 ☐ 5–9
6 ☐ 10 or more
7 ☐ Mobile home or trailer

▶ *ASK IN EACH HOUSEHOLD:*

9. (Other than the . . . business) does anyone in this household operate a business from this address?

(025)
1 ☐ No
2 ☐ Yes — **What kind of business is that?** ➚

10. Family income (cc 27)

(026)
1 ☐ Under $1,000
2 ☐ $1,000 to 1,999
3 ☐ 2,000 to 2,999
4 ☐ 3,000 to 3,999
5 ☐ 4,000 to 4,999
6 ☐ 5,000 to 5,999
7 ☐ 6,000 to 7,499
8 ☐ $ 7,500 to 9,999
9 ☐ 10,000 to 11,999
10 ☐ 12,000 to 14,999
11 ☐ 15,000 to 19,999
12 ☐ 20,000 to 24,999
13 ☐ 25,000 and over

11. Household members 12 years of age and OVER _____→

(027) Total number _____

12. Household members UNDER 12 years of age →

(028) 0 ☐ None

13. Crime Incident Reports filled _____→

(029) 0 ☐ None

CENSUS USE ONLY

(030) | (031) | (032) | (033)

PERSONAL CHARACTERISTICS

14. NAME (of household respondent)	15. TYPE OF INTER-VIEW	16. LINE NUMBER (cc 12)	17. RELATIONSHIP TO HOUSEHOLD HEAD (cc 13b)	18. AGE LAST BIRTH-DAY (cc 17)	19. MARITAL STATUS (cc 18)	20. RACE (cc 19)	21. SEX (cc 20)	22. ARMED FORCES MEMBER (cc 21)	23. What is the highest grade (or year) of regular school you have ever attended? (ASK for persons 12–24 yrs. Transcribe for 25 + yrs.) (cc 22)	24. Did you com-plete that year? (cc23)
KEYER–BEGIN NEW RECORD (034)	(035)	(036)		(037)	(038)	(039)	(040)	(041)	(042)	(043)
Last	1 ☐ Per		1 ☐ Head		1 ☐ Married	1 ☐ Wh.	1 ☐ M	1 ☐ Yes	00 ☐ Never attended or kindergarten	1 ☐ Yes
	2 ☐ Tel	____	2 ☐ Wife of head		2 ☐ Widowed	2 ☐ Neg.	2 ☐ F	2 ☐ No	____ Elem. (01–08)	2 ☐ No
	3 ☐ NI –		3 ☐ Own child		3 ☐ Divorced	3 ☐ Oth.			____ H.S. (09–12)	
First	Fill 16–21		4 ☐ Other relative		4 ☐ Separated				____ College (21–26+)	
			5 ☐ Non-relative		5 ☐ Never Mar.					

CHECK ITEM A ▶ Look at item 4 on cover page. Is this the same household as last enumeration? (Box 1 marked)
☐ Yes – SKIP to 26a   ☐ No

(044) 25a. Did you live in this house on April 1, 1970?
1 ☐ Yes – SKIP to 26a   2 ☐ No

b. Where did you live on April 1, 1970? (State, foreign country, U.S. possession, etc.)

State, etc. _____

County _____

(045) c. Did you live inside the limits of a city, town, village, etc.?
1 ☐ No   2 ☐ Yes – Name of city, town, village, etc. ⬏

(046) ☐☐☐☐ _____

(047) d. Were you in the Armed Forces on April 1, 1970?
1 ☐ Yes   2 ☐ No

Ask 26–28 for persons 16 years or older

(048) 26a. What were you doing most of LAST WEEK – working, keeping house, going to school, or something else?
1 ☐ Working – SKIP to 28a   6 ☐ Unable to work – SKIP to 28a
2 ☐ With a job but not at work   7 ☐ Retired
3 ☐ Looking for work   8 ☐ Other – Specify ⬏
4 ☐ Keeping house
5 ☐ Going to school

b. Did you do any work at all LAST WEEK, not counting work around the house? (Note: If farm or business operator in HH, ask about unpaid work.)
(049) 1 ☐ Yes – SKIP to 28a   2 ☐ No

c. Did you have a job or business from which you were temporarily absent or on layoff LAST WEEK?
(050) 1 ☐ Yes – SKIP to 28a   2 ☐ No

(051) 26d. Have you been looking for work during the past 4 weeks?
1 ☐ Yes   2 ☐ No – SKIP to 28a

27. Is there any reason why you could not take a job LAST WEEK?
(052) 1 ☐ No   Yes ➔   2 ☐ Already has a job
3 ☐ Temporary illness
4 ☐ Going to school
5 ☐ Other – Specify ⬏

Description of job or business (Current or most recent)
28a. For whom did you work? (Name of company, business, organization, or other employer)

(053) x ☐ Never worked – SKIP to 29

b. What kind of business or industry is this? (For example: TV and radio mfg., retail shoe store, State Labor Department, farm)

(054) _____

c. Were you –
(055) 1 ☐ An employee of a PRIVATE company, business or individual for wages, salary or commissions?
2 ☐ A GOVERNMENT employee (Federal, State, county or local)?
3 ☐ SELF EMPLOYED in OWN business, professional practice or farm?
4 ☐ Working WITHOUT PAY in family business or farm?

d. What kind of work were you doing? (For example: electrical engineer, stock clerk, typist, farmer)

(056) _____

e. What were your most important activities or duties? (For example: typing, keeping account books, selling cars, finishing concrete, etc.)

Notes

HOUSEHOLD SCREEN QUESTIONS		

29. Now I'd like to ask some questions about crime. They refer only to the last 12 months – between _____ 1st and _____ . During the last 12 months, did anyone break into or somehow illegally get into your (apartment/home), garage, or another building on your property?

☐ No
☐ Yes – How many times? ⟶ _____

30. (Other than the incident(s) just mentioned) Did you find a door jimmied, a lock forced, or any other signs of an ATTEMPTED break in?

☐ No
☐ Yes – How many times? ⟶ _____

31. Was anything at all stolen that is kept outside your home, or happened to be left out, such as a bicycle, a garden hose, or lawn furniture? (other than any incidents already mentioned)

☐ No
☐ Yes – How many times? ⟶ _____

32. Did anyone take something belonging to you or to any member of this household, from a place where you or they were temporarily staying, such as a friend's or relative's home, a hotel or motel, or a vacation home?

☐ No
☐ Yes – How many times? ⟶ _____

33. What was the total number of motor vehicles (cars, trucks, etc.) owned by you or any other member of this household during the last 12 months?

(057) 0 ☐ None – *SKIP to 36*
1 ☐ 1
2 ☐ 2
3 ☐ 3
4 ☐ 4 or more

34. Did anyone steal, TRY to steal, or use (it/any of them) without permission?

☐ No
☐ Yes – How many times? ⟶ _____

35. Did anyone steal or TRY to steal part of (it/any of them), such as a battery, hubcaps, tape-deck, etc.?

☐ No
☐ Yes – How many times? ⟶ _____

INDIVIDUAL SCREEN QUESTIONS		

36. The following questions refer only to things that happened to you during the last 12 months –between _____ 1st and _____ . Did you have your (pocket picked/purse snatched)?

☐ Yes – How many times?
☐ No
_____

37. Did anyone take something (else) directly from you by using force, such as by a stickup, mugging or threat?

☐ Yes – How many times?
☐ No
_____

38. Did anyone TRY to rob you by using force or threatening to harm you? (other than any incidents already mentioned)

☐ Yes – How many times?
☐ No
_____

39. Did anyone beat you up, attack you or hit you with something, such as a rock or bottle? (other than any incidents already mentioned)

☐ Yes – How many times?
☐ No
_____

40. Were you knifed, shot at, or attacked with some other weapon by anyone at all? (other than any incidents already mentioned)

☐ Yes – How many times?
☐ No
_____

41. Did anyone THREATEN to beat you up or THREATEN you with a knife, gun, or some other weapon, NOT including telephone threats? (other than any incidents already mentioned)

☐ Yes – How many times?
☐ No
_____

42. Did anyone TRY to attack you in some other way? (other than any incidents already mentioned)

☐ Yes – How many times?
☐ No
_____

43. During the last 12 months, did anyone steal things that belonged to you from inside any car or truck, such as packages or clothing?

☐ Yes – How many times?
☐ No
_____

44. Was anything stolen from you while you were away from home, for instance at work, in a theater or restaurant, or while traveling?

☐ Yes – How many times?
☐ No
_____

45. (Other than any incidents you've already mentioned) Was anything (else) stolen from you during the last 12 months?

☐ Yes – How many times?
☐ No
_____

46. Did you find any evidence that someone ATTEMPTED to steal something that belonged to you? (other than any incidents already mentioned)

☐ Yes – How many times?
☐ No
_____

47. Did you call the police during the last 12 months to report something that happened to you which you thought was a crime? (Do not count any calls made to the police concerning the incidents you have just told me about.)

☐ No   ☐ Yes – What happened?

_____

(058) ☐☐
_____
☐☐
_____
☐☐

INTERVIEWER – Was HH member 12+ attacked or threatened, or was something stolen or an attempt made to steal something that belonged to him?

☐ No   ☐ Yes – How many times? ⟶ _____

48. Did anything happen to you during the last 12 months which you thought was a crime, but did NOT report to the police?

☐ No   ☐ Yes – What happened?

_____

(059) ☐☐
_____
☐☐
_____
☐☐

INTERVIEWER – Was HH member 12+ attacked or threatened, or was something stolen or an attempt made to steal something that belonged to him?

☐ No   ☐ Yes – How many times? ⟶ _____

CHECK ITEM B ▶ Did you receive all "No's" to the Screen Questions asked of this respondent?

☐ Yes – Ask questions for next HH member on following page. End interview if last respondent.
☐ No – Fill Crime Incident Reports

Page 3

PERSONAL CHARACTERISTICS

14. NAME	15. TYPE OF INTER- VIEW	16. LINE NUMBER (cc 12)	17. RELATIONSHIP TO HOUSEHOLD HEAD (cc13b)	18. AGE LAST BIRTH- DAY (cc 17)	19. MARITAL STATUS (cc 18)	20. RACE (cc 19)	21. SEX (cc 20)	22. ARMED FORCES MEMBER (cc 21)	23. What is the highest grade (or year) of regular school you have ever attended? (ASK for persons 12–24 yrs Transcribe for 25+ yrs.) (cc22)	24. Did you com- plete that year? (cc23)
KEYER–BEGIN NEW RECORD (034)	(035)	(036)		(037)	(038)	(039)	(040)	(041)	(042)	(043)
Last	1☐ Per 2☐ Tel 3☐ NI – Fill 16–21		1☐ Head 2☐ Wife of head 3☐ Own child 4☐ Other relative 5☐ Non-relative		1☐ Married 2☐ Widowed 3☐ Divorced 4☐ Separated 5☐ Never Mar.	1☐ Wh. 2☐ Neg. 3☐ Oth.	1☐ M 2☐ F	1☐ Yes 2☐ No	00☐ Never attended or kindergarten ___ Elem. (01–08) ___ H.S. (09–12) ___ College (21–26+)	1☐ Yes 2☐ No
First										

CHECK ITEM A ▶ Look at item 4 on cover page. Is this the same household as last enumeration? (Box 1 marked) ☐ Yes – SKIP to 26a ☐ No

25a. Did you live in this house on April 1, 1970?
(044) 1☐ Yes – SKIP to 26a 2☐ No

b. Where did you live on April 1, 1970? (State, foreign country U.S. possession, etc.)

State, etc. _____

County _____

c. Did you live inside the limits of a city, town, village, etc.?
(045) (046) 1☐ No 2☐ Yes – Name of city, town, village, etc. ⤴

d. Were you in the Armed Forces on April 1, 1970?
(047) 1☐ Yes 2☐ No

Ask 26–28 for persons 16 years or older
26a. What were you doing most of LAST WEEK – working, keeping house, going to school, or something else?
(048) 1☐ Working – SKIP to 28a 6☐ Unable to work – SKIP to 28a 2☐ With a job but not at work 7☐ Retired 3☐ Looking for work 8☐ Other – Specify ⤵ 4☐ Keeping house 5☐ Going to school

b. Did you do any work at all LAST WEEK, not counting work around the house? (Note: If farm or business operator in HH, ask about unpaid work.)
(049) 1☐ Yes – SKIP to 28a 2☐ No

c. Did you have a job or business from which you were temporarily absent or on layoff LAST WEEK?
(050) 1☐ Yes – SKIP to 28a 2☐ No

26d. Have you been looking for work during the past 4 weeks?
(051) 1☐ Yes 2☐ No – SKIP to 28a

27. Is there any reason why you could not take a job LAST WEEK?
(052) 1☐ No Yes ⟶ 2☐ Already has a job 3☐ Temporary illness 4☐ Going to school 5☐ Other – Specify ⤵

Description of job or business (Current or most recent)
28a. For whom did you work? (Name of company, business, organization or other employer)

(053) x☐ Never worked – SKIP to 36

b. What kind of business or industry is this? (For example: TV and radio mfg., retail shoe store, State Labor Department, farm)
(054)

c. Were you –
(055) 1☐ An employee of a PRIVATE company, business or individual for wages, salary or commissions? 2☐ A GOVERNMENT employee (Federal, State, county or local)? 3☐ SELF EMPLOYED in OWN business, professional practice or farm? 4☐ Working WITHOUT PAY in family business or farm?

d. What kind of work were you doing? (For example: electrical engineer, stock clerk, typist, farmer)
(056)

e. What were your most important activities or duties? (For example: typing, keeping account books, selling cars, finishing concrete, etc.)

INDIVIDUAL SCREEN QUESTIONS

36. The following questions refer only to things that happened to you during the last 12 months – between ____1st and ____. Did you have your (pocket picked/purse snatched)? ☐ Yes – How many ☐ No times?

37. Did anyone take something (else) directly from you by using force, such as by a stickup, mugging or threat? ☐ Yes – How many ☐ No times?

38. Did anyone TRY to rob you by using force or threatening to harm you? (other than any incidents already mentioned) ☐ Yes – How many ☐ No times?

39. Did anyone beat you up, attack you or hit you with something, such as a rock or bottle? (other than any incidents already mentioned) ☐ Yes – How many ☐ No times?

40. Were you knifed, shot at, or attacked with some other weapon by anyone at all? (other than any incidents already mentioned) ☐ Yes – How many ☐ No times?

41. Did anyone THREATEN to beat you up or THREATEN you with a knife, gun, or some other weapon, NOT including telephone threats? (other than any incidents already mentioned) ☐ Yes – How many ☐ No times?

42. Did anyone TRY to attack you in some other way? (other than any incidents already mentioned) ☐ Yes – How many ☐ No times?

43. During the last 12 months, did anyone steal things that belonged to you from inside any car or truck, such as packages or clothing? ☐ Yes – How many ☐ No times?

44. Was anything stolen from you while you were away from home, for instance at work, in a theater or restaurant, or while traveling? ☐ Yes – How many ☐ No times?

45. (Other than any incidents you've already mentioned) Was anything else stolen from you during the last 12 months? ☐ Yes – How many ☐ No times?

46. Did you find any evidence that someone ATTEMPTED to steal something that belonged to you? (other than any incidents already mentioned) ☐ Yes – How many ☐ No times?

47. Did you call the police during the last 12 months to report something that happened to you which you thought was a crime? (Do not count any calls made to the police concerning the incidents you have just told me about.) ☐ No ☐ Yes – What happened? (058)

INTERVIEWER – Was HH member 12+ attacked or threatened, or was something stolen to steal something that belonged to him? ☐ No ☐ Yes – How many times? ⟶

48. Did anything happen to you during the last 12 months which you thought was a crime, but did NOT report to the police? ☐ No ☐ Yes – What happened? (059)

INTERVIEWER – Was HH member 12+ attacked or threatened, or was something stolen or an attempt made to steal something that belonged to him? ☐ No ☐ Yes – How many times? ⟶

CHECK ITEM B ▶ Did you receive all "No's" to the Screen Questions asked of this respondent? ☐ Yes – Ask questions for next HH member on following page. End interview if last respondent. ☐ No – Fill Crime Incident Reports

KEYER – BEGIN NEW RECORD

(101) Line number

(102) Screen question number

(103) Incident number

FORM NCS-4
(4-25-72)

U.S. DEPARTMENT OF COMMERCE
SOCIAL AND ECONOMIC STATISTICS ADMINISTRATION
BUREAU OF THE CENSUS

CRIME INCIDENT REPORT
NATIONAL CRIME SURVEY
CENTRAL CITIES SAMPLE

NOTICE – Your report to the Census Bureau is confidential by law (Title 13, U.S. code). It may be seen only by sworn Census employees and may be used only for statistical purposes.

1a. You said that during the last 12 months – *(refer to appropriate screen question for description of crime).*
In what month (did this/did the first) incident happen? *(Show flashcard if necessary. Encourage respondent to give exact month.)*

(104) ________ Month (01–12)

(105) CHECK ITEM A ▶ Is this incident report for a series of crimes?
1 ☐ No – *SKIP to 2*
2 ☐ Yes

b. In what month(s) did these incidents take place? *(Mark all that apply)*

(106)*
1 ☐ Spring (March, April, May)
2 ☐ Summer (June, July, August)
3 ☐ Fall (September, October, November)
4 ☐ Winter (December, January, February)

c. How many incidents were involved in this series?

(107)
1 ☐ Three or four
2 ☐ Five to ten
3 ☐ Eleven or more
4 ☐ Don't know

INTERVIEWER – If series, the following questions refer only to the most recent incident.

2. About what time did it happen?

(108)
1 ☐ Don't know
2 ☐ During the day (6 a.m. to 6 p.m.)
At night (6 p.m. to 6 a.m.)
3 ☐ 6 p.m. to midnight
4 ☐ Midnight to 6 a.m.
5 ☐ Don't know

3a. Did this incident take place inside the limits of this city or somewhere else?

(109)
1 ☐ Inside limits of this city – *SKIP to 4*
2 ☐ Somewhere else in the United States
3 ☐ Outside the United States – *END INCIDENT REPORT*

b. In what State and county did this incident occur?

State ________

County ________

c. Did it happen inside the limits of a city, town, village, etc.?

(110)
1 ☐ No
2 ☐ Yes – *Enter name of city, town, etc.* ➘

(111) ☐☐☐☐☐ ________

4. Where did this incident take place?

(112)
1 ☐ At or in own home/apartment, in garage or other building on property
2 ☐ At or in vacation home, hotel/motel
} *SKIP to 6a*

3 ☐ Inside commercial building such as store, restaurant, bank, gas station, public conveyance or station
4 ☐ Inside office, factory, or warehouse
} *ASK 5a*

5 ☐ Near own home; yard, sidewalk, driveway, carport
6 ☐ On the street, in a park, field, playground, school grounds or parking lot
7 ☐ Other – *Specify* ➘ ________
} *SKIP to Check Item B*

5a. Were you a customer, employee, or owner?

(113)
1 ☐ Customer
2 ☐ Employee
3 ☐ Owner
4 ☐ Other – *Specify* ________

b. Did the person(s) steal or TRY to steal anything from the store, restaurant, office, factory, etc.?

(114)
1 ☐ Yes
2 ☐ No
3 ☐ Don't know
} *SKIP to Check Item B*

6a. Did the person(s) live there or have a right to be there, such as a guest or a workman?

(115)
1 ☐ Yes – *SKIP to Check Item B*
2 ☐ No
3 ☐ Don't know

b. Did the person(s) actually get in or just try to get in the building?

(116)
1 ☐ Actually got in
2 ☐ Just tried to get in
3 ☐ Don't know

c. Was there any evidence, such as a broken lock or broken window, that the person (forced his way in/TRIED to force his way in) the building?

(117)*
1 ☐ No
Yes – **What was the evidence? Anything else?** *(Mark all that apply)*
2 ☐ Broken lock or window
3 ☐ Forced door or window
4 ☐ Slashed screen
5 ☐ Other – *Specify* ➘ ________
} *SKIP to Check Item B*

d. How did the person(s) (get in/try to get in)?

(118)
1 ☐ Through unlocked door or window
2 ☐ Had key
3 ☐ Don't know
4 ☐ Other – *Specify* ________

(119) CHECK ITEM B ▶ Was any member of this household present when this incident occurred? (If not sure, ASK)
1 ☐ No – *SKIP to 13a*
2 ☐ Yes

7a. Did the person(s) have a weapon such as a gun or knife, or something he was using as a weapon, such as a bottle, or wrench?

(120)*
1 ☐ No
2 ☐ Don't know
Yes – **What was the weapon?** *(Mark all that apply)*
3 ☐ Gun
4 ☐ Knife
5 ☐ Other – *Specify* ________

b. Did the person(s) hit you, knock you down, or actually attack you in some other way?

(121)
1 ☐ Yes – *SKIP to 7f*
2 ☐ No

c. Did the person(s) threaten you with harm in any way?

(122)
1 ☐ No – *SKIP to 7e*
2 ☐ Yes

INCIDENT REPORT

CRIME INCIDENT QUESTIONS – Continued

7d. How were you threatened? Any other way?
(Mark all that apply)

(123)
1 ☐ Verbal threat of rape
2 ☐ Verbal threat of attack (other than rape)
3 ☐ Weapon present or threatened with weapon
4 ☐ Attempted attack with weapon (for example, shot at)
5 ☐ Object thrown at person
6 ☐ Followed, surrounded
7 ☐ Other – Specify _____

SKIP to 10a

e. What actually happened? Anything else?
(Mark all that apply)

(124)
1 ☐ Something taken without permission
2 ☐ Attempted or threatened to take something
3 ☐ Harassed, argument, abusive language
4 ☐ Forcible entry or attempted forcible entry of house
5 ☐ Forcible entry or attempted entry of car
6 ☐ Damaged or destroyed property
7 ☐ Attempted or threatened to damage or destroy property
8 ☐ Other – Specify _____

SKIP to 10a

f. How did the person(s) attack you? Any other way?
(Mark all that apply)

(125)
1 ☐ Raped
2 ☐ Tried to rape
3 ☐ Shot, knifed, hit with object held in hand
4 ☐ Hit by thrown object
5 ☐ Hit, slapped, knocked down
6 ☐ Grabbed, held, tripped, jumped, pushed, etc.
7 ☐ Other – Specify _____

8a. What were the injuries you suffered, if any? Anything else? (Mark all that apply)

(126)
1 ☐ None – SKIP to 10a
2 ☐ Raped
3 ☐ Attempted rape
4 ☐ Knife or gunshot wounds
5 ☐ Broken bones or teeth knocked out
6 ☐ Internal injuries, knocked unconscious
7 ☐ Bruises, black eye, cuts, scratches, swelling
8 ☐ Other – Specify _____

b. Were you injured to the extent that you needed medical attention after the attack?

(127)
1 ☐ No – SKIP to 10a
2 ☐ Yes

c. Did you receive any treatment at a hospital?

(128)
1 ☐ No
2 ☐ Emergency room treatment only
3 ☐ Stayed overnight or longer –

(129) How many days? ➔

d. What was the total amount of your medical expenses resulting from this incident, INCLUDING anything paid by insurance? Include hospital and doctor bills, medicine, therapy, braces, and any other injury–related medical expenses.

INTERVIEWER – If respondent does not know exact amount, encourage him to give an estimate.

(130)
0 ☐ No cost – SKIP to 10a
$ _____ .00
X ☐ Don't know

9a. At the time of the incident, were you covered by any medical insurance, or were you eligible for benefits from any other type of health benefits program, such as Medicaid, Veteran's Administration, or Public Welfare?

(131)
1 ☐ No
2 ☐ Don't know
3 ☐ Yes
SKIP to 10a

9b. Did you file a claim with any of these insurance companies or programs in order to get part or all of your medical expenses paid?

(132)
1 ☐ No – SKIP to 10a
2 ☐ Yes

c. Did insurance or any health benefits program pay for all or part of the total medical expenses?

(133)
1 ☐ Not yet settled
2 ☐ None
3 ☐ All
4 ☐ Part
SKIP to 10a

d. How much did insurance or a health benefits program pay?
(Obtain an estimate, if necessary)

(134) $ _____ .00

10a. Did you do anything to protect yourself or your property during the incident?

(135)
1 ☐ No – SKIP to 11
2 ☐ Yes

b. What did you do? Anything else? (Mark all that apply)

(136)
1 ☐ Used or brandished a weapon
2 ☐ Hit, kicked, or scratched offender
3 ☐ Reasoned with offender
4 ☐ Screamed, yelled for help
5 ☐ Left scene, ran away
6 ☐ Held on to property
7 ☐ Other – Specify ➔

11. Was the crime committed by only one or more than one person?

(137)
1 ☐ Only one ➔
2 ☐ Don't know – SKIP to 12a
3 ☐ More than one ➔

a. Was this person male or female?

(138)
1 ☐ Male
2 ☐ Female
3 ☐ Don't know

b. How old would you say the person was?

(139)
1 ☐ Under 12
2 ☐ 12–14
3 ☐ 15–17
4 ☐ 18–20
5 ☐ 21 or over
6 ☐ Don't know

c. Was the person someone you knew or was he a stranger?

(140)
1 ☐ Stranger
2 ☐ Don't know
3 ☐ Know by sight only
4 ☐ Casual acquaintance
5 ☐ Well known
SKIP to e

d. Was the person a relative of yours?

(141)
1 ☐ No
Yes – What relationship?
2 ☐ Spouse
3 ☐ Parent
4 ☐ Own child
5 ☐ Brother or sister
6 ☐ Other relative – Specify ➔

e. Was he/she –

(142)
1 ☐ White?
2 ☐ Negro?
3 ☐ Other? – Specify ➔
4 ☐ Don't know
SKIP to 12a

f. How many persons?

(143) _____

g. Were they male or female?

(144)
1 ☐ All male
2 ☐ All female
3 ☐ Male and female
4 ☐ Don't know

h. How old would you say the youngest was?

(145)
1 ☐ Under 12
2 ☐ 12–14
3 ☐ 15–17
4 ☐ 18–20
5 ☐ 21 or over – SKIP to j
6 ☐ Don't know

i. How old would you say the oldest was?

(146)
1 ☐ Under 12
2 ☐ 12–14
3 ☐ 15–17
4 ☐ 18–20
5 ☐ 21 or over
6 ☐ Don't know

j. Were any of the persons known or related to you or were they all strangers?

(147)
1 ☐ All strangers
2 ☐ Don't know
SKIP to m
3 ☐ All relatives
4 ☐ Some relatives
SKIP to l
5 ☐ All known
6 ☐ Some known

k. How well were they known?
(Mark all that apply)

(148)
1 ☐ By sight only
2 ☐ Casual acquaintance(s)
3 ☐ Well known
SKIP to m

l. How were they related to you?
(Mark all that apply)

(149)
1 ☐ Spouse
2 ☐ Parents
3 ☐ Own children
4 ☐ Brothers/ sisters
5 ☐ Other – Specify ➔

m. Were all of them –

(150)
1 ☐ White?
2 ☐ Negro?
3 ☐ Other? – Specify ➔
4 ☐ Combination – Specify ➔
5 ☐ Don't know

CRIME INCIDENT QUESTIONS – Continued

(151) 12a. Were you the only person there besides the offender(s)?
1 ☐ Yes – SKIP TO 13a
2 ☐ No

(152) b. How many of these persons were robbed, harmed, or threatened? (Include only those persons 12 years of age and over)
0 ☐ None – SKIP to 13a

_____ Number of persons

(153) c. Were any of these persons members of your household?
0 ☐ No
Yes – How many? ⟶

_____

(Also mark "Yes" in Check Item H on page 12)

(154) 13a. Was something stolen or taken without permission that belonged to you or others in the household?
INTERVIEWER – If respondent was the owner or employee of a store or other commercial establishment, do not include anything stolen from the business itself, such as merchandise or cash from a register.
1 ☐ Yes – SKIP to 13f
2 ☐ No

(155) b. Did the person(s) ATTEMPT to take something?
1 ☐ No – SKIP to 13e
2 ☐ Yes

(156) c. What did they try to take? Anything else?
(Mark all that apply)
1 ☐ Purse
2 ☐ Wallet or money
3 ☐ Car
4 ☐ Other motor vehicle
5 ☐ Part of car (hubcap, tape-deck, etc.)
6 ☐ Don't know
7 ☐ Other – Specify _____

CHECK ITEM C ►
Did they try to take a purse, wallet, or money? (Box 1 or 2 marked in 13c)
☐ No – SKIP to 18a
☐ Yes

(157) d. Was the (purse/wallet/money) on your person, for instance in a pocket or being held?
1 ☐ Yes ⎫ SKIP to 18a
2 ☐ No ⎭

(158) e. What did happen? *(Mark all that apply)*
1 ☐ Attacked
2 ☐ Threatened with harm
3 ☐ Attempted to break into house or garage
4 ☐ Attempted to break into car
5 ☐ Harassed, argument, abusive language
6 ☐ Damaged or destroyed property
7 ☐ Attempted or threatened to damage or destroy property
8 ☐ Other – Specify _____

SKIP TO 18a

(159) f. What was taken? What else?
Cash: $ _____ .00
and/or

(160) Property: *(Mark all that apply)*
0 ☐ Only cash taken – SKIP to Check Item E
1 ☐ Purse
2 ☐ Wallet
3 ☐ Car
4 ☐ Other motor vehicle
5 ☐ Part of car (hubcap, tape-deck, etc.)
6 ☐ Other – Specify _____

CHECK ITEM D ►
Was a car or other motor vehicle taken? (Box 3 or 4 marked in 13f)
☐ No – SKIP to Check Item E
☐ Yes

(161) 14a. Had permission to use the (car/motor vehicle) ever been given to the person who took it?
1 ☐ No ⎫
2 ☐ Don't know ⎬ SKIP to Check Item E
3 ☐ Yes ⎭

(162) b. Did the person return the (car/motor vehicle)?
1 ☐ Yes
2 ☐ No

CHECK ITEM E ►
Is Box 0,1, or 2 marked in 13f?
☐ No – SKIP to 15a
☐ Yes

(163) c. Was the (purse/wallet/money) on your person, for instance, in a pocket or being held by you when it was taken?
1 ☐ Yes
2 ☐ No

CHECK ITEM F ►
Was only cash taken? (Box 0 marked in 13f)
☐ Yes – SKIP to 16a
☐ No

(164) 15a. Altogether, what was the value of the PROPERTY that was taken?
INTERVIEWER – Exclude stolen cash, and enter $0 for stolen checks and credit cards, even if they were used.
$ _____ .00

(165) b. How did you decide the value of the property that was stolen? *(Mark all that apply)*
1 ☐ Original cost
2 ☐ Replacement cost
3 ☐ Personal estimate of current value
4 ☐ Insurance report estimate
5 ☐ Police estimate
6 ☐ Don't know
7 ☐ Other – Specify _____

(166) 16a. Was all or part of the stolen money or property recovered, except for anything received from insurance?
1 ☐ None ⎫
2 ☐ All ⎬ SKIP to 17a
3 ☐ Part ⎭

(167) b. What was recovered?
Cash: $ _____ .00
and/or

(168) Property: *(Mark all that apply)*
0 ☐ Cash only recovered – SKIP to 17a
1 ☐ Purse
2 ☐ Wallet
3 ☐ Car
4 ☐ Other motor vehicle
5 ☐ Part of car (hubcap, tape-deck, etc.)
6 ☐ Other – Specify _____

(169) c. What was the value of the property recovered (excluding recovered cash)?
$ _____ .00

CRIME INCIDENT QUESTIONS – Continued

17a. Was there any insurance against theft?

(170)
1 ☐ No
2 ☐ Don't know } SKIP to 18a
3 ☐ Yes

b. Was this loss reported to an insurance company?

(171)
1 ☐ No
2 ☐ Don't know } SKIP to 18a
3 ☐ Yes

c. Was any of this loss recovered through insurance?

(172)
1 ☐ Not yet settled
2 ☐ No } SKIP to 18a
3 ☐ Yes

d. How much was recovered?

INTERVIEWER – If property replaced by insurance company instead of cash settlement, ask for estimate of value of the property replaced.

(173) $ _____ .00

18a. Did any household member lose any time from work because of this incident?

(174)
0 ☐ No – SKIP to 19a
Yes – How many members? _____

b. How much time was lost altogether?

(175)
1 ☐ Less than 1 day
2 ☐ 1–5 days
3 ☐ 6–10 days
4 ☐ Over 10 days
5 ☐ Don't know

19. Was anything damaged but not taken in this incident? For example, was a lock or window broken, clothing damaged, or damage done to a car, etc.?

(176)
1 ☐ No – SKIP to 20a
2 ☐ Yes

b. (Was/were) the damaged item(s) repaired or replaced?

(177)
1 ☐ Yes – SKIP to 19d
2 ☐ No

c. How much would it cost to repair or replace the damaged item(s)?

(178)
$ _____ .00 } SKIP to 20a
X ☐ Don't know

d. How much was the repair or replacement cost?

(179)
X ☐ No cost – SKIP to 20a
$ _____ .00

e. Who paid or will pay for the repairs or replacement? *(Mark all that apply)*

(180)
1 ☐ Household member
2 ☐ Landlord
3 ☐ Insurance
4 ☐ Other – Specify _____

20a. Were the police informed of this incident in any way?

(181)
1 ☐ No
2 ☐ Don't know
Yes – Who told them?
3 ☐ Household member
4 ☐ Someone else } SKIP to 21a
5 ☐ Police on scene

b. What was the reason this incident was not reported to the police? *(Mark all that apply)*

(182)
1 ☐ Nothing could be done – lack of proof
2 ☐ Did not think it important enough
3 ☐ Police wouldn't want to be bothered
4 ☐ Did not want to take time – too inconvenient
5 ☐ Private or personal matter, did not want to report it
6 ☐ Did not want to get involved
7 ☐ Afraid of reprisal
8 ☐ Reported to someone else
9 ☐ Other – Specify →

Ask only for persons 16 years or older.

21a. Did you have a job at the time this incident happened?

(183)
1 ☐ No – SKIP to Check Item G
2 ☐ Yes

b. What kind of work did you do at that job?

(184)
1 ☐ Same as described in Q. 28d of Screen Questionnaire
2 ☐ Different – Specify →

(185) ☐☐☐ _____

CHECK ITEM G ▶ BRIEFLY summarize this incident or series of incidents.

_____

_____

_____

_____

_____

CHECK ITEM H ▶ Look at 12c on Incident Report. Is there an entry for "How many?"
☐ No
☐ Yes – Be sure you have an Incident Report for each household member 12 years of age or over who was robbed, harmed, or threatened in this incident.

CHECK ITEM I ▶ Is this the last Incident Report to be filled?
☐ No – Go to next Incident Report.
☐ Yes – END INTERVIEW and enter total number of Crime Incident Reports filled for this household in Item 13 on the cover page of NCS-3.

Notes

O.M.B. No. 41-S72052; Approval Expires June 30, 1974

FORM NCS-6
(6-6-72)

U.S. DEPARTMENT OF COMMERCE
SOCIAL AND ECONOMIC STATISTICS ADMINISTRATION
BUREAU OF THE CENSUS

NATIONAL CRIME SURVEY
CENTRAL CITIES SAMPLE

ATTITUDE QUESTIONNAIRE

NOTICE — Your report to the Census Bureau is confidential by law (Title 13, U.S. Code). It may be seen only by sworn Census employees and may be used only for statistical purposes.

A. Control number

PSU	Serial	Panel	Household	Segment

B. Name of household head

C. Reason for noninterview

(310) 1 ☐ TYPE A → 2 ☐ TYPE B 3 ☐ TYPE C

Race of head
(311) 1 ☐ White
2 ☐ Negro
3 ☐ Other

TYPE Z →
Interview not obtained for —
Line number

(312) _____
(313) _____
(314) _____
(315) _____

CENSUS USE ONLY
(316) (317) (318) (319)

HOUSEHOLD ATTITUDE QUESTIONS
Ask only household respondent

Before we get to the major portion of the survey, I would like to ask you a few questions related to subjects which seem to be of some concern to people. These questions ask you what you think, what you feel, your attitudes and opinions.

1. How long have you lived at this address?
(320) 1 ☐ Less than 1 year
2 ☐ 1–2 years ⎫ Ask 2a
3 ☐ 3–5 years ⎭
4 ☐ More than 5 years — *SKIP to 5a*

2a. Why did you select this particular neighborhood? Any other reason?
(Mark all that apply)
(321) 1 ☐ Like the neighborhood
2 ☐ Good schools
3 ☐ Safe from crime
4 ☐ Only place housing could be found
5 ☐ Price was right
6 ☐ Location — close to job, family, friends, school, shopping, etc.
7 ☐ Liked the house
8 ☐ Other — *Specify* _____

(If more than one reason)
b. Which reason would you say was the most important?
(322) _____ *Enter item number*

3a. Where did you live before you moved here?
(323) 1 ☐ Outside U.S. ⎫ SKIP to 4a
2 ☐ Inside limits of this city ⎭
3 ☐ Somewhere else in U.S. — *Specify* →

_____ State
_____ County

b. Did you live inside the limits of a city, town, village, etc.?
(324) 1 ☐ No
2 ☐ Yes — *Enter name of city, town, etc.* →

(325) ☐☐☐☐ _____

4a. Why did you leave there? Any other reason? *(Mark all that apply)*
(326) 1 ☐ Location — closer to job, family, friends, school, shopping, etc., here
2 ☐ Needed larger or smaller house/apartment
3 ☐ Wanted better housing, own home
4 ☐ Wanted cheaper housing
5 ☐ Evicted, building demolished, condemned, etc.
6 ☐ Marital status changed — widowed, divorced, married
7 ☐ Old neighborhood run down, bad element moving in
8 ☐ Crime in old neighborhood, afraid
9 ☐ Other — *Specify* _____

(If more than one reason)
b. Which reason would you say was the most important?
(327) _____ *Enter item number*

5a. Is there anything you don't like about this neighborhood?
(328) 0 ☐ No — *SKIP to 6a*
(329) Yes — **What? Anything else?** *(Mark all that apply)*
1 ☐ Traffic
2 ☐ Environmental problems — trash, noise, etc.
3 ☐ Crime or fear of crime
4 ☐ Public transportation problem
5 ☐ Inadequate schools, shopping facilities, etc.
6 ☐ Neighborhood changing — bad element moving in
7 ☐ Problems with neighbors
8 ☐ Other — *Specify* _____

(If more than one answer)
b. Which problem would you say is the most serious?
(330) _____ *Enter item number*

6a. Do you do your major food shopping in this neighborhood?
(331) 0 ☐ Yes — *SKIP to 7a*
(332) No — **Why not? Any other reason?** *(Mark all that apply)*
1 ☐ No stores in neighborhood
2 ☐ Stores in neighborhood inadequate (better stores elsewhere)
3 ☐ High prices
4 ☐ Crime or fear of crime
5 ☐ Other — *Specify* _____

(If more than one reason)
b. Which reason would you say is the most important?
(333) _____ *Enter item number*

7a. When you shop for things other than food, such as clothing and general merchandise, do you USUALLY go to surburban or neighborhood shopping centers or do you shop "downtown?"
(334) 1 ☐ Surburban or neighborhood
2 ☐ Downtown

b. Why is that? Any other reason? *(Mark all that apply)*
(335) 1 ☐ Better parking
2 ☐ Better transportation
3 ☐ More convenient
4 ☐ Better selection
5 ☐ Afraid of crime
6 ☐ Store hours better
7 ☐ Better prices
8 ☐ Other — *Specify* _____

(If more than one reason)
c. Which one would you say is the most important reason?
(336) _____ *Enter item number*

▶ INTERVIEWER — *Complete interview with household respondent, beginning with Individual Attitude Questions*

INDIVIDUAL ATTITUDE QUESTIONS – *Ask each household member 16 or older*

KEYER – BEGIN NEW RECORD

(337) Line number | Name

8a. How often do you go out in the evening, or entertainment, such as to restaurants, theaters, etc.?

(338)
1 ☐ Once a week or more
2 ☐ Less than once a week – more than once a month
3 ☐ About once a month
4 ☐ 2 or 3 times a year
5 ☐ Less than 2 or 3 times a year or never

b. Do you go to these places more or less now than you did a year or two ago?

(339)
1 ☐ About the same – *SKIP to Check Item A*
2 ☐ More ⎰ **Why? Any other reason?** *(Mark all that apply)*
3 ☐ Less ⎱

(340)
1 ☐ Money situation
2 ☐ Opportunity
3 ☐ Convenience
4 ☐ Health
5 ☐ Transportation
6 ☐ Age
7 ☐ Family responsibility
8 ☐ Activities, job, school
9 ☐ Crime or fear of crime
10 ☐ Want to
11 ☐ Other – *Specify*

(If more than one reason)
c. Which reason would you say is the most important?

(341) _____ *Enter item number*

CHECK ITEM A ▶ Is box 1, 2, or 3 marked in 8a?
☐ No – *SKIP to 9a*   ☐ Yes – *Ask 8d*

d. When you do go out to restaurants or theaters in the evening, is it usually in the city or outside of the city?

(342)
1 ☐ Usually in the city
2 ☐ Usually outside of the city
3 ☐ About equal – *SKIP to 9a*

e. Why do you usually go (outside the city/in the city)? Any other reason? *(Mark all that apply)*

(343)
1 ☐ More convenient
2 ☐ Parking problems
3 ☐ Too much crime in other place
4 ☐ More to do
5 ☐ Better facilities (restaurants, theaters, etc.)
6 ☐ More expensive in other area
7 ☐ Because of friends, relatives
8 ☐ Other – *Specify* _____

(If more than one reason)
f. Which reason would you say is the most important?

(344) _____ *Enter item number*

9a. Now I'd like to get your opinions about crime in general. Within the past year or two, do you think that crime in your neighborhood has increased, decreased, or remained about the same?

(345)
1 ☐ Increased
2 ☐ Decreased
3 ☐ Same – *SKIP to c*
4 ☐ Don't know – *SKIP to c*
5 ☐ Haven't lived here that long – *SKIP to c*

b. Were you thinking about any specific kinds of crimes when you said you think crime in your neighborhood has (increased/decreased)?

(346)
0 ☐ No   Yes – What kinds of crimes? _____
☐☐

c. How about any crimes which may be happening in your neighborhood – would you say they are committed mostly by the people who live here in this neighborhood or mostly by outsiders?

(347)
1 ☐ No crimes happening in neighborhood
2 ☐ People living here
3 ☐ Outsiders
4 ☐ Equally by both
5 ☐ Don't know

10a. Within the past year or two do you think that crime in the United States has increased, decreased, or remained about the same?

(348)
1 ☐ Increased ⎰
2 ☐ Decreased ⎱ *Ask b*
3 ☐ Same ⎰
4 ☐ Don't know ⎱ *SKIP to 11a*

b. Were you thinking about any specific kinds of crimes when you said you think crime in the U.S. has (increased/decreased)?

(349)
0 ☐ No   Yes – What kinds of crimes? _____
☐☐

11a. How safe do you feel or would you feel being out alone in your neighborhood AT NIGHT?

(350)
1 ☐ Very safe
2 ☐ Reasonably safe
3 ☐ Somewhat unsafe
4 ☐ Very unsafe

b. How about DURING THE DAY – how safe do you feel or would you feel being out alone in your neighborhood?

(351)
1 ☐ Very safe
2 ☐ Reasonably safe
3 ☐ Somewhat unsafe
4 ☐ Very unsafe

CHECK ITEM B ▶ Look at 11a and b. Was box 3 or 4 marked in either item?
☐ Yes – *Ask 11c*   ☐ No – *SKIP to 12*

11c. Is the neighborhood dangerous enough to make you think seriously about moving somewhere else?

(352) 0 ☐ No – *SKIP to 12*
(353) Yes – Why don't you? Any other reason? *(Mark all that apply)*
1 ☐ Can't afford to
2 ☐ Can't find other housing
3 ☐ Relatives, friends nearby
4 ☐ Convenient to work, etc.
5 ☐ Plan to move soon
6 ☐ Other – *Specify*

(If more than one reason)
d. Which reason would you say is the most important?

(354) _____ *Enter item number*

12. How do you think your neighborhood compares with others in this metropolitan area in terms of crime? Would you say it is –

(355)
1 ☐ Much more dangerous?
2 ☐ More dangerous?
3 ☐ About average?
4 ☐ Less dangerous?
5 ☐ Much less dangerous?

13a. Are there some parts of this metropolitan area where you have a reason to go or would like to go DURING THE DAY, but are afraid to because of fear of crime?

(356) 0 ☐ No   Yes – Which section(s)? _____

(357) _____ ◀— *Number of specific places mentioned*

b. How about AT NIGHT – are there some parts of this area where you have a reason to go or would like to go but are afraid to because of fear of crime?

(358) 0 ☐ No   Yes – Which section(s)? _____

(359) _____ ◀— *Number of specific places mentioned*

14a. Would you say, in general, that your local police are doing a good job, an average job, or a poor job?

(360)
1 ☐ Good
2 ☐ Average
3 ☐ Poor
4 ☐ Don't know – *SKIP to 15a*

b. In what ways could they improve? Any other ways? *(Mark all that apply)*

(361)
1 ☐ No improvement needed – *SKIP to 15a*
2 ☐ Need more policemen
3 ☐ Patrol or investigate more
4 ☐ Be more prompt
5 ☐ Improve training, raise qualifications or pay
6 ☐ Be more courteous, concerned
7 ☐ Don't discriminate
8 ☐ Need more traffic control
9 ☐ Need more policemen in certain areas or at certain times
10 ☐ Don't know
11 ☐ Other – *Specify* _____

(If more than one way)
c. Which would you say is the most important?

(362) _____ *Enter item number*

15a. Now I have some more questions about your opinions concerning crime. Please take this card. *(Hand respondent Attitude Flashcard, NCS-574)* **Look at the FIRST set of statements. Which one do you agree with most?**

(363)
1 ☐ My chances of being attacked or robbed have GONE UP in the past few years
2 ☐ My chances of being attacked or robbed have GONE DOWN in the past few years
3 ☐ My chances of being attacked or robbed haven't changed in the past few years
4 ☐ No opinion

b. Which of the SECOND group do you agree with most?

(364)
1 ☐ Crime is LESS serious than the newspapers and TV say
2 ☐ Crime is MORE serious than the newspapers and TV say
3 ☐ Crime is about as serious as the newspapers and TV say
4 ☐ No opinion

16a. Do you think PEOPLE IN GENERAL have limited or changed their activities in the past few years because they are afraid of crime?

(365)
1 ☐ Yes   2 ☐ No

b. Do you think that most PEOPLE IN THIS NEIGHBORHOOD have limited or changed their activities in the past few years because they are afraid of crime?

(366)
1 ☐ Yes   2 ☐ No

c. In general, have YOU limited or changed your activities in the past few years because of crime?

(367)
1 ☐ Yes   2 ☐ No

▶ **INTERVIEWER** – *Continue interview with this respondent on NCS-3*

LEAA-Census National Crime Survey: Methods and Procedures [1]

The LEAA-Census National Crime Survey (NCS) refers generically to two distinct data collection efforts. The first is a continuous, nationwide panel survey; the second is a series of surveys conducted in twenty-six of the nation's largest cities. Throughout this book, the first is referred to as the NCS national sample and the second is referred to as the city samples. Because the results reported in this book deal only with the city samples, only the methods and procedures used in the city samples are discussed in this appendix. [2]

In the city samples, the samples were drawn from the central city rather than from the entire SMSA. [3] The total sample size in each of the cities surveyed was about 10,000 households and 2,000 businesses. The cities included in the NCS city samples are Atlanta, Baltimore, Boston, Buffalo, Chicago, Cincinnati, Cleveland, Dallas, Denver, Detroit, Houston, Los Angeles, Miami, Milwaukee, Minneapolis, Newark, New Orleans, New York, Oakland, Philadelphia, Pittsburgh, Portland (Oregon), St. Louis, San Diego, San Francisco, and Washington, D.C. Surveying began in these cities in the fall of 1972; follow-up surveys of households and businesses were conducted in the early months of 1975 in thirteen of the original twenty-six cities.

LEAA-CENSUS SURVEY PROCEDURES

In the survey of households there were three types of respondents: household respondents, self-respondents, and proxy respondents. The household respondent was an adult (eighteen years old or older) household member—usually the head of household or the head's spouse—who was knowledgeable about the affairs of the household. This respondent was asked such questions as whether the residence was owned or rented and the amount of income the family had. In addition to these background questions, household respondents were asked a series of screen questions regarding crimes against the entire household such as burglary and vehicle theft.

All household members fourteen years of age or older were personally interviewed to obtain background information such as age, sex, race, and educational attainment. In addition, each self-respondent was asked a series of screen questions to determine whether he or she had been the victim of a survey crime within the reference period. Proxy respondents were used to elicit the same information about household members who were twelve or thirteen years of age at the time of the interview. Proxy respondents were also used for household members who were physically or mentally unable to answer the individual questions and for household members who were temporarily absent and who were not expected to return within the enumeration period.

In the interviews with the household respondents and the self or proxy respondents, a series of victimization screen questions was asked. The survey crimes against the household were larceny of household property, burglary, and vehicle theft. The survey crimes against individual household members were rape, robbery, assault, and larceny from the person, while survey crimes against businesses were burglary and robbery. Respondents were asked to report victimization experiences occurring within a twelve-month period preceding the month of the interview.

The following are examples of household, personal, and business screen questions: "Did anyone break into or somehow illegally get into your (apartment/home), garage, or another building on your property?" "Did anyone beat you up, attack you, or hit you with something, such as a rock or bottle?" "Were you or any employee held up by anyone using a weapon, force, or threat of force on these premises?" The screen questions were phrased in everyday language rather than in legal terminology. Thus, respondents need not have organized their experiences into legal classifications.

After the respondent was asked all of the screen questions, the interviewer asked a set of detailed incident questions about any screen question that was answered in the affirmative. The incident questions ask for such information as where and when the incident happened, the extent of injury or loss, the number of offenders and victims involved, and whether the incident was reported to the police.

An attitude questionnaire was administered to every household member sixteen years old or older in a random half of all the city sample households. Questions about fear of crime, perceptions of crime trends, behavioral changes because of crime, and evaluations of local police were asked of each eligible respondent. The attitude instrument also contained a series of questions concerning household mobility, shopping practices, and so forth that were addressed to the household respondent. The attitude questionnaire can be found in Appendix A.

Most of the data that are the subject of this book are based on surveys conducted in eight of the twenty-six cities, the Impact Cities. For some of the analyses presented in this volume, especially analyses of rare phenomena, data from all twenty-six cities are used.[4]

Within each of the cities surveyed, the sampling frame was a 20 percent sample of the 1970 Census of Housing and Population, supplemented by a list of new construction building permits issued since April 1970. In each city, a stratified probability sample of housing units was selected.[5] In the eight cities, 95,173 households were selected for interview and 77,509 were actually interviewed. Of those housing units selected for study but not interviewed, most were unoccupied, demolished, or converted to nonresidential use—and hence fell outside of the scope of the study. It should be reiterated at this point that the sampling frame was composed of housing and group quarters units enumerated in the 1970 census (supplemented by new construction permits). Therefore, if the target population is defined as units occupied at the time of the survey, most of the sampled housing units that were not interviewed fall outside of the scope of the survey. When an address was sampled from the sampling frame, it may have been unoccupied (or demolished), occupied by the same family that occupied the unit in 1970, or occupied by a new family. Although unoccupied units may have disproportionately housed "mobile" families, who were missed by the survey, the new families that had recently moved into addresses selected from the 1970 Census or the new construction list—which will also be disproportionately "mobile" families—would have been picked up by the survey.

Respondents either refused to participate or were never found at home in only 4,090 households. Thus, of all households in the Impact Cities that fell within the scope of the household portion of the survey (77,509 interviewed households plus 4,090 refusals or not at home = 81,599), only 5 percent (4,090 ÷ 81,599) did not participate in the survey. Further, the 77,509 households *in which interviews were conducted* contained 168,459 persons twelve years of age or older who were eligible to be interviewed. Of these, 98 percent (165,346) were actually interviewed. Hence, in the Impact Cities, both in terms of the proportion of within scope households that participated (95 percent), and in terms of the eligible individuals in interviewed households who were interviewed (98 percent), the response rate was excellent.

WEIGHTING FACTORS

Because one important aim of the NCS victimization surveys was to make esitmates of the number of victimizations and the rate of victimization in the populations from which the samples were drawn, it was necessary to "weight" each case. In the simplest terms, if one out of ten cases in the population is selected at random to be studied, each of the cases has a weight of ten. That is, each case counts for itself and for nine other cases in the population that were not selected for study. Because both personal crimes and household crimes were estimated, it was necessary to establish both person weights and household weights.

The weighting schemes that were applied to the sample cases selected in the Impact Cities were derived from a complex general weighting procedure that the Bureau of the Census has evolved over the years.[6]

In order to account for the entire population, adjustments in the basic weights had to be made for household noninterviewees—for occupied households in which occupants were not found at home or were unavailable for some other reason (e.g., the entire household refused to participate). For example, if 10 percent of the units selected in the sample were not interviewed for some reason, the basic weights of the interviewed units would have to be increased[7] if estimates for the entire population were to be made. These household noninterview adjustments were made separately for each of the strata from which housing units were sampled. The effect of within-strata adjustments was that when a housing unit was not interviewed, interviewed housing units with characteristics similar to those of the noninterviewed housing unit were given greater weight. The reasoning here is that noninterviewed housing units are more like interviewed housing units from the same stratum than like interviewed housing units at large. Therefore, when a housing unit was not interviewed, the weights given to similar housing units were increased. Clearly, this assumes that interviewed and noninterviewed housing units from the same stratum were alike on the variables of interest. While this assumption was probably not fully warranted, noninterviewed housing units were more likely to be similar to housing units in the same stratum than housing units at large.

A further adjustment was required for noninterviewed persons in households in which at least one person was interviewed. For each city, this within-household noninterview adjustment factor was made within separate cells according to the age and race of the head of the household and the relationship of the noninterviewed person to the head of the household.[8] Thus, if 10 percent of the persons in a given cell were not interviewed, the weights of the persons in that cell who were interviewed were increased by a factor of ten-ninths.

Although other adjustments to the weights were applied,[9] the adjustments discussed above are the major weighting procedures that were used in the city samples. The result of these weighting adjustments was to reduce the biasing effects of household and person noninterviews and to produce relatively efficient estimates of the parameters under investigation. Because of the complex weighting scheme that the Bureau of the Census used to make estimates of population parameters, all of the victimization data presented in this book are population estimates. Because these data are estimates, it will be necessary to devote some attention to the standard errors of these estimates—a topic to which attention will turn shortly.

INTERVIEWING PROCEDURES

Trained Census Bureau interviewers contacted selected housing units in order to conduct personal interviews with as many of the household members (twelve years old or older) as possible. Follow-up interviews with household members who were unavailable at the time of the initial visit were made either by personal callback or by telephone; these decisions were based on the procedure that was more economical and on the preference of the respondent.

In households that were selected for administration of the attitude questionnaire, household members sixteen years old or older were asked the attitude questions before being asked about victimization experiences. In the victimization portion of the survey, all household members twelve years old or older were eligible for interview and each eligible respondent[10] answered a series of screen questions designed to ascertain whether he or she had been a victim of attempted or completed assault, rape, robbery, or personal larceny during the preceding twelve months. In addition, a household respondent was interviewed about household characteristics and was asked a series of screen questions about attempted or completed burglaries, vehicle thefts, and larcenies suffered by the household during the preceding twelve months. The personal and household screen questions can be examined in Appendix A.

After each respondent answered the series of screen questions, the interviewer asked a set of detailed incident questions for each screen question that had been affirmatively answered. These detailed questions included a brief verbal description of the incident; when and where the incident occurred; whether there was injury or loss; whether a weapon was involved; whether self-protective measures were used; what the sex, age, and race of the offender were; what the value of the stolen property was, and what property was recovered, if any; whether the loss was covered by insurance; and whether the incident was reported to the police.

There were some circumstances under which interviewers were instructed to report several incidents as a "series" of incidents on one detailed incident form rather than as separate incidents. Interviewers were instructed to use the "series" designation only as a last resort. To be reported as a "series", *all* of the following conditions had to be met:

1. The incidents must have been of a similar type.
2. There must have been at least three incidents in the series.
3. The respondent must not have been able to recall details of the individual incidents well enough to have reported them separately (U.S. Bureau of the Census, 1974a:23).

A "series" might be reported, for example, for repeated break-ins of a garage or repeated larceny of items from an automobile. By definition, "series" crimes had to be remembered only dimly (number 3, above). Thus, for these crimes, the number falling within the reference period and the precise nature of each separate victimization were likely to be unknown. In addition, the circumstances of the separate incidents must not have been known. For all of these reasons, these incident reports are of limited value. Hence, this book focuses on nonseries victimizations, although series data will occasionally be reported.[11]

CLASSIFICATION OF VICTIMIZATIONS

In constructing the detailed incident reporting form that was used to gather the specifics of each victimization elicited by the screen questions, the LEAA-Census staff included all of the elements necessary to categorize victimizations according to the UCR rules and definitions, as shown in Table B-1. For example, the UCR robbery definition is:

> Robbery . . . takes place in the presence of the victim (the owner or a person having custody of the property). To obtain the property or thing of value the robber uses force or violence on the victim or puts the victim in fear by use of threats, weapons, etc. It is like larceny but is aggravated by the element of force or threat of force. (Hoover, 1966:11)

The detailed incident questionnaires in Appendix A include questions that can be attribute-coded and tested by computer for the presence of elements required to classify all victimizations according to UCR definitions. For instance, to identify the elements of the definition of robbery one should refer to the "source code"— the circled numbers appearing to the left of each detailed incident question—in Appendix A. According to the UCR definition, robbery takes place in the presence of the victim or the person having custody of the property. Source code 119 asks, "Was any member of this household present when this incident occurred?" Next, the UCR definition requires that force, violence, threats, or the presence of a weapon be used to obtain the property. Source code 120 asks about the presence of a weapon, source code 121 about the use of force, and source code 122 about threats; source codes 154 and 155 ask whether something was actually taken or whether there was an attempt to take something. Therefore, on the basis of these attribute-coded responses, reported victimizations can be unambiguously sorted by computer into the UCR categories;[12] the victimization results are fully compatible with the UCR classification system.

COUNTING RULES

The measurement of phenomena as complex as criminal victimizations, regardless of what scheme for classifying such events is adopted, requires that a number of decisions about how to count crime occurrences be made. For example, the UCR counting rule for

Table B-1. Transformation Scheme for Converting National Crime Panel Crime Classification to Uniform Crime Report Crime Classification

Uniform Crime Report Classification	National Crime Panel Classification [a]	Condition
Rape	Rape with theft	Rape was the method of attack or the type of injury suffered *and* something was stolen or taken without permission or there was an attempt to steal or take something without permission.
	Attempted rape with theft	Verbal threat of rape or attempted rape as the method of attack or attempted rape injuries *and* something was stolen or taken without permission or there was an attempt to steal or take something without permission.
	Rape without theft	Rape was the method of attack or the type of injury suffered *and* nothing was stolen or taken without permission nor was there any attempt to steal or take something without permission.
	Attempted rape without theft	Verbal threat of rape or attempted rape as the method of attack or attempted rape injuries *and* nothing was stolen or taken without permission nor was there any attempt to steal or take something without permission.
Aggravated assault	Serious assault without theft With weapon	The offender had a weapon or something he was using as a weapon *and* the victim suffered a serious injury *and* nothing was stolen or taken without permission nor was there any attempt to steal or take something without permission.
	No weapon	The offender had no weapon *and* the victim suffered a serious injury *and* nothing was stolen or taken without permission nor was there any attempt to steal or take something without permission.
	Attempted assault with weapon without theft	The offender had a weapon *and* the victim was threatened with harm *or* was actually attacked but received no injury *and* nothing was stolen or taken without permission nor was there any attempt to steal or take something without permission.
Armed robbery	Serious assault with theft with weapon	The offender had a weapon or something he was using as a weapon *and* the victim suffered an injury *and* something was stolen or taken without permission or there was an attempt to steal or take something without permission.
	Robbery with weapon	The offender had a weapon or something he was using as a weapon *and* some-

in any way.

Category	Subcategory	Description[a]
	Attempted robbery with weapon	The offender had a weapon or something he was using as a weapon *and* the offender attempted to steal something *and* the victim was not injured in any way.
Unarmed robbery	Serious assault no weapon with theft	The offender had no weapon *and* the victim suffered a serious injury *and* something was stolen or taken without permission or there was an attempt to steal or take something without permission.
	Minor assault with theft	The offender had no weapon or the victim did not know if the offender had a weapon *and* the victim was attacked in some fashion *and* received minor injuries *and* something was stolen or taken without permission or there was an attempt to steal or take something without permission.
	Robbery no weapon	The offender did not have a weapon *and* the victim was threatened with harm or was attacked but received no injury *and* something that belonged to the victim was stolen or taken without permission.
	Attempted robbery no weapon	The offender did not have a weapon *and* the victim was threatened with harm or was attacked but received no injury *and* the offender attempted to steal something.
Simple assault	Minor assault without theft	The offender had no weapon or the victim did not know if the offender had a weapon *and* the victim was attacked in some fashion *and* the victim received minor injuries *and* nothing was stolen or taken without permission nor was there any attempt to steal or take something without permission.
	Attempted assault no weapon without theft	The offender did not have a weapon *and* the victim was threatened with harm or was actually attacked but received no injury *and* nothing was stolen or taken without permission nor was there any attempt to steal or take something without permission.
Larceny	Purse snatch without force	A purse was taken from the person *and* the offender did not have a weapon *and* the victim was not threatened with harm or actually attacked.
	Attempted purse snatch without force	An attempt was made to take a purse from the person *and* the offender did not have a weapon *and* the victim was not threatened with harm or actually attacked.
	Pocket picking	Cash or a wallet was taken from the person *and* the offender did not have a weapon *and* the victim was not threatened with harm or actually attacked.

[a]For each personal incident the victim must have been present when the incident occurred.

Source: Michael J. Hindelang, *Criminal Victimization in Eight American Cities: A Descriptive Analysis of Common Theft and Assault* (Cambridge, Mass.: Ballinger Publishing Co., 1976), p. 98-99. Reprinted by permission.

robberies is quite different from its counting rule for assaults. In the former, if ten persons in a bar are robbed of their personal belongings, only one robbery is scored; the number of persons from whom property is taken is not considered. In assault, however, if two persons are struck with a weapon, two assaults are counted. The UCR counting rules for homicide, rape, and aggravated assault all require that one offense be counted for each person victimized. However, according to UCR rules, the number of offenders in a single event does not affect the number of offenses counted for that event. If three men all forcibly rape a woman, only one UCR offense is scored. Clearly, counting rules are an important consideration in quantifying victimizations.

The NCS classification and counting rules used for personal crimes have been set forth by Turner (1973). Some highlights of these counting rules are very important to note. First, in constructing rates of *victimization* the unit of count is the victim. A single personal incident may involve two or more persons. In *personal crimes*, if two persons are victims in a single incident (e.g., robbery), two victimizations are counted.[13] Thus, the numerator of the victimization rate reflects the number of victimizations, not the number of incidents. Furthermore, if an individual is victimized at two different times during the reference period, the two victimizations against that person are counted in the same way as two victimizations against separate individuals. Therefore, the numerator of the victimization rate is not equal to the number of *different persons* who are victimized (because some persons are victimized more than once within the reference period), but the numerator is equal to the number of victimizations. Second—again because the victim is the unit of count—the number of victimizations is not affected by the number of offenders who participate in the crime. If three offenders rob two victims, two victimizations are counted. Third, if an employee of a store is robbed of the store's receipts, but does not suffer personal attack or loss of personal property "he is not categorized as having been victimized in a personal sense" (Turner, 1973:1). In this instance, the event is categorized as a business rather than a personal robbery. So that a double counting of such events would not occur, this type of robbery was counted and tabulated in the business portion, but not in the household portion of the survey.[14]

Fourth, the distinction between victimizations and incidents is relevant for personal, but not for household crimes. In household crimes the household unit is construed to be the victim. Thus, in personal robberies the number of victimizations depends on the number of persons robbed, but in household burglaries the number of victimizations depends on the number of households burglarized. Although the property of several individual household members may be stolen in a burglary, only one victimization is counted because the entire household is construed to be the victim of household crimes.

Fifth, contrary to the UCR procedure of reporting crime rates per 100,000 persons, the victimization survey data reported herein are generally shown as victimization rates per 1,000 persons twelve years old or older. When rates are presented for specific subgroups of the population (e.g., males versus females), the estimated number of persons twelve years old or older in each category is used as the base of the rate.

Sixth, tables based on the outcome or effects of incidents on victims—for example, extent of loss, extent of injury, self-protective measures used—are tabulated in terms of *victimizations* rather than incidents, because a single incident can affect two victims very differently. Thus, characteristics of the event as they pertain to specific victims use victimization[15] rather than incident counts.

STANDARD ERRORS

It was pointed out earlier in this appendix that all of the substantive results reported in this book are *estimates* of population parameters based on the samples drawn in the cities surveyed. The fact that the results are based on samples, rather than on populations of the cities means, of course, that a certain amount of sampling error has been introduced into the results. The size of this error depends on such factors as the size of the sample and the variability of the population; fortunately, the magnitude of this error can be estimated.

In the household portion of the survey, standard errors were estimated by using the random group method. In this method, each record is assigned a random group number, giving each random group about the same number of cases. For any given characteristic, the variance across the random groups is computed; the square root of that variance is a measure of the standard error of the population estimate of that particular characteristic based on the sample drawn.[16] In the Impact Cities, forty-nine random groups were designated in each city. For a large number of characteristics, the standard errors were computed using the random group method. However, because of the expense of computing standard errors for each data cell, standard errors were not calculated for all estimates. Instead, several assumptions and approximations were made by the Census Bureau's Statistical Methods Division in order to arrive at a formula of best fit that could be used for estimating standard errors of each of the major types of estimates in the household portion of the survey (e.g., personal victimization rates, household victimization rates, the number of personal incidents, and the number of household incidents).

The estimated rates of victimization and the number of victimizations, as well as the standard errors and 95 percent confidence intervals for personal crimes, were presented in Hindelang (1976: Appendix D). These data show, for example, that the rate (per 1,000 persons twelve years old or older) of total personal victimization for the eight-city aggregate was 59.97 and the standard error was 0.80. Therefore, the 95 percent confidence interval (59.97 ± 2 (.80)) is 58.37 to 61.57. Thus, with aggregate data, the results are quite reliable.

In general, the relative error of an estimate of a particular type (e.g., the rate of total personal victimization) can be expected to increase as the number of cases on which the estimate is based decreases. Generally, the more finely subdivided the sample, the greater will be the coefficient of variation (the standard error divided by the estimate).

Generally, for the results presented herein, tests of significance are not reported. There are several reasons for this. First, given the very large sample sizes drawn by the Census Bureau in these cities, many differences of little substantive import would be found to be statistically significant at conventional levels of confidence. Second, because many of the important variables to be examined—age, income, marital status—are polychotomous, the number of possible pairs for comparisons of significant differences is very large; merely to display the significance levels for all comparisons would greatly expand this book. Third, because subcategories of personal victimization—rather than total personal victimizations—are often used as the dependent variables, the number of significance tests that would have to be reported is multiplied even further. Fourth, the significance tests would not be independent; this would be true both within tables and from one table to the next, owing to the intercorrelation of the variables under investigation. Thus, repeated tests of significance—of the number that would be required herein—would have little statistical or conceptual meaning.

Finally, the lack of tests of significance in the tables presented herein does not mean that there has been no concern shown for sampling error and for the reliability of population estimates. These concerns have been carefully considered in constructing the tables reported; care has been taken not to strain beyond the limits of the data. In some cases, estimates have been suppressed because the number of unweighted cases on which they were based was too small for reliable estimates.

NOTES

1. This appendix draws heavily from Hindelang (1976:ch. 3).

2. For a discussion of the national sample methods and procedures, see Hindelang (1976:ch. 3).

3. The city samples are independent of the national panel sample.

4. As noted above, thirteen of the twenty-six cities were resurveyed in 1975. These cities include the Impact Cities and the five largest cities: Chicago, Detroit, Los Angeles, New York, and Philadelphia.

5. Prior to sampling, records for occupied housing units from the 1970 twenty percent sample tape were separated into one hundred strata by home ownership, family size, income, and race, Additional strata were created for housing units unoccupied at the time of the 1970 Census, for group quarters, and for new construction permits. See Hindelang (1976) and U.S. Bureau of the Census (1974) for details.

6. See U.S. Bureau of the Census (1974:11-19) for statistical detail.

7. More precisely, multiplied by 10/9.

8. One such cell, for example, contained persons in households headed by blacks who were fifty years old or older and in which the noninterviewed person was the spouse of the head.

9. In particular, an incident weight adjustment that corrected for the number of victims involved in an incident (to be explained below) and a "ratio estimate factor" were used. The ratio estimate factor had the effect of producing estimates that capitalized on the sampling efficiency resulting from the stratified sampling approach used. See U.S. Bureau of the Census (1974:16) for additional details.

10. As noted above, however, proxy respondents were used for all twelve and thirteen year olds and for other household members who were away from the household for the duration of the interviewing period or who, because of physical or other illnesses, were unable to respond for themselves.

11. For a discussion of the difficulties in using "series" data and some "series" results, see Hindelang (1976: Appendix F).

12. Obviously this assumes that the attribute-coded responses are accurate and unambiguous; clearly this will not always be the case.

13. Marginally involved bystanders are not counted as victims.

14. However, if two employees of a business are robbed of their personal property, two *personal* victimizations would be counted.

15. Such tables are referred to as "victim-event" tables by Turner, (1973:4).

16. This measure of variability also includes sources of nonsampling error such as interviewer effects.

✼ *Appendix C*

Variable Recoding Scheme and Source Code Identification[1]

---

1. All variables discussed throughout the book are recoded and defined as shown in this appendix, unless otherwise noted in the text. When using this appendix, refer to Appendix A for the source code identifications (the numbers that are circled on the instruments). Additionally, in order to understand the meaning of a variable, it is essential to study the skip patterns within the instruments.

HOUSEHOLD INSTRUMENT: Offense Variables

Name	Source Code	Recode Scheme
Presence of a weapon (offender)		
Gun (offender)	120	no ≠ 3, 4, or 5; yes = 3, 4, or 5
Knife (offender)	120	no = 1, 2, 4, or 5; yes = 3
"Other" weapon (offender—clubs, bottles, chains, etc.)	120	no = 1, 2, 3, or 5; yes = 4
	120	no = 1, 2, 3, or 4; yes = 5
Threats	122	no ≠ 2; yes = 2
Threat of rape	123	no ≠ 1; yes = 1
Threat of physical attack	123	no ≠ 2; yes = 2
Threat of weapon	123	no ≠ 3; yes = 3
Attempted attack with a weapon	123	no ≠ 4; yes = 4
Object thrown	123	no ≠ 5; yes = 5
Followed, surrounded	123	no ≠ 6; yes = 6
Something stolen or taken without permission	154	no ≠ 1; yes = 1
Attempt to steal something	155	no ≠ 2; yes = 2
Physical attack	121	no ≠ 1; yes = 1
Rape	125	no ≠ 1; yes = 1
Attempted rape	125	no ≠ 2; yes = 2
Shot or knifed	125	no ≠ 3; yes = 3
Hit by thrown object	125	no ≠ 4; yes = 4
Hit or slapped	125	no ≠ 5; yes = 5
Grabbed or held	125	no ≠ 6; yes = 6
Other attack	125	no ≠ 7; yes = 7
Physical injury	126	no ≠ 2–8; yes = 2, 3, 4, 5, 6, 7, or 8
Rape	126	no ≠ 2; yes = 2
Attempted rape	126	no ≠ 3; yes = 3
Knife or gunshot wounds	126	no ≠ 4; yes = 4
Broken bones or teeth	126	no ≠ 5; yes = 5

HOUSEHOLD INSTRUMENT: Offense Variables continued

Name	Source Code	Recode Scheme
Internal injuries	126	no ≠ 6; yes = 6
Bruises, black eyes, cuts, etc.	126	no ≠ 7; yes = 7
Other injury	126	no ≠ 8; yes = 8
Time of occurrence		
6 A.M. to 6 P.M.	108	no ≠ 2; yes = 2
6 P.M. to midnight	108	no ≠ 3; yes = 3
Midnight to 6 A.M.	108	no ≠ 4; yes = 4
Unknown, nighttime	108	no ≠ 5; yes = 5
Place of occurrence		
In own home	112	no ≠ 1; yes = 1
Vacation home, hotel, motel	112	no ≠ 2; yes = 2
Inside commercial building (store, restaurant, bank, public conveyance, or station)	112	no ≠ 3; yes = 3
Inside office, factory, or warehouse	112	no ≠ 4; yes = 4
Near own home (yard, sidewalk)	112	no ≠ 5; yes = 5
On the street, in a park, school grounds	112	no ≠ 6; yes = 6
Other	112	no ≠ 7; yes = 7
Inside school	112	no ≠ 7; yes = 7 (mentioned as a specific "other" place)
Property taken		
Purse	160	no ≠ 1; yes = 1
Wallet	160	no ≠ 2; yes = 2
Other	160	no ≠ 6; yes = 6
Dollar loss (sum of stolen cash and property)	159, 164	none = sum of 159 and 164 equals zero; some = sum of 159 and 164 not equal to zero
Value of stolen cash	159	none = 0; some ≠ 0
Value of stolen property	164	none = 0; some ≠ 0

Variable	Source code	Recoding scheme
requiring medical attention? (serious injury)	127	no ≠ 2; yes = 2
Was the victim hospitalized?	128	no ≠ 2 or 3; yes = 2 or 3
Victim self-protective measures	135	none ≠ 2; some measure taken = 2
Weapon	136	no ≠ 1; yes = 1
Physical force (hit, kicked, slapped)	136	no ≠ 2; yes = 2
Threatened, argued, or reasoned with offender	136	no ≠ 3; yes = 3
Tried to get help (screamed, called for help)	136	no ≠ 4; yes = 4
Left scene, ran away	136	no ≠ 5; yes = 5
Resisted without force	136	no ≠ 6; yes = 6
Other	136	no ≠ 7; yes = 7
Number of offenders	137	one = 1; more than one = 3
Number of victims	151	one ≠ 1 or more; more than one = 1 or more
Reported to the police	181	no = 1 or 2; yes = 3, 4, or 5
Victim-offender relationship (stranger–not stranger)	140, 147, 148	stranger, 140 = 1, 2, 3, or / 147 = 1, 2, or / 148 = 1 / nonstranger, 140 = 4 or 5, or / 147 = 3 or 4, or / 148 = 2 or 3
Did the offender have a right to be there	115	no ≠ 1; yes = 1
Sex of offender	138, 144	male, 138 = 1, or / 144 = 1 / female, 138 = 2, or / 144 = 2
Age of offender	139, 146	under 21, 139 = 1, 2, 3, or 4, or / 146 = 1, 2, 3, or 4
Race of offender	142, 150	white, 142 = 1, or / 150 = 1 / black/other, 142 = 2 or 3, or / 150 = 2 or 3
Total loss (including damage)	159, 164, 179	none = sum of 159, 164, and 178 or 179 equals zero / some = sum of 159, 164, and 179 not equal zero

ATTITUDE INSTRUMENT: Variables Used in Regression Analyses in Chapter 8

Name	Source Code	Definition and Coding
Sex	040	Male = 1; Female = 2
Age	037	Age at last birthday; continuous from 16 to 99
Race	039	White = 1; Black/other = 2
Household tenancy status	022	Owned or being bought = 1; Rented (cash rent or no cash rent) = 2
Family income	026	Midpoints of the thirteen original categories were used. In addition, because family income was not ascertained for about 10 percent of the respondents, an estimation procedure was employed; whites whose family incomes were not ascertained were assigned the median family income of white respondents, and black/others in the not ascertained category were assigned the median income of black/other respondents.
Total personal victimizations	NA	Sum of all series and nonseries rapes, robberies, assaults (aggravated and simple), and larcenies from the person.
Education	042	Highest number of years respondent attended school; recoded to range of 0 to 22.
Total robberies	NA	Total nonseries robbery victimizations.
Employment status	048	What respondent was doing most in week preceding interview: currently employed, keeping house, going to school, unable to work = 1; unemployed, retired, other = 2.
Marital status	038	Married = 1; Widowed, divorced, separated, never married = 2.
Total seriousness score	NA	Sum of Sellin-Wolfgang seriousness scores for all personal nonseries victimizations
Total rapes	NA	Total nonseries rape victimizations
Total aggravated assaults	NA	Total nonseries aggravated assault victimizations

Total simple assaults	NA	Total nonseries simple assault victimizations
Total larcenies from the person	NA	Total nonseries larcenies from the person
Neighborhood crime trend	345	Increased = 1 Same, don't know, haven't lived here that long = 2 Decreased = 3
Chances of being attacked or robbed	363	Gone up = 1 Haven't changed, no opinion = 2 Gone down = 3

Bibliography

Adler, Freda. *Sisters in Crime*. New York: McGraw-Hill. 1975.

Akman, D.; Figlio, Robert; and Normandeau, Andre. "Concerning Measurement of Delinquency—A Rejoinder and Beyond." *British Journal of Criminology* 7 (1967):442-49.

Amir, Menachem. *Patterns in Forcible Rape*. Chicago: University of Chicago Press, 1971.

Beasley, Ronald W., and Antunes, George. "The Etiology of Urban Crime: An Ecological Analysis." *Criminology* 11 (1974):439-61.

Becker, Howard S. *The Outsiders*. New York: Free Press. 1963.

Biderman, Albert. "Notes on Immunization Effects of Exposure and 'Risk' in Victimization Surveys." Washington, D.C.: Bureau of Social Science Research, 1975.

Biderman, Albert; Johnson, Louise; McIntyre, Jennie; and Weir, Adrianne. *Report on a Pilot Study in the District of Columbia on Victimization and Attitudes Toward Law Enforcement. Field Surveys I*. President's Commission on Law Enforcement and Administration of Justice. Washington, D.C.: Government Printing Office, 1967.

Blackstone, William. *Commentaries on the Laws of England*. 8th ed. Oxford: Clarendon Press, 1778.

Boggs, Sarah. "Urban Crime Patterns." *American Sociological Review* 30 (1965):899-908.

Boyle, Richard. "Path Analysis and Ordinal Data." *American Journal of Sociology*. 75 (1970):461-80.

Chambliss, William. *Crime and the Legal Process*. New York: McGraw-Hill. 1969.

Chapin, F. Stuart. *Human Activity Patterns in the City*. New York: John Wiley and Sons, 1974.

Chappell, Duncan, and Singer, Susan, "Rape in New York City: A Study of Rape Materials in Police Files and Its Meaning." Mimeographed. Albany: School of Criminal Justice, State University of New York at Albany, 1973.

Cho, Y.H. *Public Policy and Urban Crime.* Cambridge, Mass.: Ballinger, 1974.

Chou, Ya-lun, *Statistical Analysis.* New York: Holt, Rinehart and Winston, Inc., 1969.

Christiansen, K. "Methods of Using an Index of Crime of the Kind Devised by Sellin and Wolfgang." In *Collected Studies in Criminological Research.* Vol. 8. Strasbourg Council of Europe, 1970.

Cirino, Robert. *Don't Blame the People.* New York: Vintage Books, 1972.

Clark and Marshall. *A Treatise on the Law of Crimes.* 7th ed. Mundelein: Callaghan and Co., 1967.

Clemence, Theodore G. "Residential Segregation in the Mid-Sixties." *Demography* 4 (1967):562-68.

Cohen, Albert. *Delinquent Boys.* Glencoe, Ill.: The Free Press, 1955.

Cohen, Lawrence. "Who Gets Detained? An Empirical Analysis of the Pre-Adjudicatory Detention of Juveniles in Denver." Analytic Report SD-AR-3. U.S. Department of Justice, Law Enforcement Assistance Administration, National Criminal Justice Information and Statistics Service. Washington, D.C.: Government Printing Office, 1975.

Cohen, Stanley, and Young, Jock, eds. *The Manufacture of News: Social Problems, Deviance and the Mass Media.* London: Constable, 1973.

Conklin, John E. *The Impact of Crime.* New York: Macmillan, 1975.

——. *Robbery and the Criminal Justice System.* Philadelphia: J.B. Lippincott, 1972.

Cormack, R. "A Review of Classification." *Journal of the Royal Statistical Society,* Series A 134 (1971):321-67.

Curtis, Lynn. *Criminal Violence: National Patterns and Behavior.* Lexington, Mass.: Lexington Books, 1974.

——. *Violence, Race, and Culture.* Lexington, Mass.: Lexington Books, 1975.

DeGrazia, Sebastian. "The Uses of Time." In *Aging and Leisure,* Robert W. Kleemeier, ed. New York: Oxford University Press: 1961.

Dodge, Richard, "Analysis of Screen Questions on National Crime Survey." Mimeographed. Washington, D.C.: U.S. Department of Commerce, Bureau of the Census, Crime Statistics Analysis Staff, 1975.

Dodge, Richard, and Turner, Anthony. "Methodological Foundations for Establishing a National Survey of Victimization." Paper presented at the Annual Meetings of the American Statistical Association, Social Statistics Section, 23-26 August 1971, Fort Collins, Colorado.

Doleschal, Eugene, and Wilkins, Leslie. *Criminal Statistics.* Rockville, Md.: Center for Studies of Crime and Delinquency, National Institute of Mental Health, 1972.

Dunn, Christopher. "The Analysis of Environmental Attribute/Crime Incident Characteristic Interrelationships." Ph.D. dissertation, State University of New York at Albany, 1974.

Edwards, Ozzie L. "Patterns of Residential Segregation Within a Metropolitan Ghetto." *Demography* 7 (1970):185-92.

Ennis, Phillip. *Criminal Victimization in the United States: A Report of a*

National Survey. Field Surveys II. President's Commission on Law Enforcement and Administration of Justice. Washington, D.C.: Government Printing Office, 1967.

Erbe, Brigitte Mach. "Race and Socioeconomic Segregation." *American Sociological Review* 40 (1975):801-12.

Executive Office of the President, Office of Management and Budget. *Social Indicators, 1973.* Washington, D.C.: Government Printing Office, 1973.

Fattah, Ezzat. "Towards a Criminological Classification of Victims." *International Criminal Police Review* 22 (1967):163-69.

Figlio, Robert. "The Seriousness of Offenses: An Evaluation by Offenders and Non-Offenders." *Journal of Criminal Law and Criminology* 66 (1975): 189-200.

Freedman, Jonathan L. *Crowding and Behavior.* San Francisco: W.H. Freeman, 1975.

Garofalo, James. *Public Opinion About Crime: The Attitudes of Victims and Nonvictims in Selected Cities.* Law Enforcement Assistance Administration, National Criminal Justice Information and Statistics Service, Analytic Report SD-VAD-1. Washington, D.C.: Government Printing Office, 1977.

Gibbs, Jack P. "Suicide." In Robert K. Merton and Robert A. Nisbet, eds. *Contemporary Social Problems.* 2nd ed. New York: Harcourt, Brace and World, 1966.

Gottfredson, Don; Gottfredson, Michael; and Garofalo, James. "Time Served in Prison and Parole Outcome Among Parolee Risk Categories." *Journal of Criminal Justice* 5 (1977):1-12.

Gottfredson, Michael. "An Empirical Classification of Victims of Personal Crimes." Paper read at the annual meetings of the American Society of Criminology, Tucson, Ariz., 1976.

Gottfredson, Michael, and Hindelang, Michael. "Victims of Personal Crimes: A Methodological Disquisition." *In Proceedings of the Social Statistics Section of the American Statistical Association.* Washington, D.C.: American Statistical Association, 1975.

――. "Bodily Injury to Victims of Personal Crime." In *Sample Surveys of the Victims of Crimes,* Wesley Skogan, ed. Cambridge, Mass.: Ballinger Publishing Co., 1976.

――. " A Consideration of Memory Decay and Telescoping Biases in Victimization Surveys." *Journal of Criminal Justice* 5 (1977):205-216

Graham, Dorcas. "National Crime Survey Reinterview Results of Listing and content Check, National Sample, November 1972-June 1973." Mimeographed. Suitland, Md.: U.S. Department of Commerce, Bureau of the Census, 1974a.

――. "Reinterview Results for the First Eight Impact Cities (1972) of the National Crime Survey." Mimeographed. Suitland, Md.: U.S. Department of Commerce, Bureau of the Census, 1974b.

――. "Reasons for Differences in the Number of Crime Incidents Reported on the Original and Reinterview Survey by Type of Crime (November 1972-June 1973)." Mimeographed. Suitland, Md.: U.S. Department of Commerce, Bureau of the Census, 1974c.

———. "Preliminary Reinterview Results of Listing and Content Check for the National Crime Survey, July 1973–June 1974." Mimeographed. Suitland, Md.: U.S. Department of Commerce, Bureau of the Census, 1974d.

Griffin, Susan. "Rape: The All-American Crime." *Ramparts* 10 (September 1971):26-35.

Hale, Sir Matthew. *Pleas of the Crown: A Methodical Summary.* 1678; rprt. London: Professional Books, 1972.

Hall, Jerome. "Some Basic Questions Regarding Legal Classification for Professional and Scientific Purposes." *Journal of Legal Education* 5 (1953):329

Havighurst, Robert J., "The Nature and Values of Meaningful Free-Time Activity." In *Aging and Leisure*, Robert W. Kleemeier, ed. New York: Oxford University Press, 1961.

Hindelang, Michael. "The Uniform Crime Reports Revisited." *Journal of Criminal Justice* 2 (1974a): 1-7.

———. "Public Opinion Regarding Crime, Criminal Justice and Related Topics." *Journal of Research in Crime and Delinquency* 11 (1974b):101-16.

———. *Criminal Victimization in Eight American Cities: A Descriptive Analysis of Common Theft and Assault.* Cambridge, Mass.: Ballinger Publishing Co., 1976.

———. "Race and Involvement in Common-Law Personal Crimes: A Comparison of Three Techniques." *American Sociological Review* Forthcoming, 1978.

Hindelang, Michael; Dunn, Christopher; Aumick, Alison; and Sutton, L. Paul. *Sourcebook of Criminal Justice Statistics: 1974.* Washington, D.C.: Government Printing Office, 1975.

Hindelang, Michael; Dunn, Christopher; Sutton, Paul; Aumick, Alison. *Sourcebook of Criminal Justice Statistics: 1975.* Washington, D.C.: Government Printing Office, 1976.

Hindelang, Michael, and Gottfredson, Michael. "The Victim's Decision Not to Invoke the Criminal Justice Process." In *The Victim and the Criminal Justice System*, W. McDonald, ed. Beverly Hills: Sage Publications, Inc., 1976.

Hindelang, Michael; Gottfredson, Michael; Dunn, Christopher; and Parisi, Nicolette. *Sourcebook of Criminal Justice Statistics: 1976.* Washington, D.C.: Government Printing Office, 1977.

Hoover, J. Edgar. *Crime in the United States: Uniform Crime Reports— 1965.* Washington, D.C.: Government Printing Office, 1966.

Horton, John. "Time and Cool People." In *Life Styles: Diversity in American Society*, Saul D. Feldman and Gerald W. Thielbar, eds. Boston: Little, Brown, and Company, 1972.

Hovland, Carl I.; Lumsdaine, Arthur A.; and Sheffield, Fred D. "A Baseline for Measurement of Percentage Change." In *The Language of Social Research*, Paul F. Lazarsfeld and Morris Rosenberg, eds. New York: The Free Press, 1955.

Hubbard, Jeffrey C.; DeFleur, Melvin L.; and DeFleur, Lois B. "Mass Media Influences on Public Conceptions of Social Problems." *Social Problems* 23 (1975):22-34.

Kelley, Clarence. *Crime in the United States: Uniform Crime Reports—1973.* Washington, D.C.: Government Printing Office, 1974a.

——. *Uniform Crime Reporting Handbook.* Washington, D.C.: Government Printing Office, 1974b.

——. *Crime in the United States: Uniform Crime Reports—1975.* Washington, D.C.: Government Printing Office, 1976.

Kerlinger, Fred N. *Foundations of Behavioral Research.* 2nd ed. New York: Holt, Rinehart and Winston, 1973.

Kerlinger, Fred N., and Pedhazur, Elazar. *Multiple Regression in Behavioral Research.* New York: Holt, Rinehart and Winston, 1973.

Labovitz, Sanford. "Some Observations on Measurements and Statistics." *Social Forces* 56 (1967):151-60.

Lamborn, LeRoy. "Toward a Victim Orientation in Criminal Theory." *Rutgers Law Review* 22 (1968):733-68.

Lander, Bernard. *Toward an Understanding of Juvenile Delinquency: A Study of 8,464 Cases of Juvenile Delinquency in Baltimore.* New York: Columbia University Press, 1954.

Laumann, Edward O. *Prestige and Association in an Urban Community.* Indianapolis: Bobbs-Merrill, 1966.

Law Enforcement Assistance Administration. "The Cleveland-Akron Commercial Victimization Feasibility Test." Statistics Division Technical Series, Report No. 2. Mimeographed. Washington, D.C.: U.S. Department of Justice, Law Enforcement Assistance Administration, Statistics Division, n.d.

——. U.S. Department of Justice, National Institute of Law Enforcement and Criminal Justice, Statistics Division. *San Jose Methods Test of Known Crime Victims.* Statistics Technical Report No. 1. Washington, D.C.: Government Printing Office, 1972.

——. U.S. Department of Justice, National Criminal Justice Information and Statistics Service. *Crimes and Victims: A Report on the Dayton–San Jose Pilot Survey of Victimization.* Washington, D.C.: Government Printing Office, 1974.

——. U.S. Department of Justice, National Criminal Justice Information and Statistics Service. *Criminal Victimization Surveys in the Nation's Five Largest Cities.* Washington, D.C.: Government Printing Office, 1975a.

——. U.S. Department of Justice, National Criminal Justice Information and Statistics Service. *Criminal Victimization in the United States: 1973 Advance Report.* Washington, D.C.: Government Printing Office, 1975b.

——. U.S. Department of Justice, National Criminal Justice Information and Statistics Service. *Criminal Victimization Surveys in 13 American Cities.* Washington, D.C.: Government Printing Office, 1975c.

——. U.S. Department of Justice, National Criminal Justice Information and Statistics Service. *Criminal Victimization in the United States: A Comparison of 1973 and 1974 Findings.* Washington, D.C.: Government Printing Office, 1976.

——. U.S. Department of Justice, National Criminal Justice Information and

Statistics Service. *Survey of Inmates of Local Jails*, 1972. Washington, D.C.: Prepublication report, 1977.

Letkemann, Peter. *Crime as Work*. Englewood Cliffs, N.J.: Prentice-Hall, 1973.

Levine, James. "The Potential for Crime Overreporting in Criminal Victimization Surveys." *Criminology* 14 (1976):307-30.

Liebow, Elliot. *Talley's Corner*. Boston: Little, Brown and Company, 1967.

MacDonald, John M. *Rape Offenders and Their Victims*. Springfield, Ill.: Charles C. Thomas, 1971.

Macnaughton-Smith, P. "The Classification of Individuals by the Possession of Attributes Associated with a Criterion." *Biometrics* 19 (1963):364-66.

——. *Some Statistical and Other Numerical Techniques for Classifying Individuals*. Home Office Research Unit Report. London: Her Majesty's Stationery Office, 1965.

Maltz, Michael. "Crime Statistics: A Mathematical Perspective." *Journal of Criminal Justice* 3 (1975):177-94.

McClintock, F., and Gibson, Evelyn. *Robbery in London*. London: MacMillan and Co., 1961.

McNemar, Quinn. *Psychological Statistics*. 4th ed. New York: John Wiley and Sons, 1969.

Mulvihill, Donald; Tumin, Melvin; and Curtis, Lynn. *Crimes of Violence, Volume 11: A Staff Report Submitted to the National Commission on the Causes and Prevention of Violence*. Washington, D.C.: Government Printing Office, 1969.

Murphy, Linda. "Effect of Attitude Supplement on NCS-Cities Sample Victimization Data." Mimeograph. U.S. Department of Commerce, Bureau of the Census, 1976.

Nie, Norman H.; Hull, C. Hadlai; Jenkins, Jean G.; Steinbrenner, Karin; and Bent, Dale H. *Statistical Package for the Social Sciences*. 2nd ed. New York: McGraw-Hill, 1975.

Normandeau, Andre. "Trends and Patterns in Crimes of Robbery." Ph.D. dissertation, University of Pennsylvania, 1968.

Pittman, David, and Handy, William. "Patterns in Criminal Aggravated Assault." *Journal of Criminal Law, Criminology and Police Science* 55 (1964): 462-70.

Pokorny, Alex. "Human Violence: A Comparison of Homicide, Aggravated Assault, Suicide, and Attempted Suicide." *Journal of Criminal Law, Criminology and Police Science* 56 (1965):488-97.

Pollock, Sir Frederick, and Maitland, Frederic. *The History of English Law*. 2nd ed. 1898; rprt. Cambridge: University Press, 1968.

Pope, Carl. "Dimensions of Burglary: An Empirical Examination of Offense and Offender Characteristics." Ph.D. dissertation, State University of New York at Albany, 1975.

President's Commission on Crime in the District of Columbia. *Report*. Washington, D.C.: Government Printing Office, 1966.

President's Commission on Law Enforcement and Administration of Justice. *The Challenge of Crime in a Free Society.* Washington, D.C.: Government Printing Office, 1967.

Quinney, Richard. *The Social Reality of Crime.* Boston: Little, Brown, and Company, 1970.

———. *Critique of Legal Order.* Boston: Little, Brown, and Company, 1973.

Reiss, Albert, Jr. *Studies in Crime and Law Enforcement in Major Metropolitan Areas. Volume I. Field Surveys III.* President's Commission on Law Enforcement and Administration of Justice. Washington, D.C.: Government Printing Office, 1967.

Reppetto, Thomas A. *Residential Crime* Cambridge, Mass.: Ballinger Publishing Co., 1974.

Riedel, Marc. "Perceived Circumstances, Inferences of Intent, and Judgements of Offense Seriousness." *Journal of Criminal Law and Criminology* 66 (1975):201-208.

Robison, Sophia. "A Critical View of the Uniform Crime Reports." *Michigan Law Review* 69 (1966):1031-54.

Schmid, Calvin. "Urban Crime Areas: Part I." *American Sociological Review* 25 (1960a): 527-42.

———. "Urban Crime Areas: Part II." *American Sociological Review* 25 (1960b):655-78.

Schmid, Calvin, and Schmid, Stanton. *Crime in the State of Washington.* Olympia: Law and Justice Planning Office, Washington State Planning and Community Affairs Agency, 1972.

Schreiner, Irwin. "Preliminary Reinterveiw Results from the First Eight Cities (1972) of the National Crime Survey (NCS)." Mimeographed. Suitland, Md.: U.S. Department of Commerce, Bureau of the Census, 1974.

Sellin, Thorsten. *Culture Conflict and Crime.* New York: Social Science Research Council, 1938.

———. "The Significance of Records of Crime." *Law Quarterly Review.* 67 (1951):489-504.

Sellin, Thorsten, and Wolfgang, Marvin. *The Measurement of Delinquency.* New York: John Wiley and Sons, 1964.

Shaw, Clifford, and McKay, Henry. *Juvenile Delinquency and Urban Areas.* Chicago: The University of Chicago Press, 1942.

Silverman, Robert. "Victim Typologies: Overview, Critique, and Reformulation." In *Victimology*, Israel Drapkin and Emilio Viano, eds., Lexington, Mass.: D.C. Heath and Co., 1974.

Simon, Frances. *Prediction Methods in Criminology.* London: Her Majesty's Stationery Office, 1971.

Simpson, G. *Principles of Animal Taxonomy.* New York: Columbia University Press, 1961.

Sneath, P., and Sokal, R. *Numerical Taxonomy.* San Francisco: Freeman, 1973.

Sokal, R. "Classification: Purposes, Principles, Progress, Prospects." *Science* 185 (1974):1116-23.

Somers, Robert. "A New Asymmetric Measure of Association for Ordinal Variables." *American Sociological Review* 27 (1962):799-811.

Spector, Paul E. "Population Density and Unemployment: The Effects on the Incidence of Violent Crime in the American City." *Criminology* 12 (1975): 399-401.

Stephen, J.F. *A History of the Criminal Law of England.* London: Methuen and Co., 1883.

Taeuber, Karl E. "The Effect of Income Redistribution on Racial Residential Segregation." *Urban Affairs Quarterly* 4 (1968):5-14.

Taeuber, Karl E., and Taeuber, Alma F. *Negroes in Cities.* Chicago: Aldine, 1965.

Toch, Hans. *Violent Men.* Chicago: Aldine, 1969.

Turner, Anthony. "Classification and Counting Rules Employed for Personal Crimes in the National Crime Panel." Mimeographed. Washington, D.C.: U.S. Department of Justice, Law Enforcement Assistance Administration, National Criminal Justice Information and Statistics Service, 1973.

Turner, Stanley. "The Ecology of Delinquency." In *Delinquency: Selected Studies,* Thorsten Sellin and Marvin E. Wolfgang, eds. New York: John Wiley and Sons, 1969.

U.S. Bureau of the Census. "Supplemental Tables Measuring Accuracy of Recall for About 360 Police Record Cases of Businesses in the Dayton Area Known to Have Been Victimized During 1970." Mimeographed. Suitland, Md: U.S. Bureau of the Census, Business Division, n.d.

——. "The Index of Inconsistency for an L-Fold Classification System, L > 2" in *Technical Notes No. 2* U.S. Bureau of the Census. Washington, D.C., 1969.

——. "Victim Recall Pretest (Washington, D.C.): Household Survey of Victims of Crime." Mimeographed. Suitland, Md.: U.S. Bureau of the Census, Demographic Surveys Division, 1970a.

——. "Household Survey of Victims of Crime: Second Pretest (Baltimore, Maryland)." Mimeographed. Suitland, Md.: U.S. Bureau of the Census, Demographic Surveys Division, 1970b.

——. "National Crime Survey: Central Cities Sample, Impact Cities, 1972 Survey Documentation." Mimeographed. Suitland, Md.: U.S. Department of Commerce, Social and Economic Statistics Administration. 1974a.

——. *Statistical Abstract of the United States: 1974.* 95th ed. Washington, D.C.: Government Printing Office, 1974b.

——. "National Crime Survey, Central Cities Sample—Impact Cities, Interviewer's Manual." Mimeographed. Suitland, Md.: U.S. Department of Commerce, Social and Economic Statistics Administration, March 1975.

U.S. Department of Justice, Federal Bureau of Investigation. *Uniform Crime Reporting Handbook.* Washington, D.C.: Government Printing Office, 1966.

von Hentig, Hans. *The Criminal and His Victim.* New Haven: Yale University Press, 1948.

Wellford, Charles, and Wiatrowski, Michael, "On the Measurement of Delinquency." *Journal of Criminal Law and Criminology* 66 (1975):157-88.

Whyte, William F. *Street Corner Society.* Chicago: University of Chicago Press, 1943.

Wilkins, Leslie. "New Thinking in Criminal Statistics." *Journal of Criminal Law, Criminology and Police Science* 56 (1965):277-84.

Wilkins, Leslie, and Macnaughton-Smith, Peter. "New Prediction and Classification Methods in Criminology." *Journal of Research in Crime and Delinquency*, 1 (1964):19-32.

Wolfgang, Marvin. *Patterns in Criminal Homicide.* New York: John Wiley and Sons, 1958.

———. "Uniform Crime Reports: A Critical Appraisal." *University of Pennsylvania Law Review* 111 (1963):708-38.

Wolfgang, Marvin, and Ferracuti, Franco. *The Subculture of Violence: Toward an Integrated Theory in Criminology.* London: Tavistock Publications, 1967.

Wolfgang, Marvin; Figlio, Robert; and Sellin, Thorsten. *Delinquency in a Birth Cohort.* Chicago: University of Chicago Press, 1972.

Author Index

Subject Index

injury, 63-66, 115-116
lifestyle, 246, 248, 253-254, 269
loss, 96-100, 118-120
roles, 188, 211, 242, 248, 269
victimization, 8, 9-10, 110-114,
  121-123, 136-138, 142-143,
  145-146, 254, 269
Shopping, 222-224
Structural constraints, 242-244

Time of occurrence, 41, 46, 61, 77,
  88, 252-255

Uniform Crime Reports, 1-2, 19-26,
  36, 38, 40, 48, 71-72, 75-77
  limitations of, 25, 74
  offender characteristics in, 257-258
U.S. Bureau of the Census, xxi, 3, 14n,
  227, 229, 230-232, 287, 289, 291

Vehicle theft, 22, 133-135, 272, 292
Victim precipitation, 135, 267-268
Victim typologies
  theoretical, 105-106, 126-129, 148-
    149
  empirical, 109-123
Victimization, demographic correlates
  of
  age, 6-8, 9-10, 13-15, 63-66, 96-
    101, 109-111, 114, 116, 121-123,
    136-141, 253-254
  areal characteristics, 148-149, 160
  employment status, 121-122
  income, 5, 11-12, 13, 63-66, 96-
    101, 111, 114, 116, 119, 123,
    138-141, 254
  major activity, 111-112, 116
  marital status, 8, 14-15, 63-66,
    96-101, 111, 114, 116, 121, 123,
    136-141, 254
  race, 5, 9-10, 11-12, 13, 63-66, 96-
    101, 119, 123, 138-141
  sex, 8, 9-10, 63-66, 96-101, 111,
    114, 121-123, 136-141, 254
  vocation, 254
Victimization likelihoods
  behavioral changes, 217-218

clustering within households, 144-
  146
conditional and unconditional, 130-
  135
fear of crime, 189-191
interdependence for persons and
  households, 136-146, 149
lifestyle, 250-266
predictive attribute analysis of,
  109-114, 121-123
versus victimization rates, 125, 180
Victimization surveys
  attitude subsample, 142, 155, 289
  classification of victimizations,
    294-295
  counting rules, 293-297
  early surveys, 2-3
  eight Impact Cities, xxii, 1, 3, 14n,
    127, 155, 231-232, 275-292
  five largest cities, 33, 58, 127, 299n
  household respondent, 3, 141-144,
    287-288
  incident questions, 288-289, 292
  instruments, 237-238, 277-286
  limitations, 227-233, 237-238
  memory biases, 3, 228-230
  national sample, 231, 236, 287
  National Crime Survey 1, 3, 19, 107,
    230, 275-292
  proxy respondent, 144, 287-288
  reinterviews, 230-233
  reliability, 227-228, 230-233
  response rate, 289-290
  sampling, 289
  screen questions, 2-3, 142, 288, 292
  self-respondent, 3, 144, 287-288
  standard errors, 297-299
  tests of significance, 298-299
  twenty-six cities, 127, 287
  validity, 227-230
  weighting factors, 290-291
Vocation, 241, 245, 253, 254, 256,
  263-264, 270

Weapons
  injury, 42-43, 46, 61-62, 81, 88
  loss, 72, 80-82, 85, 95

About the Authors

Michael J. Hindelang received his doctorate in criminology from the University of California, Berkeley, and is currently Professor of Criminal Justice at the State University of New York, Albany. His research interests include criminal justice statistics and juvenile delinquency. He is co-editor of the annual *Sourcebook of Criminal Justice Statistics* and co-director of research projects involving the utilization of criminal justice statistics, criminal victimization, and the methodology of self-reported delinquency techniques, all at the Criminal Justice Research Center, Albany, New York.

Michael R. Gottfredson received his doctorate in criminal justice from the State University of New York, Albany. He is currently the Director of the Criminal Justice Research Center in Albany, New York, and Visiting Assistant Professor in the School of Criminal Justice, State University of New York, Albany. He co-directs a research project on the utilization of criminal justice statistics and co-edits the annual *Sourcebook of Criminal Justice Statistics*. His research interests include criminal justice decisionmaking and the interpretation of crime statistics.

James Garofalo also received his doctorate in criminal justice from the State University of New York, Albany. He is currently the co-director of a research project involving analysis of criminal victimization data at the Criminal Justice Research Center, Albany, New York. His research interests are in the areas of public opinion and the mass media as they relate to crime.